# EU COMPETITION LITIGATION

All EU Member States have now transposed Directive 2014/104/EU on damages actions for breaches of competition law into national law. The Directive (and the soft-law instruments accompanying it) not only marks a new phase for private enforcement of competition law but also, more generally, provides a novel and thought-provoking instance of EU harmonisation of aspects of private law and civil litigation.

Following up on a previous volume in the Swedish Studies in European Law series, published in 2016, this book offers contributions from top practitioners and scholars from all over Europe, who present and discuss first experiences from the implementation of the new damages regime in various jurisdictions.

Topics covered include theoretical and practical reflections on the state of private enforcement in Europe, the balancing of conflicting interests pertaining to public and private enforcement of competition law respectively, and specific legal issues such as causation and the estimation of harm. The authors explore problems solved, problems created, and future challenges in the new regime of private enforcement of competition law in Europe, offering predictions as to issues that may have to be settled through recourse to the European Court of Justice.

# EU COMPETITION LITIGATION

All EU Member States have now transposed Directive 2014/104/EU on damages actions for breaches of competition law into national law. The Directive (and the soft-law instruments accompanying it) not only marks a new phase for private enforcement of competition law but also, more generally, provides a novel and thought-provoking instance of EU harmonisation of aspects of private law and civil litigation.

Following up on a previous volume in the Swedish Studies in European Law series, published in 2016, this book offers contributions from top practitioners and scholars from all over Europe, who present and discuss first experiences from the implementation of the new damages regime in various jurisdictions.

Topics covered include theoretical and practical reflections on the state of private enforcement in Europe, the balancing of conflicting interests pertaining to public and private enforcement of competition law respectively, and specific legal issues such as causation and the estimation of harm. The authors explore problems solved, problems created, and future challenges in the new regime of private enforcement of competition law in Europe, offering predictions as to issues that may have to be settled through recourse to the European Court of Justice.

# EU Competition Litigation

## *Transposition and First Experiences of the New Regime*

Swedish Studies in European Law
Volume 12

Edited by
Magnus Strand
Vladimir Bastidas Venegas
Marios C Iacovides

•HART•
OXFORD • LONDON • NEW YORK • NEW DELHI • SYDNEY

HART PUBLISHING

Bloomsbury Publishing Plc

Kemp House, Chawley Park, Cumnor Hill, Oxford, OX2 9PH, UK

HART PUBLISHING, the Hart/Stag logo, BLOOMSBURY and the Diana logo are trademarks of Bloomsbury Publishing Plc

First published in Great Britain 2019

Reprinted 2019



A catalogue record for this book is available from the British Library.

Library of Congress Cataloging-in-Publication data

Names: EU Competition Law and the New Private Enforcement Regime: First Experiences from Its Implementation (Conference) (2017 : Uppsala universitet). | Strand, Magnus, editor. | Bastidas Venegas, Vladimir, 1974- editor. | Iacovides, Marios C., editor. | Swedish Network for European Legal Studies, sponsoring body.

Title: EU competition litigation : transposition and first experiences of the new regime / edited by Magnus Strand, Vladimir Bastidas Venegas, Marios C Iacovides.

Other titles: European Union competition litigation

Description: Oxford, UK ; Chicago, Illinois : Hart Publishing, 2019. | Series: Swedish studies in European law | "All the topical contributions included here spring from the conference, EU Competition Law and the New Private Enforcement Regime: First Experiences from Its Implementation, which was held in Uppsala on 13 and 14 May 2017 at the initiative of the Network [Swedish Network for European Legal Studies] and in collaboration with Uppsala University"—ECIP editorial preface. | Includes bibliographical references and index.

Identifiers: LCCN 2018057168 (print) | LCCN 2018058979 (ebook) | ISBN 9781509922024 (EPub) | ISBN 9781509922017 (hardback)

Subjects: LCSH: Antitrust law—European Union countries—Congresses. | Actions and defenses—European Union countries—Congresses. | Damages—European Union countries—Congresses. | International and municipal law—European Union countries—Congresses. | European Parliament. Directive 2014/104/EU of the European Parliament and of the Council of 26 November 2014 on certain rules governing actions for damages under national law for infringements of the competition law provisions of the member states and of the European Union—Congresses.

Classification: LCC KJE6456.A8 (ebook) | LCC KJE6456.A8 E9 2017 (print) | DDC 343.2407/21—dc23

LC record available at https://lccn.loc.gov/2018057168

ISBN: HB: 978-1-50992-201-7
ePDF: 978-1-50992-203-1
ePub: 978-1-50992-202-4

Typeset by Compuscript Ltd, Shannon
Printed and bound in Great Britain by TJ International Ltd, Padstow, Cornwall

To find out more about our authors and books visit www.hartpublishing.co.uk. Here you will find extracts, author information, details of forthcoming events and the option to sign up for our newsletters.

# Foreword

WHAT IS THE most appropriate way to enforce competition law? How can public and private enforcement best be combined to combat practices distorting free competition efficiently? What role should private enforcement, and in particular actions for damages by private parties, play in deterring anti-competitive behaviour? Those fundamental questions, and the way they are tackled, are of crucial importance for the functioning of any legal system sanctioning breaches of competition law. Because of their importance, questions linked to private enforcement of competition law have attracted considerable attention in literature.

One of the most influential and ground-breaking texts on the subject is the Opinion of the late Advocate General Van Gerven in *Banks v British Coal Corporation*,[1] an Opinion that inspired me as a young scholar to contribute to the discussion on damages for breaches of competition rules almost 20 years ago. Since then, however, significant developments have occurred in this field, many of which are recorded comprehensively in this book.

The seminal judgments in *Courage*[2] and *Manfredi*,[3] where the Court of Justice of the European Union (the Court) laid the groundwork for a system of private enforcement in the European Union, deserve special mention. On the basis of the need to ensure the full effectiveness of EU law, the Court held that it should be possible for private claimants to claim damages for losses caused by infringements of EU competition law before national courts. Against that jurisprudential backdrop, the EU legislature enacted Directive 2014/104/EU on certain rules governing actions for damages under national law for breaches of EU or national competition law,[4] the legislative instrument that lies at the very heart of this book.

The contributions to this unique volume edited by Magnus Strand, Vladimir Bastidas and Marios C Iacovides address a wide range of issues that touch upon a myriad of difficulties arising in the harmonisation of private enforcement of competition law in the European Union from the perspective of Directive 2014/104. Those difficulties stem, in particular, from the reliance on domestic

[1] Case C-128/92 *Banks & Co v British Coal Corporation* EU:C:1994:130, Opinion of AG Van Gerven EU:C:1993:860.

[2] Case C-453/99 *Courage Ltd v Bernard Crehan* EU:C:2001:465.

[3] Joined cases C-295/04 to 298/04 *Vincenzo Manfredi and Others* EU:C:2006:461.

[4] Directive 2014/104/EU of the European Parliament and of the Council of 26 November 2014 on certain rules governing actions for damages under national law for infringements of the competition law provisions of the Member States and of the European Union [2014] OJ L349/1.

private law and procedural rules in order to resolve issues not expressly dealt with by the Directive. As this book aptly illustrates, the enactment of the Directive constitutes only a first step in the process of harmonisation: despite the principle of full compensation laid down in the Directive, many central questions pertaining to the attribution of damages by national courts remain to be clarified, either by the Court within the framework of the preliminary ruling procedure under Article 267 TFEU or by further legislative texts. Those questions include, for example, guidance on the interpretation of the concepts of harm or causation and types of damage to be compensated – concepts that are arguably of crucial importance in any action for damages. Moreover, as the critical examination of the current state of private enforcement in this book suggests, the full potential of private enforcement is yet to be reached by the EU regulatory regime. This is due to, in particular, the way rules regarding discovery are applied and the decision-making practice of public enforcers, which does not adequately take into account the needs of private enforcement.

As it approaches the issue of private enforcement from a broad variety of perspectives, this book is a welcome addition to the existing literature. It is also undoubtedly an important addition to the scholarly work on EU law published in this series.

Nils Wahl
*Advocate General at the Court of Justice of the European Union*

# *Editorial Preface*

It is with pride and satisfaction that we present this twelfth volume in the series *Swedish Studies in European Law*, which has been issued under the auspices of the Swedish Network for European Legal Studies since 2006.

All the topical contributions included here spring from the conference 'EU Competition Law and the New Private Enforcement Regime: First Experiences from Its Implementation', which was held in Uppsala on 13 and 14 May 2017 at the initiative of the Network and in collaboration with Uppsala University. The idea for the conference was to collect and discuss the EU Member States' first experiences of the transposition and implementation of Directive 2014/104 on certain rules governing actions for damages for infringements of competition law,[1] as well as the soft-law instruments accompanying it.[2] The transposition period for the Directive had expired only a few months before the conference (on 27 December 2016), meaning that speakers and guests were able to benefit from comparative discussions of problems encountered and solutions chosen. As it was generally felt that such discussions were very rewarding, we decided to collect the papers presented at the conference in this edited volume. The 2017 conference was a follow-up event to the 2014 Uppsala conference 'EU Competition Law and the Emerging Harmonization of Private Enforcement: The Upcoming Directive and Beyond', which anticipated the final adoption of the Directive by a few months.[3] That conference also resulted in an edited volume in this series, published in 2016: *Harmonising EU Competition Litigation: The New Directive and Beyond*. There are abundant references to that volume in this one, and interested readers are warmly recommended to treat the two volumes as complementary.

We have divided the contributions to this edited volume into three parts. The first part addresses certain general issues regarding the Directive and its

[1] Directive 2014/104/EU of the European Parliament and of the Council of 26 November 2014 on certain rules governing actions for damages under national law for infringements of the competition law provisions of the Member States and of the European Union [2014] OJ L 349/1.

[2] The private enforcement package adopted in 2013 also included Commission, 'Communication from the Commission on quantifying harm in actions for damages based on breaches of Art 101 or 102 of the Treaty on the Functioning of the European Union' [2013] OJ C167/19; Commission, 'Commission Staff Working Document – Practical Guide on quantifying harm in actions for damages based on breaches of Art 101 or 102 of the Treaty on the Functioning of the European Union', SWD(2013) 205; and (with a broader scope) Commission Recommendation 2013/396/EU of 11 June 2013 on common principles for injunctive and compensatory collective redress mechanisms in the Member States concerning violations of rights granted under Union Law [2013] OJ L201/60.

[3] The political compromise text from which the final text was drafted became available just as the conference was arranged.

transposition into national law. In the opening contribution, 'EU Competences and the Damages Directive: The Continuum between Minimum and Full Harmonisation', Max Hjärtström and Julian Nowag analyse the Directive from a constitutional perspective and explain how the allocation of competences between the EU and Member States affects the interpretation of individual provisions. Subsequently, Ulrich Classen and Martin Seegers of the CDC Cartel Damages Claims offer insights from their day-to-day experiences of private enforcement litigation in 'The State of Private Enforcement of Competition Law: A Practitioner's Perspective'. This is followed by Magnus Strand, who uses the Directive as a point of departure for some reflections on 'Managing Transposition and Avoiding Fragmentation: The Example of Limitation Periods and Interest', including a critique of certain aspects of the Swedish transposition of the Damages Directive. The first part of the book ends with a more detailed account of the transposition process in 'A First Look at the Portuguese Act 23/2018 Transposing the Private Enforcement Directive' by Sofia Pais.

The second part consists of contributions focusing on the interrelationship between public and private enforcement, an intensely debated topic in recent years. This part opens with Lars Henriksson, who asks 'Privately Enforcing Public Mandatory Law – an Inconsistent Approach to Remedies?'. Henriksson looks in particular at a unique feature of the Swedish private enforcement regime, the right for a company that has tipped off the Swedish Competition Authority (SCA) regarding a potential competition law violation to launch an action against the alleged infringer in the competent Swedish court when the SCA chooses not to pursue the matter further. Torbjörn Andersson then offers a critique of the complex issue of 'The Binding Effect of Decisions and Judgments under EU Competition Law', and highlights the inconsistencies created by the Directive, especially when it comes to decisions or rulings finding the defendant non-liable for the alleged competition law violation. Katharina Voss wonders whether the Directive is truly 'Facilitating Follow-on Actions? Public and Private Enforcement of EU Competition Law after Directive 2014/104', highlighting the potential of the so-called hybrid settlement decisions and questioning the wisdom behind the numerous settlements the Commission enters into with defendants. Using the example of recently concluded follow-on actions against TeliaSonera in Sweden for the well-known margin squeeze abuse that resulted in the *TeliaSonera* preliminary ruling from the European Court of Justice,[4] the section continues with Per Karlsson, who examines 'The Practical and Legal Effect(s) of National Decisions in Subsequent Damages Actions'. Karlsson exposes the reasons behind the Swedish courts' seeming inconsistencies in the follow-on actions against TeliaSonera and illustrates how the Directive might have led to entirely different results. The second part concludes with Helene Andersson who addresses what has been a hot potato both before and after the

[4] Case C-52/09 *Konkurrensverket v TeliaSonera Sverige* EU:C:2011:83.

adoption of the Directive: 'The Quest for Evidence – Still an Uphill Battle for Cartel Victims?' The diverging views of authors in this second part as to the optimal relationship between public and private enforcement demonstrate that it is likely that the topic will continue to be intensely debated in the foreseeable future.

In the third part of the volume, we have collected contributions focusing more specifically on private enforcement issues as such, mostly but not entirely concentrating on classic damages law issues. This part begins with Assimakis Komninos' 'Damages Actions and Article 102 TFEU Cases: The New Frontier for Private Enforcement', in which he explains the practical challenges encountered in the private enforcement of damages in abuse cases in different Member States. This is followed by Anna Piszcz, who explores 'Implementing the Rules of the Damages Directive on Joint and Several Liability: The SME Derogation', focusing in particular on certain problematic issues concerning small and medium-sized enterprises. This third part continues with Katri Havu who investigates 'Causation and Damage: What the Directive Does Not Solve and Remarks on Relevant EU Law', exploring, for example, the implications of notions such as 'effective judicial protection' and 'full compensation' on the assessment of causation in competition damages. Aspects related to the problematic assessment of harm in competition litigation are examined by Pieter van Cleynenbreugel in his contribution 'The Presumption of Harm and Its Implementation in the Member States' Legal Orders', in which he specifically explores interpretation problems accompanying the presumption of harm and the room for varying interpretations in the Member States. This part of the book is concluded by Marios C Iacovides and his chapter 'Article 17(3) of the Directive and the Interaction between the Swedish Competition Authority and Swedish Courts', which focuses on the transposition of Article 17 of the Directive into Swedish law and the possibility for competition authorities to assist in the quantification of harm.

Allow us to finish this introduction with a few words on what may lie ahead. Although a great deal has happened since its adoption in 2014, it is the view of the undersigned that the *Wirkungsgeschichte* of the (still) new private enforcement regime in EU competition law is only now beginning to become apparent. As cases where the new regime is applicable are finding their way to courts in the Member States, the first reference for a preliminary ruling has been submitted by the Tribunal Judicial da Comarca de Lisboa[5] (a first hint of drizzle, let us see if it starts to pour) and the Commission has published a first draft of its Guidelines on passing-on after a public consultation.[6] Furthermore, the first Commission

[5] Registered as Case C-637/17 *Cogeco Communications Inc v Sport TV Portugal and Others*.

[6] Commission, 'Draft guidelines for national courts on how to estimate the share of cartel overcharges passed on to indirect purchasers and final consumers', public consultation available at: ec.europa.eu/competition/consultations/2018_cartel_overcharges/index_en.html.

review of the Directive is coming up soon, in 2020. All this promises new and interesting developments down the road.

On that note, there will surely be a need to return again to this interesting field of EU law, private law and civil procedure. Here, some of the ancient common roots of European law meet the most recent harmonising efforts of late modernity – what better place to meet again?

Magnus Strand, Vladimir Bastidas & Marios C Iacovides
*Uppsala and Stockholm, 30 September 2018*

# *Table of Contents*

# *Table of Cases*

**European Court of Justice**

**European Commission Decisions**

**European Court of Human Rights**



**National Courts**

*Austria*



*France*



*Germany*



*Greece*



*Netherlands*

*Spain*



*Sweden*



*United Kingdom*

# Table of Legislation

**European Instruments**

*Treaties and Conventions*

*EU Regulations*

*EU Directives*

**National Legislation**

*Austria*



*Belgium*



*Denmark*



*Estonia*



*Finland*

*Portugal (numbered Acts ordered by date)*



*Spain*

*Sweden*

*United Kingdom*

# Part I

# Rolling Out the New Private Enforcement Regime

# 1

# *EU Competences and the Damages Directive: The Continuum Between Minimum and Full Harmonisation*

MAX HJÄRTSTRÖM* AND JULIAN NOWAG**

## I. INTRODUCTION

The Damages Directive[1] (the Directive) constitutes the first Directive adopted within the field of Union competition law.[2] This novelty may seem surprising for two opposing reasons. First, competition falls within the exclusive competence of the European Union.[3] Second, following the principle of conferral,[4] issues of remedies and damages have traditionally been left to the Member States – labelled as the *principle of national procedural autonomy*[5] – and only been subjected to the principles of effectiveness and equivalence.[6] That principle is reaffirmed by Article 4 of the Directive, which provides that all national rules and procedures relating to the exercise of claims of damages are subject to the conditions of equivalence and effectiveness.

* Doctoral Candidate Lund University.

** Associate Senior Lecturer Lund University. The authors have contributed equally to this chapter.
We would like to thank Steven Weatherill, Xavier Groussot, the participants of the conference in Uppsala in summer 2017 as well as the editors of this volume for their invaluable comments. All error remain ours.

[1] Directive 2014/104/EU of the European Parliament and of the Council on certain rules governing actions for damages under national law for infringements of the competition law provisions of the Member States of the European Union [2014] OJ L349/1.

[2] U Bernitz, 'Introduction to the Directive on Competition Damages Actions' in M Bergström, M Iacovides and M Strand *Harmonisation EU Competition Litigation: The New Directive and Beyond*, Swedish Studies in European Law 8 (Oxford, Hart, 2016) 5.

[3] TFEU, Art 3(1)(b).

[4] TFEU, Art 5(2).

[5] Also referred to as 'judicial autonomy'. See Case C-33/76 *Rewe* EU:C:1976:188; Case C-312/93 *Peterbroeck* EU:C:1995:437, para 12; Case C-13/01 *Safalero* EU:C:2003:447, para 49.

[6] eg Case 199/82 *San Giorgio* EU:C:1983:318, para 12.

This competence constellation, according to which the Union law depends upon the domestic judiciary to give effect to its substantive rights and obligations, has been described as a fundamental principle within the Union.[7]

The *rationale* of national procedural autonomy appears to be the distinction between *substantive* and *procedural* matters. This dichotomy is pivotal in competition law, where the Union has *exclusive* competence to regulate substantive issues.[8] Yet, this distinction is not always clear-cut. The European Court of Justice (ECJ) has developed a substantive EU right to damages, which has not merely impinged on, but even substantially shaped, national procedural law. It has been argued that within this competence allocation, it is for the EU legal order to lay down substantive rights and obligations for its legal subjects, whilst conversely, the determination of rules of liability, procedure and remedies belongs to the national legal orders.[9]

This chapter examines the Directive and the issue of competence allocation between the Union and the Member States, by analysing the degree of comprehensiveness and detail of the Directive as well as future perspectives of full harmonisation on EU level. It is argued that the distinction between minimum and full harmonisation is not particularly helpful. Instead, we suggest an alternative understanding of harmonisation in the area, based on a continuum. This continuum emerges between Union competences on the one side of the spectrum, and national procedural autonomy on the other. This new perspective allows for a better understanding of the current and future functioning of the Directive, and shows that in certain areas, EU competence provides a firmer ground for comprehensive regulation, whilst in other areas, more deference to the Member States' legal orders is necessary. We further argue that such an analysis is useful since the substantive right to damages, recognised by the ECJ, is broader than the provisions of the Directive. Accordingly, the ECJ's case-law will continue to regulate situations that are not covered by the Directive itself.

The first part of this chapter examines the EU right to compensation, and the Directive as a form of minimum harmonisation. The second part then highlights why this characterisation seems problematic, introduces the continuum and explains the rationale for greater or lesser intrusion on the part of the EU. The concluding section finally provides an outlook as to what action could be expected from the EU based on the continuum approach.

[7] D Ashton and D Henry, *Competition Damages Actions in the EU: Law and Practice* (Cheltenham, Edward Elgar, 2013) 8.

[8] TFEU, Art 3(1)(b).

[9] V Milutinovic, The 'Right to Damages' under EU Competition Law: from Courage v Crehan to the White Paper and Beyond, European Monographs 73 (Aphen aan den Rijn, Kluwer, 2010) 306.

## II. THE DIRECTIVE AS MINIMUM HARMONISATION OF THE RIGHT TO DAMAGES

This section will first explore the *acquis communautaire* resulting from the case-law of the ECJ, which the Directive allegedly endorses. It will be shown that the right to damages stems from the effectiveness of EU law, and that the *acquis* reaffirms the principle of national procedural autonomy. Second, it will explain the Directive in the light of the concept of minimum harmonisation.

### A. From Effectiveness to an EU Right to Competition Law Damages

At the heart of the Directive is the right to damages for the breach of EU competition law. An EU right to damages constitutes the linchpin for an efficient private enforcement regime. The EU had not seen until recently any substantial legislation in the field of private enforcement; action took the form of notices, white papers and the like.[10] The decentralisation of EU competition law[11] accentuated the relationship between public and private enforcement.[12] Besides public enforcement, an effective system of private enforcement was deemed necessary; and the latter was to complement rather than hinder the former.[13]

The right to damages in the Directive stems from the direct effect of Union law.[14] Articles 101 and 102 TFEU have long been recognised as directly effective.[15] Here, the effectiveness of judicial protection is essential, and Article 19(1) TFEU requires the Member States to 'provide remedies sufficient to ensure effective legal protection in the fields covered by Union law'.

However, the private enforcement of EU competition law, in the absence of harmonised EU rules, has always been left, in the spirit of national procedural autonomy, to the legal orders of the Member States. Although a right to

[10] I Lianos, P Davis and P Nebbia, *Damages Claims for the Infringement of EU Competition Law* (Oxford, Oxford University Press, 2015) 13–14.

[11] Through Council Regulation (EC) No 1/2003 of 16 December 2002 on the implementation of rules on competition laid down in Articles 81 and 82 of the Treaty [2002] OJ L1/1.

[12] Speech by former Director-General of the Directorate-General for Competition (DG Comp) Alexander Italianer during the 5th International Competition Conference in Brussels 17 February 2012, 'Public and private enforcement of competition law', available at: http://ec.europa.eu/competition/speeches/text/sp2012_02_en.pdf.

[13] ibid. The effectiveness of EU competition needs to be ensured within this twofold framework, see also, European Commission, 'Staff Working Document Impact Assessment Report, Damages actions for breach of the EU antitrust rules Accompanying the proposal for a Directive of the European Parliament and of the Council on certain rules governing actions for damages under national law for infringements of the competition law provisions of the Member States and of the European Union' (SWD/2013/0203 final), para 30.

[14] Milutinovic, The 'Right to Damages' under EU Competition Law (n 9) 47.

[15] Case 127/73 *Belgische Radio en Televisie v SV SBAM and NV Fonior* EU:C:1974:6, para 16. And even direct *horizontal* effect. See Recital 3 of the Damages Directive.

damages for an infringement of an EU right by a Member State has been clearly established since the *Francovich* judgment,[16] the creation of a substantive right to remedies in actions between private parties was more contentious.[17] Moreover, the area is found within a sensible cross-section of judicial competences,[18] and the post-decentralisation regulatory landscape is divided between NCAs and the Commission; national courts and the ECJ; and more generally domestic law and EU law. The lack of legislative and judicial intervention at an EU level ultimately led to a lack of clarity as to the actual rights that Articles 101 and 102 conferred upon individuals, and, consequently, what type of remedies they could perform.[19]

The Court first broke ground in the *Courage* judgment,[20] where it recognised a substantive EU right to damages in competition law cases. The case has been described as 'one of the most remarkable reforms in the five decades of EU competition law enforcement', making damages an important part of the private enforcement regime.[21]

The Court, building upon the *Francovich* principle and the on the direct effect of Articles 101 and 102 TFEU,[22] held that *effectiveness* entails that there cannot be an absolute bar to bringing an action for damages.[23] It is precisely the direct effect and effectiveness that generated this new EU right to compensation.[24] A directly effective right, conferring rights upon individuals which they can invoke before a national court, demands the existence of effective remedies to protect that very right.[25] However, as long as the principles of effectiveness and equivalence are respected, there is nothing preventing national courts from curtailing that right in order to, for instance, protect parties against unjust enrichment via the exercise of Union rights.[26]

After the *Courage* judgment, Regulation 1/2003 proceeded with the 'modernisation' of EU competition law, and the decentralisation of competition enforcement. A first attempt to bring the right to damages into the legislative

[16] Joined Cases C-6/90 and C-9/90 *Francovich* EU:C:1991:428.

[17] Ashton and Henry, Competition Damages Actions in the EU (n 7) 10.

[18] Which gives rise to ancillary question such as subsidiarity; see eg C Petrucci, 'Subsidiarity in Directive 2014/104 EU on Damages Actions for Breach of EU Competition Law' (2017) 23(2) *European Public Law* 395.

[19] A Jones and B Sufrin, *EU Competition Law: Text, Cases, and Materials*, 6th edn (Oxford, Oxford University Press, 2016) 1055.

[20] Case C-453/99 *Courage Ltd v Crehan* EU:C:2001:465.

[21] Lianos, Davis and Nebbia, Damages Claims for the Infringement of EU Competition Law (n 10) 3.

[22] *Courage* (n 20) para 23.

[23] ibid, para 28.

[24] The effectiveness and requirement to protect rights conferred on individuals was emphasised by the Court in Case 26/62 *Van Gend den Loos* EU:C:1963:1.

[25] This argument can be seen in *Courage* (n 20) para 26, and *Francovich* (n 16) paras 31–33.

[26] R Nazzini, *Competition Enforcement and Procedure*, 2nd edn (Oxford, Oxford University Press, 2016) 88. *Courage* (n 20) paras 30–31.

realm came in 2005, when the Commission adopted a Green Paper on damages actions for breach of the EU antitrust rules.[27] The Commission stated that:

> Facilitating damages claims for breach of antitrust law will not only make it easier for consumers and firms who have suffered damages arising from an infringement of antitrust rules to recover their losses from the infringer but also strengthen the enforcement of antitrust law.[28]

The conditions of the right to damages were further developed in the *Manfredi*[29] judgment, where the Court held that:

> It follows that any individual can claim compensation for the harm where there is a causal relationship between that harm and an agreement or practice prohibited under Article [101 TFEU].[30]

The Court recalled that it is the responsibility of the domestic legal systems to designate the competent courts and to lay down the procedures governing such actions.[31] Nonetheless, the Court took an additional step in shaping the interpretation and application of the right to damages. It clarified that for the purposes of EU competition law, actionable loss encompasses both actual loss and loss of profit, plus interest.[32] Further, the right to compensation is not only available to parties to an anticompetitive contract,[33] but also to third parties.[34] The case was followed by a Commission White Paper,[35] which, in contrast to the Green Paper,[36] appears to elevate full compensation as the guiding rationale for a right of damages.[37]

Following *Courage* and *Manfredi*, this right to damages appears to be subject to three cumulative criteria, essentially based on those following those of the state liability case-law:[38] (i) an infringement of Union competition law;[39]

[27] Commission, 'Green Paper on damages actions for breach of the EC antitrust rules' COM (2005) 672 final.

[28] ibid, 3.

[29] Joined Cases C-295/04 to C-298/04 *Manfredi* EU:C:2006:461.

[30] ibid, para 61.

[31] ibid, para 62.

[32] ibid, para 95.

[33] As was the case in *Courage* (n 20).

[34] Petrucci 'Subsidiarity in Directive 2014/104' (n 18) 399.

[35] Commission, 'White Paper on damages actions for breach of the EC antitrust rules' COM (2008) 165 final. The White Paper was accompanied by a Commission, 'Staff working paper accompanying the White Paper on damages actions for breach of the EC antitrust rules' SEC (2008) 404.

[36] Commission, 'Green Paper on Damages actions' (n 27).

[37] Lianos, Davis and Nebbia (n 10) 18, 25; Commission, 'White Paper on Damages Actions' (n 35) 3. Yet, the Court appears to maintain a deterrence rationale. See eg Case C-557/12 *Kone and Others* EU:C:2014:1317, para 23.

[38] See Case C-46/93 *Brasserie du pêcheur (Factortame III)* EU:C:1996:79, para 51.

[39] *Courage* (n 20) para 24.

(ii) a quantifiable loss;[40] and (iii) a causation requirement between the breach of law and the loss suffered.[41]

The content of the right to damages was further elaborated in *Kone*.[42] The Court further extended the reach of the right to damages to cover claims based on the existence of umbrella pricing, although such claims could not be made under national law due to insufficient causal links with the cartel.[43] Once again, the ECJ based its judgment on the full effectiveness of Article 101 TFEU[44] and it appears to be a 'deviation from the general principle of national procedural autonomy'.[45]

## B. The Directive as Minimum Harmonisation

The following paragraphs will explore in what way the Directive is generally seen as minimum harmonisation. In essence, minimum harmonisation is apparent in two respects: the Directive endorses the case-law without precluding the further development thereof, and lays down (mostly) minimum standards to be implemented at the national level.

The current form of the Directive appears to be the result of negotiations and compromises. The Court's case-law, together with the Commission's papers, were followed by a legislative proposal in 2009. Subsequent to political pressure, the proposal was, however, removed from the agenda.[46] After years of renegotiation, the Directive was finally adopted in 2014.

Being the first Directive adopted in the area and given the long negotiations, it appears that the Directive ensures the respect of national procedural autonomy.[47] In principle, it endorses the *acquis*[48] laid down by the case-law and the established principles on liability for infringements of EU law.[49] Yet, the

[40] *Manfredi* (n 29) para 95. Which comprises not only actual loss (*damnum emergens*) but also loss of profit (*lucrum cessans*) plus interest.

[41] In *Manfredi* (n 29) para 61. Although the ECJ provides little guidance as to causality, see to this effect, FG Wilman 'The End of the Absence? The Growing Body of EU Legislation on Private Enforcement and the Main Remedies it Provides for' (2016) 53 *Common Market Law Review* 887, 902.

[42] Kone and Others (n 37).

[43] ibid, paras 30–34.

[44] ibid, para 33.

[45] Lianos, Davis and Nebbia (n 10) 30.

[46] Ashton and Henry (n 7) 4.

[47] See eg N Dunne, 'Courage and Compromise: the Directive on Antitrust Damages' (2015) 40(4) *European Law Review* 581, 592, who points out that 'the Directive is decidedly non-exhaustive in terms of the range of issues covered; for issues outside its scope, national procedural autonomy – and thus divergence – remains the rule'. See also P van Cleynenbreugel, 'Embedding Procedural Autonomy: The Directive and National Procedural Rules' in Bergström, Iacovides and Strand (eds), *Harmonising EU Competition Litigation* (n 2) 99, 116.

[48] Commission 'Staff working paper accompanying the White Paper on damages actions' (n 35); Commission 'White Paper on Damages Actions' (n 35) 3.

[49] Lianos, Davis and Nebbia (n 10) 4.

full effect of the case-law has been hampered by 'procedural and substantive deficiencies at national level that have inhibited the growth of a competition culture within the EU to date'.[50] Thus, the rationale of effectiveness and the right to effective judicial protection is a central ground for the adoption of the Directive.[51] The Directive also mentions effectiveness of enforcement and the need for both effective public and private enforcement.[52] Moreover, Recital 7 of the Directive advances a claim for harmonisation based on the internal market rationale: disparate possibilities of damages claims across the different Member States would lead to uneven enforcement, produce competitive advantages, and would ultimately be detrimental to the internal market.

Minimum harmonisation generally sets out mandatory thresholds, without precluding Member States from affording a stronger protection to the rights concerned. However, the dichotomy of minimum and full harmonisation appears elusive. Weatherill provides an explanation of this distinction as follows:

> A minimum model allows more space and diversity and local autonomy; a maximum model seems to promise greater uniformity in the pattern of regulatory intervention chosen for the internal market. A minimum model preserves to a degree the independence of relevant institutions at State level; the maximum model transfers regulatory responsibility to the EU's legislative institutions – and to its Court too.[53]

Thus, looking at the Directive, it could be expected to set out thresholds and minimum standards thereby achieving minimum harmonisation at the national level.[54] Accordingly, the Member States should remain free to afford a stronger protection to the right to damages.[55] Examining the provisions of the Directive, these paradigms of minimum harmonisation appear to hold true. This can for instance be observed with regard to limitation periods. The Directive imposes a minimum period of five years[56] but the Member States remain free to set longer periods. Other provisions also provide respect for national variations, and therefore autonomy. Article 5(8) leaves it open to the Member States to maintain in force or enact new rules mandating a greater disclosure of evidence than the minimum standards set by the Directive.

Thus, it is not surprising that the Directive is seen as minimum harmonisation, by merely setting minimum procedural standards in a limited number of

[50] Dunne, 'Courage and Compromise: the Directive on Antitrust Damages' (n 47) 582. See also Green Paper on Damages Actions (n 27). See also Commission, 'White Paper on Damages Actions' (n 35).

[51] Damages Directive, Recital 4.

[52] ibid, Recital 5.

[53] S Weatherill, 'Maximum versus Minimum Harmonization: Choosing between Unity and Diversity in the Search for the Soul of the Internal Market' in NN Shuibhne and LW Gormley (eds), *From a Single Market to Economic Union: Essays in Memory on John A. Usher* (Oxford, Oxford University Press, 2012) 176.

[54] As is argued by Dunne (n 47) 601.

[55] Nazzini, Competition Enforcement and Procedure (n 26) 239.

[56] Damages Directive, Art 10.

areas. Moreover, the Directive expressly reaffirms the principles of effectiveness and equivalence,[57] as a testimonial of a respect for national procedural autonomy. However, as will be examined, in certain areas the Directive appears to go beyond minimum harmonisation, to impose far more comprehensive rules.

## III. THE MEMBER STATES' COMPETENCE CONTINUUM

This section first highlights issues that do not fit the concept of minimum harmonisation. Subsequently, it introduces the idea of a continuum between the EU's and Member States' competences, and applies this approach to the right to damages. Finally, we apply the continuum to questions concerning damages for the breach of EU competition law within and outside the immediate scope of the Directive.

### A. Problems in Qualifying the Directive as Minimum Harmonisation

Even if the Directive reaffirms the *acquis* without pre-empting any further developments thereof,[58] this regulatory intervention in national procedural law raises questions. Admittedly, certain key issues, such as rules on causation, costs or conflict of laws, discussed in the Commission's Green Paper, have been excluded from the Directive.[59] Nevertheless, the fact that the Directive is non-exhaustive in terms of the scope of the issues covered, does not mean that it corresponds with the concept of minimum harmonisation adequately nor that it is in line with national procedural autonomy. In fact, the issues governed by the Directive are often prescribed in far more detail than the mere setting of minimum thresholds.

Here, Article 288(3) TFEU and the nature of the Directive as a legal act is relevant. That Article stipulates that a Directive[60] is binding *only* as to the result to be achieved;[61] however, it leaves the Member States *free to determine the means* by which that result is to be achieved. Additionally, in the case of minimum harmonisation, Member States should also be free to determine the desired level of protection, provided that the minimum threshold is met. Bearing these limitations in mind, two main points can be advanced to potentially contest the qualification of the Directive as a minimum harmonisation.

First, minimum harmonisation appears *insufficient* in order to ensure a level playing field, and the effectiveness of damages actions.[62] The internal

[57] ibid, Art 4.
[58] ibid, Recital 12.
[59] Dunne (n 47) 583.
[60] In contrast to a Regulation which is binding in its entirety.
[61] In the case of minimum harmonisation, a threshold.
[62] See Damages Directive, Recital 8.

market rationale demands, for instance, that the limitation period (Article 10) is governed by a uniform set of standards throughout the Union. Only uniform standards can ensure that there are no substantial disparities as to the possibility to bring a claim for antitrust damages in the different Member States.[63] This type of 'uniform harmonisation'[64] of procedural conditions of a substantive right does not fit well within the meaning of minimum harmonisation.

In the spirit of uniformity Article 1(1) provides that the Directive ensures 'equivalent protection throughout the Union for anyone who has suffered [harm from an infringement of the antitrust provisions]'. This Article highlights the tension between equivalent protection – which demands a certain degree of uniformity – and minimum harmonisation – which demands respect for national regulatory diversity.[65] Accordingly, the imperative of removing national procedural discrepancies leads to a Directive which appears to go beyond what could be described as minimum harmonisation. Equivalent protection[66] does not fit well with the concept of minimum harmonisation. There are only a limited number of ways in which the desired result of equivalent protection can be achieved. In other words, full compensation and the establishment of a level playing field might require full harmonisation in certain matters. The Directive provides numerous examples of such detailed rules which limit national procedural autonomy to such an extent that it appears non-existent in certain areas.[67]

Second, it seems difficult to use minimum harmonisation by means of a Directive with regard to a substantive right, as the distinction between procedural and substantive issues may be delicate to draw. The controversy is attached to the difficulty of clearly distinguishing between rights and remedies.[68] If a right refers to the legal position of a legal subject, a remedy ensures enforcement of that right through an action before a court of law.[69] A connection between rights and remedies can be seen as inherent in the existence of a *directly effective* right itself.[70] The 'effectiveness approach' thus demands a substantive right to damages.[71] Union law lays down rights and obligations for private parties, which

[63] Art 10(2) and (3) thus lays down rather detailed conditions governing when the limitation period begins to run, and circumstances under which it is interrupted or suspended.

[64] This term is here used to design quasi-uniform rules. On the distinction between uniformity and maximum harmonisation, see eg A de Vries, 'The Aim for Complete Uniformity in EU Private Law: An Obstacle to Further Harmonization' (2012) 4 *European Review of Private Law* 913, 926.

[65] Art 1(1) bases the rule of equivalent protection on the requirement of undistorted competition and removing obstacles to the proper functioning of the internal market.

[66] In other words, effectiveness and uniformity.

[67] Which will be further examined in the subsequent section.

[68] eg Ashton and Henry (n 7) 11. See also W Van Gerven, 'Of Rights Remedies and Procedures' (2000) 37 *Common Market Law Review* 501, 502.

[69] For a similar interpretation, see Van Gerven, 'Of Rights Remedies and Procedures' (n 68) 502. Although Van Gerven points out that a general distinction is impossible to make.

[70] ibid, 13.

[71] For similar views, see Lianos, Davis and Nebbia (n 10); Milutinovic (n 9) 75.

subsequently must be effectively protected at the national level.[72] Whenever a right or an obligation is created, a 'right to enforce' must also arise, ie 'an effective means for the injured party to enforce compliance with the behaviour required'.[73] Thus, remedies are a necessary consequence of the creation of rights or obligations, without which a right would have no effective legal existence.[74] The division of competences between the Union and the Member States illustrates this difficulty. The EU provides for a right and for ensuring its effective enforcement, while the *national procedural provisions* applicable to that right should be left within the national competence.

Thus, the question of minimum or full harmonisation should rather be understood as a *matter of degree*. The dichotomy between full and minimum harmonisation remains elusive. In particular, the scope for national authorities under the Directive appears surprisingly narrow. This seems to follow from the idea that the harmonisation of a substantive right to remedies necessarily demands a certain degree of uniformity.[75] Therefore, to understand the competence allocation between the Union and the Member States, we suggest abandoning this dichotomy in favour of a continuum approach.

### B. A Continuum Approach

In the following section we develop the idea of a continuum. This continuum is based on the division of competences between the EU and the Member States and aims to explain harmonisation attempts concerning the EU right to antitrust damages. One end of the continuum is marked by the Court's declaration of EU competence in establishing the EU right to damages, and the other end by the Member States' competence in the form of national procedural autonomy.

#### *i. An EU Substantive Right to Damages*

As explained above, the ECJ in *Courage*,[76] based on its judgments in *Francovich*[77] and *Brasserie du Pêcheur*,[78] and on the idea of effectiveness,[79] established this EU right to antitrust damages. While the Court's rulings might be problematic in terms of the initial establishment of the general right to damages for the breach of EU law,[80] *Courage* seems to be a mere extension of the earlier case-law

[72] *Van Gend en Loos* (n 24) para 5.

[73] Ashton and Henry (n 7) 14.

[74] eg ibid, 11.

[75] Uniformity seen as corollary to effectiveness in a pluralistic legal order.

[76] *Courage* (n 20).

[77] *Francovich* (n 16).

[78] *Brasserie du pêcheur (Factortame III)* (n 38).

[79] *Courage* (n 20) para 28.

[80] On the usurpation of competence via *Francovich* (n 16), see eg C Harlow, 'Francovich and the Problem of the Disobedient State' (1996) 2(3) *European Law Journal* 199.

to the area of competition law, an area of exclusive EU competence. With the Directive, this competence and the EU right to antitrust damages is thus recognised by the EU legislature, and with it the Member States too.

Four lines of arguments beyond effectiveness can be advanced in support of the EU's detailed involvement in protecting the right to damages. First, as already mentioned, according to Article 3(3) TFEU, the EU has exclusive competence to protect competition within the internal market. Second, this competence does not need to be interpreted narrowly. As witnessed in the area of environmental crimes, the EU's competence for the protection of the environment also includes the competence to impose criminal sanctions;[81] the same argument has been advanced within the field of criminal procedures generally.[82] If the EU's shared competence in the area of environmental protection includes criminal sanctions, the inclusion of civil compensation in the area of competition, which is an exclusive competence, seems even more justified. Third, the Directive is based on Article 103 and 114 TFEU. This legal basis entailed greater power for the Council, and therefore the Member States, in the adoption of the Directive. Moreover, the dual legal basis means that the Directive has a double nature where the harmonisation addresses divergences and thereby improves the functioning of the internal market which in turn improves competition enforcement by means of increased deterrence.[83] Finally, a common route to justify detailed EU rules relates to the EU Charter of Fundamental Rights. Where EU law, for example, in the form of a Directive, occupies parts of the area, effective judicial protection as protected by Article 47 of the Charter provides for another route to justify EU competence and detailed involvement in the establishment of the right to EU antitrust damages.[84]

### *ii. National Procedural Autonomy as an Expression of Member State Competence*

National procedural autonomy requires that in the absence of Union legislation, it is national law that lays down procedural rules for the protection of the rights of individuals stemming from directly applicable EU law.[85] This autonomy is qualified by the principles of equivalence and effectiveness.[86] A national procedural autonomy 'focus', affirmed by the Court in its case-law, thus leaves the enforcement of EU law within national rules to the Member States.[87]

[81] See Case C-176/03 *Commission v Council* EU:C:2005:542; C-440/05 *Commission v Council* EU:C:2007:625.

[82] Van Gerven (n 68) 501.

[83] For such an argument in the context of public health and the internal market, see Case C-547/14 *Philip Morris Brands and Others* EU:C:2016:325.

[84] See eg Case C-239/14 *Tal* EU:C:2015:824.

[85] See n 5.

[86] eg *Kone and Others* (n 37) para 30.

[87] Yet, it also empowers the ECJ to impose negative or positive obligations upon national legal orders' see Cleynenbreugel, 'Embedding Procedural Autonomy: The Directive and National Procedural Rules' (n 47) 99–119.

Nevertheless, it is generally difficult to determine where procedural autonomy stops and where the principle of effectiveness and uniform application of EU law prevails.[88] Although the notion of national procedural autonomy is controversial,[89] it is commonly accepted that the national legal context in which EU law is inserted and enforced 'is a matter of the Member States' autonomy'.[90] However, that autonomy is not absolute, and even perhaps 'non-justiciable as a division of competences'.[91] Nonetheless, it is submitted that a certain ideal of national procedural autonomy is generally recognised.[92] However, as can be observed within the field of antitrust damages, the ECJ and the EU legislator have increasingly moved away from defining the substantive right to enter the realm of procedures. Accordingly, although national procedural autonomy only exists in the absence of harmonised EU law, this does not necessarily mean that that autonomy should be completely reduced[93] – even more so in the case of minimum harmonisation.

### *iii. The Continuum*

With the EU's competence on the one side, it is the principle of national procedural autonomy that constitutes its other side. With these two poles of competence established, the following picture emerges. The EU has general competence over the substantive right to compensation for the breach of EU competition law. It could be expected that this competence includes the elements of *who* can receive *what* from *whom* under which *conditions*. In contrast, the Member States have the competence to determine how compensation could be obtained once the conditions of the right are fulfilled. They can, for example, decide whether damages are to be claimed by means of a judicial process or whether the competition authority can directly issue a compensation order as part of its decision. Similarly, Member States should in principle decide what rules of procedure, and in particular, what rules of evidence apply in such cases.

However, the contours of the competence just described only serve as a starting point of the continuum and they are not clear-cut. Bearing in mind the

[88] IS Forrester, 'The Role of the CJEU in Interpreting Directive 2014/104/EU on Antitrust Damages Actions' (2017) ERA Forum, docs no, 67, 76.

[89] To the point that some authors deny its existence; see to this effect, CN Kakouris 'Do the Member States Possess Judicial Procedural "Autonomy"?' (1997) 34 *Common Market Law Review* 1389.

[90] S Prechal 'Community Law in National Courts: The Lessons from Van Schijndel' (1998) 35 *Common Market Law Review* 681, 682.

[91] Milutinovic (n 9) 310.

[92] Which Art 4 appears to make clear. Dunne (n 47) 583, sees it at the basis for the Directive alongside the right to full compensation for losses arising from breach of EU competition law.

[93] In this respect, Nazzini (n 26) 239, points out that that is not the case. See also, Cleynenbreugel (n 48) 109: 'the positive obligations imposed do not – and cannot – deviate from the key features offered by a "national procedural autonomy" focus'.

tension between *effectiveness* and *national procedural autonomy*,[94] the blurred nature becomes evident. On the one hand, the procedural autonomy is limited by the requirement that national procedures need to ensure effectiveness and equivalence, which is clearly stipulated in Article 4 of the Directive. On the other hand, the EU's competence concerning the substantive right is also not always clear. In particular, it is not always easy to identify whether issues fall within the scope of the right, that is to say whether the issue is part of the *who* can receive *what* from *whom* under which *conditions*. For example, the statute of limitations, seems to be rather difficult to fit within this category. While it has a clear relation to the substantive right to compensation, questions concerning limitations can equally be related to procedural limitations as these rules establish how long a claim can be brought to court. Thus, it appears that procedural elements which could be said to be *intrinsically linked* to the effectiveness of the substantive right does not fit well with the idea of minimum harmonisation and national procedural autonomy. This difficulty of drawing a line between the substantive and procedural relates back to the difficult relationship between rights and remedies.[95] If rights and remedies are themselves linked, the existence of an EU right seems to lead to the conclusion that rather comprehensive harmonisation of the very conditions of the exercising of the right is necessary and justifiable. These core procedural elements demand a more comprehensive harmonisation and a more uniform application.

However, such an interpretation would completely negate the idea of national procedural autonomy. Thus, it is within this uneasy distinction between the right and questions intrinsically linked to the right, and national procedural autonomy that the Directive is operating. We submit that it might therefore be beneficial to think about the provisions of the Directive as being part of the continuum between the EU's competences to determine the contours of the right and the national procedural autonomy.

### C. Applying the Continuum

This continuum is mirrored both in the case-law of the Court and in the Directive itself. A sliding scale thus emerges: the closer the issue regulated is related to the EU right to damages itself, the more detailed the prescriptions are; sometimes leaving no room for national variation. In contrast, the closer the issue regulated is to national procedural autonomy, the more room is left for the Member States in the implementation.

The *nucleus* of the substantive EU right to remedies is found in Article 3 of the Directive which lays down a right to full compensation. Looking back

[94] As discussed in the previous section.
[95] See n 68.

at the *Manfredi* judgment,[96] the core of the right to compensation is set out in an especially detailed fashion, which entails compensation for actual loss and the loss of profit plus interest. The right to compensation was subsequently incorporated into Article 3(2) of the Directive, which sets the premises for calculation of the loss, and the type of loss that should be compensated, whilst the third paragraph prohibits any kind of overcompensation. This right was later further elaborated in *Kone and Others*.[97] On the one hand, the judgment highlights national procedural autonomy which in the absence of EU legislation would only be limited by the requirements of equivalence and effectiveness.[98] On the other hand, it is prescriptive and detailed concerning what follows from the requirement of effectiveness. First, the Court finds that effectiveness requires that losses made due to umbrella pricing should be covered because cartel members could have foreseen such effects.[99] Second, the Court not only holds that national rules preventing umbrella pricing would hinder effectiveness,[100] but goes further and sets out the details of a causation test to be applied in such cases.[101] While these are detailed rules regarding the substance of the right to damages as developed by the Court, such detailed rules regarding the substance of the right can also be found in the Damages Directive.[102]

The Directive is very detailed with regard to scope and content of the right, that is to say the *who* can receive *what* from *whom* under which *conditions*. Concerning the persons able to claim damages, Articles 12 to 15 set out in detail the conditions under which indirect purchasers and claimants from different levels in the supply chain are entitled to claim damages. In this regard, the Directive even ventures into areas that would usually be seen as part of procedural autonomy by setting out detailed rules with regard to the burden of proof.[103] These detailed prescriptions may seem necessary to ensure that the core of the right, ie the question of *who* can claim damages, is not undermined by national procedural rules. The difficulty in obtaining compensation for indirect purchasers and other claimants from different levels of the supply chain emerges in two aspects. First, there is the question of whether such cartel victims are, in principle, allowed to bring a claim before a national court. Second, and possibly more importantly, of whether such victims will encounter difficulties in proving loss due to the indirect nature of their relationship with the cartel members.

[96] *Manfredi* (n 29).

[97] Kone and Others (n 37).

[98] ibid, para 30.

[99] ibid, para 30.

[100] ibid, para 33.

[101] ibid, para 34, explaining that in the market circumstances the cartel was 'liable to have the effect of umbrella pricing being applied by third parties' and those market circumstances 'could not have be ignored by cartelists'.

[102] See eg Damages Directive, Arts 3, 13, 14.

[103] See eg ibid, Arts 13, 14(1), 17(1).

Comprehensive prescriptions also exist concerning the question from *whom* damages can be claimed. Article 11 sets out, in detail, the issue of joint and several liability, covering areas such as immunity and small and medium-sized enterprises. Finally, precise rules can also be observed regarding the actual damages that need to be compensated, in other word the *how much*. The Damages Directive, beyond setting a pure minimum standard, prohibits overcompensation and punitive damages in Article 3(3). Such comprehensive prescriptions are closer to full harmonisation than to minimum harmonisation. This level of detail can be explained by the fact that the compensation level relates to the core of the right to compensation, the *what*. The same applies to Article 13 which also addresses the level of compensation by regulating in great detail the passing-on defence.

Beyond the core of the right to compensation, the Directive makes further inroads towards national procedural autonomy in two other areas. First, Article 15 requires the taking into account of other damages proceedings concerning the competition law infringement. This requirement, while clearly related to procedure, also has a connection to the right as such. This coordination requirement has direct consequences on the amount of obtainable compensation. Only coordination between different proceedings can ensure the absence of over- or under-compensation. The second area that the Directive regulates is the area which is found between the substantive right and national procedural autonomy. This area includes limitation periods, presumptions and the estimation of harm. Some deference is notable in this area. Article 10 uses the minimum harmonisation approach by setting a minimum limitation period of five years and thus leaving the Member States room for regulatory preferences. Yet, the national margin is limited in as much as the Article regulates both the beginning and the suspension of this period. In fact, the five years set as a minimum will quite likely be a form of full harmonisation, as nearly all Member States have chosen that period.[104] The same deference by means of setting a minimum can be observed in Article 17. This Article limits the national procedural autonomy by introducing a presumption of harm and the requirement that an estimation of harm must be allowed. Both of these requirements aim at the core of safeguarding the amount of compensation available to victims of competition law infringements. Yet, the details are left to national procedural law while addressing national procedures.

## IV. CONCLUSIONS AND OUTLOOK

In this chapter it has been argued that the concept of minimum harmonisation is insufficient to explain the modus operandi of the Damages Directive,

[104] See eg Baker and McKenzie 'A Multi-jurisdictional Survey on the Implementation of the EU Antitrust Damages Directive (2014/104/EU)' (Jun 2017), available at: www.bakermckenzie.com/en/insight/publications/2017/06/a-multijurisdictional-survey/.

as the Directive goes beyond minimum harmonisation. Therefore, a continuum approach has been suggested. This continuum exists between Union and national competences and should not merely be understood as a tool gradually blurring the division of competences between the EU and the Member States, but as an interpretative tool to understand the expanding involvement of the EU in national procedural law. Issues intrinsically linked to a right – and thus the one side of the continuum – are more likely to be subject to comprehensive harmonisation, whilst deference can be expected for procedural issues only remotely connected to the right to claim damages itself. It has further been argued that this continuum approach, which generally delineates the competence between the EU and Member States, can also be applied to matters within scope of the Directive. The continuum approach facilitates the understanding of the functioning of the Directive and provides a justification for closer EU involvement in procedural matters.

It is to be expected that this trend of increased EU involvement will only be reinforced in the future. In this respect, it can be assumed that the increasing imposition of general procedural obligations on the Member States paves the way for a more comprehensive harmonisation of national procedural law.[105] Article 20 contains a review clause, requiring the Commission to establish a report of the functioning of the Directive by the end of 2020. Although that Article limits the issues that the Commission is required to review, it is likely that further discrepancies and national hurdles could lead to a new legislative proposal further harmonising the area. In this respect, the continuum also provides a tool to examine the future harmonisation of issues, such as, fault, causation and interest which seem to be very closely linked to the EU right to antitrust damages. Consequently, issues that are outside the scope of the Directive, but attached to the broader substantive right to damages, may well be subject to future EU harmonisation.

Another important issue will be the interpretation of the Directive by the ECJ. The Court is likely to intervene with closer scrutiny into the national legal orders of the Member States. The Court could equally be expected to engage fully with questions linked closely to the substantive right, such as fault, causation and interest. Moreover, as argued in this chapter, harmonisation entails the applicability of the Charter. Consequently, and again, procedural issues not covered by the Directive could be scrutinised by the ECJ.[106] Here, it is likely that effective judicial protection might play a key role in the Court's future case-law.[107]

[105] Cleynenbreugel (n 47) 99.
[106] See Case C-617/10 *Åkerberg Fransson* EU:C:2013:105, para 21.
[107] Cleynenbreugel (n 47) 117.

# 2

# *The State of Private Enforcement of Competition Law: A Practitioner's Perspective*

ULRICH CLASSEN AND MARTIN SEEGERS*

## I. INTRODUCTION

THE RIGHT TO compensation for damages resulting from the infringement of European and/or national competition law is currently being put into practice, albeit slowly. More than 15 years after the European Court of Justice (ECJ) confirmed in its judgments *Courage* and *Manfredi* that any person may claim compensation for the harm caused by an infringement of European competition law, actions for damages are today a reality in Europe. We see an increasing number of cross-border damages actions against cartel members in many (EU) Member States. The judiciary, claimants, plaintiffs and the lawyers involved are discovering a new era. Many cases involve complex and novel legal questions. Furthermore, economic issues in the context of quantifying harm, the question of how to best select and transform concepts of economic theory into real life, are of paramount importance. From the very beginning, the decision of damaged companies whether to assess and pursue claims resulting from antitrust infringements is closely connected to the prospects of a successful outcome. The likelihood of an investment in effort, manpower, financial resources for lawyers, economists and court fees, combined with adverse cost risks associated with a potential legal action, depends not only on the question of calculating damages. For a cartel victim, justice is not an abstract or merely academic concept. At the end of the day, it all comes down to the question of whether the associated efforts and costs will be justified by the likely realised awards.

*Dr Ulrich Classen is Director and Dr Martin Seegers Legal Counsel at CDC Cartel Damage Claims Consulting SCRL, Brussels. The views expressed by the authors are strictly personal, based on publicly available information, and do not engage the entity they served, serve or might serve in the future.

However, answering this question and finding solutions is not straightforward, especially in view of Europe-wide infringements with cartel members domiciled and/or active in multiple countries and damages suffered by victims in many different jurisdictions. Follow-on damages actions, for example, have been brought against participants of the Europe-wide cartels in *Air Cargo*, *Hydrogen Peroxide*, *Sodium Chlorate*, *Paraffin Wax* and *Trucks*. All of them relate to infringements committed prior to the adoption of EU Directive 2014/104/EU on damages actions for infringements of competition law of the Members States and of the European Union (Damages Directive)[1] by the Member States. These cases, as well as further legal actions that have been filed, mostly in the Netherlands, Germany, Austria and the United Kingdom, have often been regarded as a first source of guidance. The same, however, holds true for cartel-related damages actions that have been brought in the meantime before the courts in, for example, Finland, Italy, Belgium, Spain, Portugal and France.

The European Commission assumes that business and consumer victims forgo up to an estimated EUR 23 billion in compensation every year.[2] In the period from 2006 to 2012, no damages actions following Commission decisions were reported in more than two-thirds of the Member States.[3]

The Damages Directive reaffirms the *acquis communautaire* as established by the ECJ and introduces a minimum standard of rules to facilitate antitrust damages actions. Even before its transposition, courts in some Member States referred to it when interpreting national laws. While the Damages Directive has optimistically been regarded as a milestone, it should rather be seen as a first but important step of a long journey. It rests with the Member States' legal systems, especially their procedural framework and the court realities in these jurisdictions, to put the idea of full compensation into practice. In the meantime, first experiences gained under the new regime give rise to concern that perhaps the Damages Directive has not only solved but also increased the complexity of the private enforcement of competition law.

## II. DAMAGE QUANTIFICATION AND INTEREST

The quantification and proof of damages caused by an infringement is a key challenge in cartel damages actions. In fact, the assessment of the value of a (potential) case is already a decisive factor for the pre-trial decision whether to pursue damages claims at all.

[1] Directive 2014/104/EU of the European Parliament and of the Council of 26 November 2014 on certain rules governing actions for damages under national law for infringements of the competition law provisions of the Member States and of the European Union [2014] OJ L349/1.

[2] Commission, Competition Policy Brief 2015-1, p. 2, available at: http://ec.europa.eu/competition/publications/cpb/2015/001_en.pdf.

[3] Commission, Competition Policy Brief 2015-1 (n 2).

Pursuant to Articles 1(1) and 3(2) of the Damages Directive, cartel victims have 'the right to claim full compensation for that harm', which includes the right to compensation for actual loss and for loss of profit, plus the payment of interest.[4] In this context, cartel members are, at least as a rule (Article 11(6) Damages Directive), also liable for so-called umbrella damages, namely damages resulting from the fact that non-cartel members active in the same market under the 'umbrella' of the cartel and its market-wide price effects have set their prices higher than would have been possible under competitive conditions.[5] The Damages Directive itself does not address the complex issues relating to the quantification of damages.[6] Instead, Article 17 stipulates a rebuttable presumption that cartels cause harm and empowers national courts to estimate the amount of the harm according to national procedural law. While the statutory laws of most of the Member States so far do not include a presumption,[7] some courts have assumed prima facie that at least long-lasting cartels have led to inflated prices. In addition, several national courts have assumed prima facie that a cartel has actually had an effect on any purchase of cartelised products during the cartel period within its geographic scope. The presumption reflects economic realities. Empirical studies suggest that more than 90 per cent of cartels artificially increase prices.[8] Cartel members may rebut the presumption by showing that their infringement had no effect on the given market or claimant.

Notwithstanding such presumption, plaintiffs have to submit to the court evidence regarding the specific amount of the damage sought. The procedural requirements for establishing the basis of the court's estimation of the damage are still far from clear. In any event, Article 17(1) of the Damages Directive stipulates that 'neither the burden nor the standard of proof required for the quantification' of damages shall render the exercise of the right to full compensation practically impossible or excessively difficult. UK courts already adopt a rather pragmatic approach to the assessment of damages in competition cases. They recognise that the quantification of damages often needs to be accomplished 'by the exercise of a sound imagination and the practice of the broad axe'.[9]

[4] See Damages Directive, Recital 12; Joined Cases C-295/04 to C-298/04 *Manfredi* EU:C:2006:461, para 95.

[5] See also Case C-557/12 *Kone AG and Others v ÖBB-Infrastruktur AG* EU:C:2014:1317.

[6] But see on this Commission, 'Quantifying harm in actions for damages based on breaches of article 101 or 102 of the Treaty on the Functioning of the European Union' SWD(2013) 205; Communication on quantifying harm in actions for antitrust damages, [2013] OJ C 167/19.

[7] A rare example is contained in § 88/C Hungarian Competition Act with a rebuttable presumption that hardcore cartels result in a price increase of 10%, see István Nagy, WuW 2010, p 902.

[8] Oxera, 'Quantifying Antitrust Damages' (2009), study prepared for the Commission, 91, available at: http://ec.europa.eu/competition/antitrust/actionsdamages/quantification_study.pdf.

[9] England and Wales Court of Appeal, *Devenish Nutrition Ltd v Sanofi-Aventis SA (France) & Ors* [2008] EWCA Civ 1086 at para 13, quoting the judgment in *Watson Laidlaw & Co Ltd v Pott, Cassells and Williamson* (1914) 31 RPC 104 at 117–18 (per Lord Shaw).

The quantification of cartel damages is complex, particularly in cases with cross-border elements, for example, purchases of cartelised products in several Member States. It requires specific expertise in economics, and it regularly builds upon a large set of data and information regarding the victims' purchases of the product and the affected market in general. Article 3(2) of the Damages Directive stipulates that full compensation shall place a person who has suffered harm caused by an infringement of competition law in the position in which that person would have been without the infringement. The calculation of the scenario but for a cartel, the so-called but-for scenario, leads to the hypothetical market price of the cartelised product. As a further step, the price difference due to the infringement is multiplied by the quantity purchased in the relevant period, which results in the total net price overcharge. However, in the event of hardcore cartels, the damage usually consists of two parts. Such cartels do not only have a direct price effect, but regularly also a volume effect, caused by a reduction in production or sales output due to higher prices charged by the victim downstream to its own customers.

A major obstacle for the quantification of cartel damages is that claimants are generally disadvantaged vis-à-vis infringers in terms of access to relevant information and data. The main reasons are (i) an existing information asymmetry due to the secret nature of the cartel and infringement; and (ii) the limited and inadequate information contained in non-confidential cartel decisions by the Commission or national competition authorities. While cartels typically have market-wide effects, a potential claimant is usually not in possession of aggregated market-wide data. The availability and securing of evidence to prove damages is difficult notably in the case of long-lasting cartels. The lapse of years is regularly accompanied by a deterioration of evidence, limited availability of electronic data and changes in accounting systems. In addition, the statutory obligation to retain documents and records under commercial or tax law is limited, and it varies across Europe. For example, the obligation to retain company records in Germany and Italy is ten years while in the Netherlands and Sweden it is seven years. Therefore, disclosure orders vis-à-vis cartel members might often fall short due to the lapse of time.

Cartel effects can often be best demonstrated through a so-called 'before-during-after analysis'. In this context, not only the individual victim's procurement data will be relevant. To correctly assess and account for the influence of non-cartel related factors on the pricing of goods, and to distinguish such factors from cartel effects, data from other victims of the cartel are also helpful. Even cartel members might often not know everything about the real world, ie the pricing details of their co-infringers vis-à-vis their customers. Cheating among cartelists is considered as a destabilising factor and might offer an insight into the overall effects of a cartel. The Damages Directive has identified the information asymmetry and requests that the Member States introduce rules for the provision of required information *inter partes* and even from third parties (see under section IV). Striking the right balance

between justified information requests and an undue delay of proceedings is of utmost importance.

A further important factor from a practical viewpoint is interest. Although it has long been recognised as part of the cartel members' obligation to fully compensate for the damage resulting from competition law infringements, judgments containing information about the calculation of interest are scarce. Pursuant to Article 3 of the Damages Directive and the ECJ, interest shall be due from the time when the damage occurred until the time when compensation is paid.[10] In the case of long-lasting cartels, interest might lead to a very substantive increase, even to a multiplication of the damages awarded. EU law does neither distinguish between compensatory or default interest nor further specifies and describes how to calculate interest with the Member States following the principle of effectiveness and adequacy. In cross-border follow-on cases, multiple national interest regimes often need to be considered in parallel, depending on where the damage occurred. The calculation of interest on antitrust damages is complex, as changes in the applicable interest regimes may have taken place during the relevant time. A recent study by the European University Institute (EUI)[11] offers a useful overview of interest regimes in certain European jurisdictions and how they are applied in antitrust cases.

## III. PASSING-ON DEFENCE AND INDIRECT PURCHASERS

Articles 12 to 15 of the Damages Directive set forth the legal consequences of the situation where direct purchasers of an infringer fully or partly forward the price overcharge they had to pay due to the infringement by increasing the prices they charge to their own customers ('indirect purchasers'). Firstly, it recognises the passing-on defence under which, for example, a cartel member argues that the direct purchaser sustained no or reduced damage because he passed on the overcharge. Secondly, it recognises the standing of indirect customers to bring damages actions against the infringers. While the burden of proof regarding the passing-on defence shall rest on the infringers (Article 13), indirect customers shall enjoy a rebuttable presumption of pass-on (Article 14(2)).

With regard to indirect purchaser claims, the Damages Directive might require major changes to the existing laws of the Members States. While their standing has already been acknowledged by the ECJ,[12] national laws did not – but often do now – stipulate a presumption of pass-on to their benefit. In the past, indirect purchasers in own actions for damages against cartel members

[10] *Manfredi* (n 4) para 97, with reference to Case C-271/91 *Marshall* EU:C:1993:335.

[11] G Monti (ed), 'EU Law and Interest on Damages for Infringements of Competition Law: A Comparative Report', Florence, EUI Working Paper Law 2016/11.

[12] Case C-453/99 *Courage v Crehan* EU:C:2001:6297, para 26.

had to substantiate and prove that, and the extent to which, a pass-on of overcharges took place from direct purchasers to their market level. However, it is unclear how and to what extent defendants in the future will rebut the new presumption of pass-on. They will have to demonstrate to the satisfaction of the court that the overcharge was not, or not entirely, passed on to the indirect purchaser plaintiff.

In contrast, it corresponds to the law of most of the Member States, that in actions of direct purchasers, the defendant bears the burden of proof when relying on the passing-on defence. However, the Damages Directive leaves the conditions for the passing-on defence to the Member States' legal orders and their procedural autonomy respectively.[13] According to Article 13 of the Damages Directive, the Members States have to ensure that defendants can invoke the defence, for whose application Article 12 contains guiding principles. Article 12 states that not only should a plaintiff's overcompensation be avoided, but also the 'absence of liability of the infringer'.

Recent case-law of the highest courts in several Member States, notably Germany, the Netherlands and the UK, indicates a common understanding of the passing-on defence and its conditions. Firstly, the defendant, in addition to the pass-on itself, has to show an adequate causal link between the infringement and the increase in prices charged to the indirect customers. Similar to the German Federal Court of Justice in its *ORWI* judgment of 28 June 2011, allowing the passing-on defence under the principles of the setting-off of benefits ('*Vorteilsausgleich*'),[14] the Supreme Court of the Netherlands in its judgment of 8 July 2016 in the case *TenneT v ABB*[15] held that under the passing-on defence, the only benefits that can be taken into account, are those that were adequately caused by the cartel. Equally, the UK Competition Appeal Tribunal (CAT) in its judgment of 14 July 2016 in *Sainsbury's v Mastercard* required a sufficient causal link between the price increase towards indirect customers and the infringement. The CAT notably made a distinction between the economic and the legal concept of pass-on:

> First, whereas an economist might well define pass-on more widely (i.e. to include cost savings and reduced expenditure), the pass-on defence is only concerned with identifiable increases in prices by a firm to its customers. Secondly, the increase in price must be causally connected with the overcharge, and demonstrably so.[16]

[13] See on the Member States' procedural autonomy when implementing Directives, TFEU, Art 288; Damages Directive, Recital 11; Case C-530/11 *Commission v UK* EU:C:2014:67, para 46; Case C-601/15 *J. N. v Staatssecretaris van Veiligheid en Justitie* EU:C:2016:84, para 60; Case C-260/11 *Edwards und Pallikaropoulos* EU:C:2013:221, para 37; Case C-421/12 *Commission v Belgium*, EU:C:2014:2064, para 46.

[14] Bundesgerichtshof, KZR 75/10, BGHZ 190, 145 – *ORWI*, allowing the passing-on defence under the principles of the setting-off of benefits ('*Vorteilsausgleich*').

[15] Hoge Raad, ECLI:NL:HR:2016:1483 – *TenneT v ABB*, No 4.3.1 to 4.4.5.; followed by Rechtbank Gelderland, judgment of 29 March 2017, C/05/244194/HA ZA 13-373, No 4.13. to 4.22.

[16] CAT, [2016] CAT 11, Ref. 1241/5/7/15, para 484(4)(ii) – *Sainsbury's v Mastercard*.

Secondly, the application of the passing-on defence shall not lead to an undue relief of the infringer, namely an absence of liability. According to the *ORWI* case-law of the German Federal Court of Justice, benefits received from indirect purchasers can only be taken into account provided that this offsetting is in line with the purpose of the damages claim and the infringers' liability for the antitrust infringement, namely which 'do not unduly relief the infringers'[17] from liability. Likewise, the Supreme Court of the Netherlands in *TenneT*, states that the passing-on defence can only succeed where the setting-off of benefits in the case at hand is 'appropriate'.[18] The CAT in *Sainsbury's* explicitly requires of defendants, while referring to the Damages Directive, that they show the existence also of claiming indirect purchasers:

> Given these factors, we consider that the pass-on 'defence' ought only to succeed where, on the balance of probabilities, the defendant has shown that there exists another class of claimant, downstream of the claimant(s) in the action, to whom the overcharge has been passed on. Unless the defendant (and we stress that the burden is on the defendant) demonstrates the existence of such a class, we consider that a claimant's recovery of the overcharge incurred by it should not be reduced or defeated on this ground.[19]

According to the case-law of some Member States, an infringer must show, in addition, that the direct purchaser, when passing-on price overcharges, did not suffer a decrease in demand, which offset any benefits received through higher prices charged to the indirect customers.[20] Such a volume effect leads to a loss of profit to the disadvantage of the direct purchaser. Of course, Article 12(3) of the Damages Directive confirms that its provisions 'shall be without prejudice' to the right of the injured party to claim and obtain compensation for loss of profits due to a full or partial passing-on. However, this should not affect the above-mentioned case-law on the passing-on defence. The relation of the passing-on of overcharges and countervailing volume effects is confirmed by the Commission's Study on the Passing-on of Overcharges published in 2016.[21] In any event, claimants should be ready to show and quantify potential volume effects to offset a passing-on defence when potentially raised by defendants.

Although the defendants have the burden of proof when relying on the passing-on defence, the Damages Directive in Article 13 stipulates that they 'may reasonably require disclosure from the claimant and from third parties'. There is

[17] *ORWI* (n 14), para 58; see as well, instructive, Regional Court (Landgericht) Dortmund, judgment of 27 June 2018, 8 O 13/17 [Kart], ECLI:DE:LGDO:2018:0627.8O13.17KART.00, paras 146 to 175 – *Trucks cartel*.

[18] Hoge Raad, *TenneT*, (n 15), No 4.4.3, referring to the Damages Directive and the effectiveness principle.

[19] *Sainsbury's* (n 16), 484(5).

[20] See eg *ORWI* (n 14), para 69.

[21] Commission, Study on the Passing-on of Overcharges, Final Report written by RBB Economics and Cuatrecasas, 2016, available at: http://ec.europa.eu/competition/publications/reports/KD0216916ENN.pdf.

a risk that this right to disclosure in practice results in voluminous information requests for claimants and third parties. Practically, it also raises the question of the consequence of limited availability of information, given potentially long-lasting cartel infringements and short document retention periods. It may be assumed that defendants will use the right to disclosure to try to delay already lengthy and complex damages proceedings. However, the wording of Article 13 of the Damages Directive requires a balancing of interests and suggests a rather restrictive approach when ordering disclosure, in as much as the burden of proof (of the defendants) would otherwise de facto be turned around.

## IV. THE DISCLOSURE OF EVIDENCE *INTER PARTES*

The success of antitrust damages actions widely depends on the data and information a (potential) plaintiff has access to. Sufficient data and information, as seen above, are required for quantifying damages and evidencing the causality of the infringement for the damage. In this respect, the burden of proof generally lies with the claimant. However, as mentioned, there exists an information asymmetry between victims and cartel members. The operations of cartels are secret and complex, and from the outset, victims do not know the details of the cartel agreements and/or practices, the exact scope of the cartel, its implementation and what cartel-related evidence exists. The Damages Directive makes it easier for claimants to gain access to evidence by introducing possibilities for court-controlled disclosure.

Pursuant to Article 5 of the Damages Directive, a claimant may under certain conditions request the court to order the defendant or third parties to disclose evidence which is in their control. At the same time, the provision allows the defendant to request for such disclosure by the claimant or third parties. Article 5 is probably the most innovative and crucial provision of the overall Damages Directive. This is at least true from a Continental perspective, as courts and judges in common law countries (eg the UK and Ireland) have a tradition of dealing with disclosure requests. In practice, it will be decisive how the courts will apply and interpret the conditions set forth in Article 5(1) to (3) and the national implementing rules respectively. This encompasses the notions of 'reasonably available facts and evidence to substantiate the plausibility of its claim for damages', or the defence, the 'evidence circumscribed as precisely and as narrowly as possible', to exclude fishing expeditions, and to 'limit the disclosure of evidence to that which is proportionate'.

Although victims usually require disclosure to overcome the information asymmetry towards infringers, Article 5 only provides for access to documents 'in' court proceedings. However, victims need the information already before the filing of a damages action, to assess the affected product and geographical market, the scope of damages, prospect of success, the costs and risks, and strategies for enforcement measures. This includes the identification of competent

courts and the applicable law. Against this background, Member States provide for or have recently introduced pre-trial disclosure procedures. While some Member States offer confidentiality rings between the parties or their lawyers (eg in the UK), others have extended the Damages Directive's disclosure to allow for early, but separate proceedings (eg Germany), or allow for rather poorly substantiated actions for damages with the prospect of information gathering (eg Austria).

In practice, lengthy and costly proceedings for access to evidence and unnecessary litigation could be avoided if competition authorities were obliged to publish meaningful, non-confidential versions of infringement decisions shortly after their adoption. The decisions should not only identify all addressees, but also details of the affected market and – most importantly – the concrete content of the cartel agreements and/or practices. This allows victims to assess in due time whether they have suffered damage, and against whom and where a damages claim might be brought to court. It would significantly improve both the efficiency of the judicial system and the effectiveness of the private enforcement of competition law.

Article 5(5) of the Damages Directive codifies case-law according to which the infringers' interest in avoiding follow-on damages actions is not protected. In the *Hydrogen Peroxide* case, the EU General Court (GC) confirmed that the facts of antitrust infringements do not constitute protected information.[22] It emphasised that the re-publication of the hydrogen peroxide cartel decision envisaged by the Commission would include details of affected products, prices as fixed and implemented, and concrete information on the allocation of market shares. The Court considered that such information would facilitate damages actions and, thus, strengthen the competition rules.[23] The EU Court of Justice, with its *Evonik Degussa* judgment of 14 March 2017, a parallel case, essentially confirms the GC line of reasoning. According to the Court, the publication of a meaningful non-confidential version of infringement decisions enables victims to assess and support damages actions. Their interest in specific information must be weighed against the protection of rights of the undertakings concerned (eg the protection of professional secrecy and business secrecy) and of the individuals concerned (eg the protection of personal data).[24] However, information which has been classified as secret or confidential, but which is over five years old, must as a rule be considered historical and as having lost its secret or confidential nature.[25] The EU Court of Justice also confirmed that the publication of verbatim quotations from documents provided by an undertaking to the Commission in support of a leniency statement differs from the publication

[22] Cases T-341/12 *Evonik Degussa v Commission* [2015] EU:T:2015:51 and T-345/12 *Akzo Nobel & Ors v Commission* [2015] EU:T:2015:50.

[23] Case T-345/12 *Akzo Nobel & Ors v Commission* [2015] EU:T:2015:50, para 75.

[24] Case C-162/15 P *Evonik Degussa v Commission* [2017] EU:C:2017:205, para 78.

[25] ibid, para 64.

of verbatim quotations from the leniency statement itself. Whereas the publication of the first is in general possible, any publication of the second is not permitted.[26]

## V. ACCESS TO INFORMATION FROM COMPETITION AUTHORITIES

Equally, the Damages Directive facilitates a claimant's access to the documents included in the files of competition authorities. Such disclosure is considered subsidiary to disclosure *inter partes*. Article 6(10) of the Damages Directive states that the disclosure of evidence from a competition authority should only be ordered where that evidence 'cannot reasonably be obtained from another party or from a third party'. It sets forth rules on the disclosure of documents categorised in three lists.

Pursuant to Article 6(5) of the Damages Directive (the so-called 'grey list'), documents which have been specifically prepared by natural or legal persons for the administrative proceedings (eg cartelists' replies to requests for information), or which the competition authority has drawn up and sent to the parties during the proceedings, shall only be disclosed after the authority has closed its proceedings. According to recent EU court decisions, rendered in different contexts, proceedings are not considered closed before the last appeal has been decided.[27] In many cases, only some cartel participants appeal their fining decision while others decide not to appeal (eg because of settlements with the Commission). Here, the documents prepared for the administrative proceedings regarding the non-appealing infringers should be accessible, irrespective of a pending action by a co-cartelist seeking the decision's annulment. This is in line with the wording of Article 6(5) and the judgment issued by the GC in *CDC Hydrogen Peroxide*.[28] Both imply that proceedings should be considered as closed once the competition authority has adopted its decision, irrespective of whether the decision might later be annulled. Similarly, the Commission specified in its observations of 18 February 2014 to the UK Supreme Court (pursuant to Article 15(3) Regulation 1/2003) in a follow-on action, that a cartel decision becomes final for claims against an infringer who has not appealed the administrative decision.[29]

In contrast, Article 6(6) of the Damages Directive (the 'black list') fully exempts two categories of evidence from disclosure, namely leniency statements and settlement submissions of the infringers. However, absolute protection of these documents might conflict with primary EU law. According to

[26] ibid, para 87.

[27] Case T-534/11 *Schenker v Commission* EU:T:2014:854, para 72.

[28] Case T-437/08 *CDC Hydrogen Peroxide v Commission* [2011] ECR II-8251, para 62.

[29] Available at: http://ec.europa.eu/competition/court/amicus_curiae_morgan_crucible_observations_en.pdf.

the *Donau Chemie* case-law of the ECJ so far, the disclosure of any leniency material has to be subject to a balancing exercise by the national court in each individual case.[30] In any event, annexes to leniency statements and settlement submissions are not covered by the absolute protection of the black list. They fall under Article 6(9) of the Damages Directive (the 'white list'), pursuant to which the disclosure of evidence in the file of the competition authorities that does not fall under the other provisions of the Article may be ordered/requested at any time in actions for damages.

## VI. JOINT AND SEVERAL LIABILITY AND CHOICE OF DEFENDANTS

The choice of the (potential) defendants against which an action for damages may be filed has important implications. Several factors play a role, such as the identity and financial strength of the defendants or the protection of commercial relationships with suppliers. In addition, the number of defendants is important from a practical point of view, as a higher number of, for example, defending cartel members may later facilitate separate and independent settlements with each of them. However, on the other hand, this will usually increase the number of court submissions and thus complicate court procedures.

The background of any decision on the choice of defendants is the joint and several liability of all infringers. Pursuant to the principle of joint and several liability enshrined in the laws of all Member States[31] and in Article 11(1) of the Damages Directive each victim has the right to claim full compensation for the damage resulting from the infringement of competition law from any and all of the cartel members until the victim is fully compensated. The freedom of choice implies that the liability of cartel members does not depend on direct contractual relationships with the damaged victim.[32]

This includes the liability of parent companies for damages resulting from cartel meetings in which employees of their subsidiaries participated. Pursuant to the clarification in Article 1(1) of the Damages Directive, the victims of an infringement of competition law 'by an undertaking' can claim compensation 'from that undertaking'. In addition, Article 2(2) specifies that 'infringer' means the 'undertaking' that has committed an infringement of competition law. In EU competition law, the concept of undertaking means an economic unit operating in the market, even if that unit in law consists of several natural or legal persons. When such a unit infringes competition law it falls, pursuant to the principle of personal responsibility, on that economic unit to answer

[30] Case C-536/11 *Donau Chemie & Ors* EU:C:2013:366.

[31] AG Opinion in Case C-352/13 *CDC Hydrogen Peroxide* EU:C:2014:2443, para 70.

[32] See Damages Directive, Recital 12; and Case C-557/12 *Kone and Others* ECLI:EU:C:2014:1317, para 34.

for that infringement. The ECJ in its *Akzo Nobel* judgment[33] held that a parent company, as a part of the economic unit, is jointly and severally liable for the infringement with the other persons constituting that unit, including its subsidiaries.[34] In the past, some national courts denied liability of parent companies for damages resulting from cartel meetings in which employees of their subsidiaries participated.[35] However, the ECJ had already pointed to the civil liability of the 'undertaking' and not only its entities directly participating in the illegal meetings.[36] According to this case-law, it is 'manifestly unfounded' to preclude a parent company from liability for the infringement committed by its subsidiaries by reference to corporate law principles, such as the limited liability of entities or the separate personality of companies.[37] The Austrian Supreme Court of Justice confirmed the civil liability of parent companies by reference to EU law.[38] The same applies to courts in the Netherlands and the UK.[39] Where EU competition law applies, the liability of the undertaking should be established across Europe.

However, the Damages Directive sets forth two exceptions to the principle of joint and several liability. Firstly, pursuant to Article 11(2), a small or medium-sized enterprise (within the meaning of the Recommendation C(2003) 1422[40]) is liable only to its own direct and indirect purchasers if its market share in the relevant market was always below 5 per cent during the cartel period, and the application of joint and several liability would 'irretrievably jeopardize its economic viability and cause its assets to lose all their value'. The exception does not apply if the enterprise in question led the cartel or coerced others to participate, or if it is a repeated infringer of competition law. All these conditions, which are only roughly defined, contribute to an even greater complexity in the private enforcement regime. It is also questionable whether the exception is adequate in view of the Damages Directive's objective to strengthen the victim's right to compensation, or whether it unilaterally favours cartel members, namely the infringers, at the sole expense of the victims. Secondly, pursuant to Article 11(4) of the Damages Directive, as a rule, the liability of an immunity

[33] Case C-516/15 P *Akzo Nobel & Ors v Commission* EU:C:2017:314, para 56.

[34] Case C-97/08 P *Akzo Nobel & Ors v Commission* [2009] ECR I-8237, paras 54–56 and 77.

[35] Regional Court of Berlin [2014] 16 O 193/11 (Kart), and Düsseldorf [2016] 37 O 27/11 (Kart), at first instance.

[36] *Kone* (n 5), para 37.

[37] Case C-508/11 P *Eni v Commission* EU:C:2013:289, paras 81–82.

[38] Austrian Supreme Court of Justice (*Oberster Gerichtshof*), Cases [2012] 5 Ob 39/11p and [2012] 4 Ob 46/12m.

[39] Amsterdam Court of Appeal, *CDC v Kemira* [2015] ECLI:NL:RBAMS:2014:3190; England and Wales High Court, *Provimi Ltd v Roche Products Ltd & Ors* [2003] EWHC 961.

[40] Commission Recommendation 2003/361 of 6 May 2003 concerning the definition of micro, small and medium-sized enterprises, [2003] OJ L 124/36. Art 2 of the Annex to the Recommendation defines SMEs as follows: '1. The category of micro, small and medium-sized enterprises (SMEs) is made up of enterprises which employ fewer than 250 persons and which have an annual turnover not exceeding EUR 50 million, and/or an annual balance sheet total not exceeding EUR 43 million'. The figures are maximum values, which is why Member States may fix lower ceilings, see Art 2 of the Recommendation.

recipient is also limited to the damage caused to its direct and indirect purchasers, or, in the case of purchasing cartels, to direct and indirect providers. These two liability privileges have been unknown to most national laws until now. They provide uncertainty to claimants and remove potentially solvent debtors. The EU Court of Justice, in previous cases at least, formulated doubts regarding the acceptance, and thus lawfulness, of provisions which unduly restrict the possibilities of cartel victims to effectively enforce their claims for damages.[41]

## VII. JURISDICTION AND APPLICABLE LAW

Given the dimension of infringements of EU competition law, all with cross-border elements, it is important to know where, for example, a follow-on damages action can be brought to court. Equally, it is necessary to know which law the court seized will apply. A cartel might have covered the whole or part of the EU territory, or have affected the cross-border trade by foreclosing national and/or regional markets. Regularly, several undertakings with parent and subsidiary companies with seats in different Member States participated in the infringement. The same is/holds true for many corporate victims damaged by anticompetitive conduct, having parent and subsidiary companies in several European countries.

In the European context, the international competence of courts is determined by Regulation 1215/2012 ('Brussels I bis'), as well as the Lugano Convention which has similar rules and covers the EEA countries and Switzerland.[42] The ECJ, in its judgment in *CDC Hydrogen Peroxide* of 21 May 2015, adjudicated central aspects of the application of the Brussels I Regulation in antitrust damage cases.[43] It confirmed that claimants have a choice between a variety of competent courts. First, each cartel member can, pursuant to the common rule in Article 4(1) Brussels I bis, be sued at the place of its domicile. Article 60(1) Brussels I bis specifies that the 'domicile' of legal persons is where they have their statutory seat, central administration or principal place of business. Plaintiffs can at this place of jurisdiction enforce their full damages claim, including damages sustained outside the forum state.

Secondly, pursuant to Article 7(2) Brussels I bis, claimants may sue cartel members in the courts at the place where the harmful event occurred (*forum delicti*). The special head of jurisdiction encompasses both the place where the

[41] *Kone* (n 5) para 36; Case C-536/11 *Donau Chemie* ECLI:EU:C:2013:366, paras 32, 38, 46 et seq: refusing of victim's access to each (leniency) document must 'be based on overriding reasons relating to the protection of the interest relied on'; as well as *Courage* (n 12) paras 26 et seq; *Manfredi* (n 4) paras 60 et seq, 78; Case C-360/09 *Pfleiderer* EU:C:2011:389, paras 28 et seq.

[42] Regulation (EU) No 1215/2012 of the European Parliament and of the Council of 12 December 2012 on jurisdiction and the recognition and enforcement of judgments in civil and commercial matters [2012] OJ L 351/1; Lugano Convention of 30 October 2007 on jurisdiction and the recognition and enforcement of judgments in civil and commercial matters [2007] OJ L 339/3.

[43] Case C-352/13 *CDC Hydrogen Peroxide* ECLI:EU:C:2015:335.

tortious conduct was committed and the place where the damage occurred. The ECJ clarified that in antitrust cases, claimants might choose between (i) the courts of the place in which the overall cartel was definitely concluded; (ii) the courts of the place in which one cartel agreement in particular was made which is identifiable as the sole causal event giving rise to a specific damage, or (iii) the courts of the place where the victim's own registered office is located.[44] Importantly, the first and latter allow victims to enforce claims for the whole damage they have sustained by the cartel.[45]

Thirdly, the ECJ held that under Article 8(1) Brussels I bis, several cartel members can be sued together – for the full damage sustained by the plaintiff – at the courts of the place where one of them, the so-called anchor defendant, has its domicile. The rule requires that the claims are so closely connected that it is expedient to hear and determine them together to avoid the risk of irreconcilable judgments resulting from separate proceedings. It is not sufficient that there be a divergence in the outcome of the dispute, but that divergence must also arise in the context of the same situation of fact and law.[46] The ECJ confirmed that this is fulfilled in the event of a jointly committed single and continuous infringement by cartel members which are jointly and severally liable for the same damage. Thus, each addressee of infringement decisions can be a potential anchor defendant. This includes, as courts in, for example, the UK, Austria and the Netherlands have already held,[47] a parent company found to have participated in the infringement. UK courts have also held that even subsidiary companies of cartel members, without being addressees themselves but active in the same market, might be anchor defendants.[48]

Regarding jurisdiction clauses in supply contracts, pursuant to Article 25 Brussels I bis, the ECJ ruled that they only cover tortious antitrust claims for damages provided this becomes sufficiently clear from the wording of the clause agreed upon. Given that it is impossible for victims to either have knowledge or foresee such unlawful acts, ie secret cartels, a reference to disputes concerning liability resulting from an infringement of competition law is required. However, even then such clauses are not applicable vis-à-vis the – jointly and severally liable – other cartel members. The arguments apply mutatis mutandis to arbitration clauses, as also held by the Amsterdam Court of Appeal in *Sodium Chlorate* and the majority opinion in literature.[49]

[44] ibid, para 56.

[45] ibid, para 54.

[46] ibid, para 20; Case C-98/06 *Freeport* EU:C:2007:595, para 40; Case C-145/10 *Painer* EU:C:2011:798, para 79; Case C-645/11 *Sapir and Others*, EU:C:2013:228, para 43.

[47] See eg England and Wales High Court, *Provimi Ltd v Roche Products Ltd & Ors* [2003] EWHC 961; Austrian Supreme Court of Justice (*Oberster Gerichtshof*) in [2012] 5 Ob 39/11p and [2012] 4 Ob 46/12m; Amsterdam Appeal Court, *CDC v Kemira* [2015] ECLI:NL:RBAMS:2014:3190.

[48] See *Provimi Ltd* (n 47).

[49] Amsterdam Court of Appeal, *CDC v Kemira* (n 47); England and Wales High Court, *Microsoft Mobile v Sony Europe* [2017] EWHC 374.

The choice of forum also has consequences on the applicable law. Whereas courts always apply the procedural law of the forum state, the situation might be different regarding substantive law. Following the private international law of the forum state, a court might, for example, apply the law of the place where the damage occurred. Thus, where a plaintiff has sustained damages in several countries, the court might, in part and in parallel, apply a multitude of different laws on the overall damages claims. However, some national conflict of law rules might allow for the application of one law. Also, the harmonised EU conflict of law rule in Article 6(3)(b) Regulation 864/2007 (Rome II),[50] allows the application of *lex fori* on the whole claim under certain conditions, regardless of where the damage occurred. Where an infringement of competition law affects the market in more than one country, the plaintiff seeking compensation for the damage resulting from this infringement may choose to base his claim on the law of the court seized, if the market in that Member State is among those directly and substantially affected by the infringement. This also applies where the claimant, in accordance with the rules on jurisdiction, sues several defendants in that court. A uniform application of *lex fori* on Europe-wide cartels is in line with the EU law effectiveness principle as it significantly reduces the complexity of cross-border antitrust cases.

In practical terms, a reduced level of complexity regarding the applicable law facilitates also the calculation of interest by the courts. Outside the application of Article 6(3)(b) Rome II, in cross-border follow-on cases, multiple national interest regimes might be applicable in parallel. However, in such cases the calculation of interest is complex. With a view to further clarifying and informing about the situation of the interest regimes in several European jurisdictions, which may have changed over time, the recent study by the EUI[51] offers a useful overview and guidance for practitioners in antitrust damage cases.

## VIII. CONSIDERATIONS ON THE CHOICE OF FORUM

Given that in Europe-wide antitrust damage cases, particularly cartel cases, private international law allows – and asks – the claimant to choose between alternative competent jurisdictions, the question arises as to where a legal action should be brought to court. At first glance, the answer looks simple, as a claimant should 'exercise that option in a manner he considers most suitable

[50] Regulation (EC) No 864/2007 of the European Parliament and of the Council of 11 July 2007 on the law applicable to non-contractual obligations (Rome II) [2007] OJ L 199/40, which pursuant to Arts 31 and 32 is applicable to infringements causing damage which occur after the entry into force on 11 January 2009.

[51] Monti, *EU Law and Interest on Damages for Infringements of Competition Law* (n 11).

and advantageous'.[52] So-called forum shopping is not only 'undoubtedly permitted',[53] it is also highly complex in practice. The features to be considered are manifold and the differences between the Member States are significant in this respect, while the consequences of the plaintiff's choice are far-reaching.

Many of the aspects which may be decisive for successful claims enforcement are not even addressed by the Damages Directive. The choice of forum might be, as mentioned, relevant for the applicable law, which is crucial for important aspects such as limitation periods or interest rates. In many cases, the national law pre-Damages Directive remains applicable, as pursuant to Article 22(1), the 'substantive provisions' of the Damages Directive do not apply retroactively. Of course, such national law provisions shall comply with the EU effectiveness principle, which is questionable, for example, for many absolute limitation periods (eg under Swedish, Finnish or Spanish law) which start to run as from the day the damage occurred and which are not suspended during the administrative cartel proceedings. Subsequently, the rules or regimes have to be interpreted and applied in line with EU law, as confirmed by the ECJ in *Manfredi*.[54]

However, probably the most important factor is an effective and independent judicial system. In the field of the private enforcement of competition law, specialised courts or chambers sufficiently staffed and equipped, with skilled and/or adequately trained judges, ideally with economic expertise and IT competence, are not only a mere advantage. The availability of a judiciary with adequate personnel, technical and organisational resources is in practice indispensable. Only this will comply with the ECJ's and the Damages Directive's (Article 4) requirement pursuant to which Member States shall ensure that all national rules and procedures relating to the exercising of claims for damages are designed and applied in a way that they do not render 'practically impossible or excessively difficult' the exercising of the right to full compensation for harm caused by an infringement of competition law. The duration of proceedings, the approach of judges in managing complex antitrust cases and existing precedents are further crucial factors. Equally, the appropriateness of the rules on evidence and disclosure, and the fact that the parties may submit electronic data and documents in foreign languages are decisive factors. In practice, also early and well-structured case management hearings by courts as already held in some Member States (eg the Netherlands, UK, Finland) followed by a tight schedule for the further agenda are also helpful, as they reduce the costs and duration of proceedings, while increasing their efficiency.

From this perspective, there still remains a great deal of work to be done in many Member States. For example, it is not proportionate that, while parties

[52] AG Jääskinen, Opinion in Case C-352/13 *CDC Hydrogen Peroxide* EU:C:2015:335, para 89.

[53] AG Mengozzi, Opinion in Case C-98/06 *Freeport* EU:C:2007:302, para 38; see also Amsterdam Court of Appeal, *CDC v Kemira* (n 47).

[54] *Manfredi* (n 4) paras 72–82.

invest thousands of hours and financial means in lawyers and economists in the preparation of a solid damages action, the budget for courts is limited to a small number of hours for the adjudication of a case. A German judge reports of the resource planning of a court foreseeing 23 hours for judges to resolve a competition law case, from its preparation, to hearings and finally the judgment.[55] There are also significant differences as to whether evidence in electronic form may be submitted or not. Under current rules in some Member States, plaintiffs may have to submit thousands of invoices and other documents in paper form to substantiate a claim. This obstacle to effective claims enforcement could and should be avoided. The lack of personnel, technical and organisational resources – sufficient to cope with the complexities of antitrust cases – is the reason why the effectiveness of the judiciary in many Member States is not always a given. This has an impact particularly on the length of procedures, as illustrated by the *CDC Hydrogen Peroxide* case pending before the Regional Court of Dortmund, Germany, since 2009. More than three years have elapsed since the ECJ rendered its judgment. The delay is probably due to insufficient resources, and thus the Court has not proceeded further with the case. Considering the fact that the cartel duration lasted from at least 1994 until 2000, as found and established by the Commission, over 20 years have already elapsed without any expectation of when and to what extent compensatory justice will be granted. In addition, it is fair to ask the question, why procedural rules of some Member States even encourage defendants to artificially delay procedures, instead of setting incentives for judges to take a more active or pragmatic role in managing antitrust cases efficiently. Indisputably, the lapse of years, if not decades, is regularly accompanied by a deterioration of (witness) evidence and, thus, has negative effects on the prospects of successful claims enforcement. Overall, the right to an effective remedy, as protected by Article 47 of the EU Charter of Fundamental Rights,[56] is crucial. Its practical effect is reflected by the old maxim: 'Justice delayed is justice denied'.

For victims and most practitioners, the choice of forum will also relate to the costs and cost risks associated with antitrust litigation. The applicable cost rules play a further key role in practice. Moreover, there are considerable differences between the Member States in this area. While the loser pays rule is standard across Europe, the absolute amounts that may come into play differ significantly. Cost risks of the parties are often not evenly distributed in cartel cases. Given that cartels are multi-party infringements, a plaintiff typically does not only face significantly higher efforts and costs in pursuing the case than each of the (potentially) several defendants. On the contrary: if the outcome is negative, he will be confronted with multiple adverse cost orders in relation to

[55] G Klumpe and T Thiede, 'Regierungsentwurf zur 9. GWB-Novelle: Änderungsbedarf aus Sicht der Praxis' (2016) 50 *Betriebs-Berater* 3011, 3015.

[56] Charter of Fundamental Rights of the European Union [2012] C 326/02.

all the defendants. In addition, in many Member States, also cartel members not sued by a plaintiff may join the court proceedings as third-party interveners on the side of the defendant(s), and thus create additional costs and cost risks. In financial terms, the success or risk ratio for a plaintiff relating to costs per unit is fourfold for two defendants, ninefold for three defendants, 16-fold for four defendants etc. While some countries foresee a cap in respect of adverse cost risks, other countries do not have such a mechanism. For example, the costs and cost risks of a damages action in the Netherlands or Belgium are less than 10 per cent of comparable costs and cost risks in Germany.[57] In the UK, the costs and cost risks may be even higher. In an opt-out class action against *Mastercard*, the plaintiff placed a security for adverse cost risks of GBP 10 million.[58] However, too high upfront costs and non-proportional cost risks effectively deter many victims from pursuing their legitimate claims in court. As a further consequence for some cases, litigation funding by third parties will only be feasible in certain Member States.

Overall, the factors a plaintiff has to take into account when choosing the jurisdiction and court for an antitrust action are wide in scope. Some Member States clearly perceived the differences in the attractiveness of jurisdictions which, as a matter of fact, in the EU lead to a competition of jurisdictions. In this light, certain Member States have adopted further rules facilitating antitrust actions which go beyond the Damages Directive's minimum standard (eg the Netherlands and the UK). In this context, the literature even assesses whether 'forum selling' exists, namely an interest from judges or court administrators to attract follow-on antitrust cases to their courts.[59]

## IX. LITIGATION FUNDING AND CLAIMS BUNDLING

The funding of private antitrust enforcement cases is particularly important given that the main obstacles are quite often the high costs and cost risks combined with the uncertainty of the outcome of potentially long-lasting litigation processes. In practice, alternative solutions exist to ensure the funding of antitrust damage cases. Some of which significantly increase the likelihood of

[57] In Germany, upfront court fees to be paid by a plaintiff, capped at a claims value of EUR 30 million, amount to approximately EUR 300,000 in the 1st instance, EUR 440,000 in the 2nd instance and EUR 550,000 in the 3rd instance. The adverse cost risk per defendant amounts to approximately EUR 835,000 (three instances). The cost risks regarding third-party interveners must also be added. In the Netherlands, court fees amount to approximately EUR 7,500 per instance, and adverse costs are capped at approximately EUR 25,000 per counterpart and instance. Contribution proceedings following third-party notifications are separate, ie without implying additional cost risks for plaintiffs.

[58] *Walter Hugh Merricks v Mastercard Incorporated & Ors*, CAT 1266/7/7/16.

[59] See S Bechtold, J Frankenreiter and D Klerman, 'Forum Selling Abroad', *Southern California Law Review* (forthcoming).

establishing evidence and proof of cartel damages in court and consequently increase the likelihood of obtaining fair compensation in out-of-court settlements.

With a view to pursuing own enforcement activities, a claimant might first opt to cooperate with a third-party litigation funder. This alleviates the cost risks associated with filing a legal action against (several) cartel members. Law firms are also increasingly offering contingency and/or success fee arrangements, often in combination with or in parallel to litigation funders, where the respective bar rules of Member States allow it. Claimants interested in external funding should particularly take into account transparent and clear commercial conditions of litigation funders. Otherwise there is a risk that the largest part of a potential compensation award does not go to the victim, but to the litigation funder and law firm. Another way is to cooperate with a specialised company under the assignment model. The concept, which was developed by CDC Cartel Damage Claims in 2002 for claims in Continental Europe, results from a victims' perspective in a full outsourcing of the overall complex process of both evidencing cartel damages and of enforcing claims. Ideally, a multitude of corporate victims of a cartel assign under claims purchase agreements their damages claims to a specialised firm, which then enforces the bundled claims in its own name in and out of court. The model is not a form of collective redress, as the firm is the sole plaintiff. However, it may ensure the overall funding of the case, while at the same time creating economies of scale and synergies for both the damage quantification (eg data collection and analysis) and the claims enforcement (eg cost reductions, increased negotiation power, separation of enforcement and business). Furthermore, an advantage is that in Europe-wide cases the model enables the enforcement of claims in the best-placed jurisdiction.[60] Both the ECJ in *CDC Hydrogen Peroxide*[61] and Article 2(4) of the Damages Directive acknowledge that persons having acquired antitrust claims are entitled to file a damages action.[62] Previously, national courts in several Member States (eg Austria, Germany, the Netherlands and Finland) recognised the model, even though some courts set requirements as to the financial resources of the plaintiff.

In any event, victims of antitrust infringements considering whether to cooperate with a litigation funder, law firm or professional specialised company should ensure as far as possible an alignment of interests. This is not only relevant for structuring business terms, but also for the choice of forum. As most lawyers seem to have an understandable interest in litigating in their home jurisdiction, this, in a given case, might not necessarily be the best-placed jurisdiction.

[60] See on cross-border assignments Regulation (EC) No 593/2008 on the law applicable to contractual obligations (Rome I), Art 14.

[61] AG Jääskinen, Opinion in Case C-352/13 *CDC Hydrogen Peroxide* EU:C:2015:335, para 29.

[62] See on the model also Commission, Collective Redress in Antitrust, 2012, available at: www.europarl.europa.eu/document/activities/cont/201206/20120613ATT46782/20120613ATT46782EN.pdf, 37.

## X. CONCLUSION

The Damages Directive indeed facilitates the private enforcement of competition law, particularly for indirect cartel victims. With its implementation, a minimum standard of rules will be harmonised across Europe. While for some jurisdictions (eg the UK), the changes required are modest, for other jurisdictions, notably Continental European Member States, without a tradition of disclosure rules and corresponding procedures, changes are more significant.

However, many aspects, which in practice are crucial for a truly effective private enforcement regime have not been addressed by the Damages Directive. In this context, a great deal of work remains to be done in many Member States to allow for an effective enforcement of antitrust damages claims, which are complex from a factual, legal and financial perspective. Probably the most important factor is the availability of an effective judicial system with specialised courts or chambers with a sufficient number of skilled or adequately trained judges, ideally with economic expertise. The lack of personnel, technical and organisational resources – sufficient to cope with the complexities of antitrust damage cases – is the reason why the effectiveness of the judiciary in many Member States is not always a given. This impacts on the length of court procedures which in several countries are much too long. In addition, the approach of judges to manage complex antitrust cases, the possibility of the parties to submit electronic data and documents in foreign languages are important factors. Further, it is only in Member States with balanced cost rules, which duly take into account the structural disadvantage of a single plaintiff (facing much higher cost risks) vis-à-vis several cartel members, that the right to compensation can be effective at all. Otherwise, many victims are in practice deterred from enforcing their legitimate claims.

Therefore, in Europe-wide cartel cases where claimants can choose between equally competent jurisdictions and courts, victims have to consider a broad set of differences between the Member States. This challenge will remain after the Damages Directive's implementation and the existing competition of jurisdictions in Europe – some authors even speak of 'forum selling'[63] – will continue. Some Member States have perceived the potential to attract international antitrust cases to their courts and in the implementation process have gone beyond the minimum standard of rules in the Damages Directive. This also applies regarding the possibility of the enforcement of bundled claims (acknowledged in its Article 2(4). Some Member States provide for forms of group actions or class actions, also following the Commission Recommendation on common principles for collective redress mechanisms in Europe.[64] Victims may opt in

[63] See Bechtold, Frankenreiter and Klerman, 'Forum Selling Abroad' (n 59).

[64] Commission Recommendation 2013/396/EU of 11 June 2013 on common principles for injunctive and compensatory collective redress mechanisms in the Member States concerning violations of rights granted under Union Law [2013] OJ L 201/60.

(eg France and Italy) or opt out (eg the UK and Portugal) or even both, depending on the case (eg Belgium). Although these mechanisms have not yet, with the exception of the UK, played a role in the context of antitrust litigation, they are practically indispensable in allowing the enforcement of end-consumer mass claims.

Regarding the success of the Damages Directive much depends on the application of the new rules by the courts which have to, as always, fill the gaps in the Damages Directive and/or the implementation provisions and to consider the details of each individual case. There is reason enough to hope and trust that the future under the new regime will bring significant improvements for the private enforcement of competition law. Judges with a great interest in the field and committed to the often complex issues of antitrust damage cases will be the real key players safeguarding the path to individual and collective justice.

3

# *Managing Transposition and Avoiding Fragmentation: The Example of Limitation Periods and Interest*

MAGNUS STRAND*

## I. LIMITATION PERIODS AND INTEREST IN COMPETITION DAMAGES

THE UPHILL CLIMB for competition damages claimants is steep, and particularly so for those who attempt stand-alone actions. They must prove there was an infringement of competition law, with all the difficulties connected to either Article 101 or Article 102 TFEU as well as to establishing a relevant market. Notwithstanding whether the action is a follow-on or stand-alone action, claimants must further prove they have suffered harm that was factually and legally caused by the infringement at issue, and prove the extent of that harm (dodging the pitfalls of the passing-on problem[1]). Of course all these issues are surrounded by further complexities and details that must be overlooked here. However, there are two specific details that I wish to address, details that must be taken into account in any competition damages action. The details I have in mind are those of limitation periods and interest. It will be demonstrated that the transposition of Directive 2014/104[2] in Sweden will likely increase the awards of damages payable by reason of an infringement of

* Associate Professor of European law and senior lecturer in commercial law, Uppsala University. An earlier version of this chapter, in Swedish, is available as 'EU och civilrättens splittring: Exemplet preskription och ränta vid skadestånd' (2017) 130 *Tidsskrift for Rettvitenskap* 313–346. Thanks are due to Tore Alméns Minnesfond, Assistant Professor Katri Havu (Helsinki), Associate Professor Mikael Hansson (Gothenburg), Professor Bengt Domeij, senior lecturer Kjell Adolfsson and Jonatan Schytzer (all at Uppsala). Any and all misconceptions are my own.

[1] Examined by this author in M Strand, *The Passing-On Problem in Damages and Restitution under EU Law* (Cheltenham, Elgar European Law and Practice Series, Edward Elgar Publishing, 2017).

[2] Directive 2014/104/EU of the European Parliament and of the Council of 26 November 2014 on certain rules governing actions for damages under national law for infringements of the competition law provisions of the Member States and of the European Union [2014] OJ L349/1.

competition law very significantly. In light of this change in Swedish law, which pertains to competition damages only, it will be discussed critically whether it is well-advised to create such special regimes for particular instances of damages, and what other strategies were available to the transposing Swedish legislator.

Much has been said, and written, on the fragmentation of national private law under the pressure of EU law harmonisations.[3] The aim of this chapter is not to add to the theoretical discussions on, for instance, what constitutes coherence or to trace the various causes for or consequences of fragmentation. Suffice it here to note that there is a *perception of pressure*. Under this view, which this author has encountered not only in legal writings but (and in particular) among government officials with the task of transposing EU law directives into national law, EU law gives rise to a fragmentation of national private law and there is little or nothing that can be done about it. It will be submitted that such defeatism can and should be nuanced. To that end, the aim of this contribution is to demonstrate that the common Swedish response to this 'external pressure', which has been to resort to minimum transposition, is liable to bring adverse consequences and that there are options to that response. Issues pertaining to limitation periods and interest on an award of damages payable due to a breach of competition law will be used to illustrate the point.

A few years ago I was very privileged to take part in a comparative study concerning interest on competition damages in the Member States, where the rules on interest in not all, but many Member States were studied.[4] The analysis was focused on whether national rules were compatible with Directive 2014/104.[5] The comparative interest project used a hypothetical scenario where harm had been caused by cartel-inflated prices. It was assumed that harm to an amount of 100 units had been suffered by a cartel victim in 1993, 1998, 2006 and 2008 (in sum 400 units of harm). In the scenario, the cartel was exposed in 2009, a final judgment ruling that the cartelists must pay damages was delivered in

[3] Significant contributions include P Letto-Vanamo and J Smits (eds), *Coherence and Fragmentation in European Private Law* (Munich, Sellier – de Gruyter, 2012); several contributions in R Brownsword, H-W Micklitz, L Niglia and S Weatherill (eds), *The Foundations of European Private Law* (Oxford, Hart Publishing, 2011); L Niglia, 'Of Harmonization and Fragmentation: The Problem of Legal Transplants in the Europeanization of Private Law' (2010) 17 *Maastricht Journal of European and Comparative Law* 116–36; and P Legrand, 'Antivonbar' (2006) 1 *Journal of Comparative Law* 13–40. A critique of this line of thinking (going beyond the European sphere) can be found in P Holmes, 'The Rhetoric of "Legal Fragmentation" and its Discontents: Evolutionary Dilemmas in the Constitutional Dilemmas of Global Law' (2011) 7 *Utrecht Law Review* 113–40. Of course, the phenomena discussed are not specific to private law, *cf* eg H Petersen and H Zahle (eds), *Legal Polycentricity: Consequences of Pluralism in Law* (Aldershot, Dartmouth, 1996) and T Andersson (ed), *Parallel and Conflicting Enforcement of Law* (Stockholm, Institute for Legal Research, Norstedts Juridik/Martinus Nijhoff Publishers, 2005). From Swedish discourse I must mention B Bengtsson, 'Om civilrättens splittring' in L Gorton, J Ramberg and J Sandström (eds), *Festskrift till Kurt Grönfors* (Stockholm, Norstedts Juridikförlag, 1991) 29–46.

[4] The results have been published in G Monti (ed), 'EU Law and Interest on Damages for Infringements of Competition Law – A Comparative Report', EUI Working Papers LAW 2016/11, available at: http://cadmus.eui.eu/handle/1814/40464.

[5] Directive 2014/104 (n 2). The details on interest in the Directive will be described below.

2013 and final payment was made in 2014. The simplified question asked in this situation was how large an amount of interest on those damages was payable in the respective Member States. Calculations varied wildly, from a nominal amount that would under certain circumstances be payable under French law to an amount of interest equivalent to the original amount of damages payable under Dutch law.[6] If national limitation periods had been taken into account, I am convinced that new and partly other variations would have come into play.

In the context of this work, I became aware of the significance of interest in competition damages actions. That issue, which at first sight seemed a small detail, is a major concern for litigants. It also became apparent that the issue of limitation periods, not addressed in the interest project, was equally important and almost inseparable from the issue of interest. On closer scrutiny, these issues (and others related to the Directive that will not be discussed here) also became a striking example of the pitfalls of the minimum transposition of directives, which was the strategy chosen by the Swedish legislator with regard to Directive 2014/104. Therefore, I decided to study in some detail the approaches of the Nordic countries,[7] and of Sweden in particular, to limitation periods and interest on competition damages in the process of transposing Directive 2014/104 into Swedish law.

The relevant details of Nordic laws will be described below. It is nevertheless useful to point out here that under all four systems studied, interest payable on an award of damages is traditionally categorised as interest for delay. Consequently, the interest rate is set comparatively high: a reference rate increased by 7 or 8 per cent is applied in all four countries studied. At such a rate, the amount of interest payable will typically rise quickly, even though the reference rates have followed the current global tendency towards lower interest rates. Before the transposition of Directive 2014/104, the high rate was balanced by a comparatively short period of interest accrual. As will be described below, the combination of this high traditional interest rate and the new EU rules on the period for interest accrual and on the limitation period caused some concern in the transposition of the Directive. In Sweden, at least, this combination threatened to give rise to draconian levels of interest. At the end of the day, this risk was largely avoided, but the amounts of interest payable have nevertheless been significantly increased – with regard to damages for an infringement of competition law, not for other infringements of market-related law. Amounts were increased in the other Nordic countries too, albeit to a lesser extent. In section IV, I will attempt to explain the choices made by

[6] See Monti, 'EU Law and Interest on Damages for Infringements of Competition Law – A Comparative Report' (n 4) 18–19 for a table of the amounts of interest payable.

[7] I have studied Danish, Finnish, Norwegian and Swedish rules, but the language barrier has kept me from including Icelandic law. Thanks are due to Assistant Professor Katri Havu for helping out with Finnish law material not available in Swedish or English.

the Swedish legislator. It is beyond the scope of this contribution to present any detailed analysis of the transposition in the other Nordic countries, but there will be some comparisons.[8] Before plunging into the details of national law, however, the relevant passages in Directive 2014/104 will be presented in the following section.

## II. DIRECTIVE 2014/104 ON LIMITATION PERIODS AND INTEREST

### A. Limitation Periods

The relevant provision on limitation periods in the Directive is its Article 10. The complete wording of the Article will not be repeated here, but it should be highlighted that the limitation period for bringing an action for damages under the Directive is 'at least five years' under Article 10(3). It is accordingly possible for the Member States to enact longer limitation periods than five years. Moreover, and very importantly, Article 10(2) stipulates that the limitation period may

> not begin to run before the infringement of competition law has ceased and the claimant knows, or can reasonably be expected to know:
>
> (a) of the behaviour and the fact that it constitutes an infringement of competition law;
> (b) of the fact that the infringement of competition law caused harm to it; and
> (c) the identity of the infringer.

These are far-reaching criteria, suggesting that there will be little room for defendants in competition litigation to argue that the limitation period has elapsed. However, Article 10(2) is somewhat checked by Recital 36, which in the relevant part includes a statement that

> Member States should be able to maintain or introduce absolute limitation periods that are of general application, provided that the duration of such absolute limitation periods does not render practically impossible or excessively difficult the exercise of the right to full compensation.[9]

Recital 36 thus implies that absolute limitation periods in national law, ie comparatively long limitation periods that begin to run, for example, at the

[8] More detailed comparisons were presented in Strand, 'EU och civilrättens splittring: Exemplet preskription och ränta vid skadestånd' (n *). The transposition of the rules on limitation in Directive 2014/104 in Central and Eastern European Member States has been discussed in an interesting article by A Vlahek and K Podobnik, 'Provisions of the Damages Directive on Limitation Periods and their Implementation in CEE Countries' (2017) 10(15) *Yearbook of Antitrust and Regulatory Studies* 147–75.

[9] Denmark and Norway have used this window of opportunity to include an absolute limitation period in their transposing legislation, while Finland and Sweden have not.

first harmful event or first occurrence of harm, should be considered compatible with the Directive as such. However, they will be subject to scrutiny under the EU law principle of effectiveness.[10]

## B. Interest

By contrast, there is no specific provision on interest in Directive 2014/104. It is only stated in Article 3(2) that the concept of 'full compensation', to which anyone who has suffered harm by reason of an infringement of competition law shall be entitled, includes 'compensation for actual loss and for loss of profit, plus the payment of interest'. This echoes a holding of the Court of Justice in *Manfredi*, but no further details can be found there.[11] To find further guidance, one should instead turn to Recital 12 of the Directive, which includes the following passage:

> Anyone who has suffered harm caused by such an infringement can claim compensation for actual loss (*damnum emergens*), for gain of which that person has been deprived (loss of profit or *lucrum cessans*), plus interest, irrespective of whether those categories are established separately or in combination in national law. The payment of interest is an essential component of compensation to make good the damage sustained by taking into account the effluxion of time and should be due from the time when the harm occurred until the time when compensation is paid, without prejudice to the qualification of such interest as compensatory or default interest under national law and to whether effluxion of time is taken into account as a separate category (interest) or as a constituent part of actual loss or loss of profit. It is incumbent on the Member States to lay down the rules to be applied for that purpose.

It should be noted that this is not an article of the Directive but only a recital, and thus the Member States are not formally compelled to transpose its semi-legal contents into their national laws. Even if Member States choose to follow its recommendations, it should further be noted that Recital 12 intends to leave a certain margin of appreciation to them. National classifications of the type of interest do not matter. It does not even matter if compensation for

[10] The many-splendoured case-law and literature on this principle will not be cited extensively here. The development of this principle began in Case 33/76 *Rewe* EU:C:1976:188 and Case 45/76 *Comet* EU:C:1976:191. Central case-law includes Case C-312/93 *Peterbroeck* EU:C:1995:437 and Joined Cases C-317/08, C-318/08, C-319/08 and C-320/08 *Rosalba Alassini* EU:C:2010:146. An overview of the case-law and literature by this author is available in Strand (n 1) ch 2.

[11] Joined Cases C-295/04 to 298/04 *Vincenzo Manfredi and Others* EU:C:2006:461, para 97. The Court has discussed certain details on how to establish the amount of interest payable under EU law in other contexts, however, and it is a matter of some debate whether these holdings can be transplanted into the competition damages context. The holdings at issue include Case C-271/91 *Marshall* EU:C:1993:335, para 31 and Case C-481/14 *Jørn Hansson* EU:C:2016:419, para 53. This author would generally recommend caution against such analogies between EU law contexts.

the effluxion of time is awarded by alternative means. Moreover, Recital 12 is entirely silent with regard to the rate of interest.

Having said that, it remains clear that Recital 12 includes a very specific recommendation on the period of time during which interest should accrue. This recommendation that interest 'should be due from the time when the harm occurred until the time when compensation is paid', albeit more vaguely phrased, was in fact intended by the Commission to be part of what is now Article 3 of Directive 2014/104.[12] In the legislative process this was transferred to a recital, diminishing the legal force of the text which should now be read as a recommendation rather than as a rule of EU law which is to be transposed into national law. Further, the legal essence of the recital runs contrary to Nordic legal tradition, according to which interest on damages does not usually begin to accrue until the claim has been presented to the defendant. Under such circumstances it is somewhat surprising to see that all Nordic legislators have chosen (without discussing it in their *travaux préparatoires*, which is otherwise the custom regarding important legislative choices) to follow this recommendation. It may be that Recital 12 was taken as an indication of where EU case-law would eventually lead us irrespective of national choices. If so, that conclusion is debatable.[13] For the purposes of this chapter, however, it is the choice as such which is interesting. I find it hard to shake off the impression that the Nordic legislators took the view that there was no choice. This *perception of inevitable compulsion* to comply even with a recital of an EU directive has inspired the discussion below.

## III. TRANSPOSING THE RELEVANT PASSAGES INTO SWEDISH LAW

### A. Swedish Law before Transposing Directive 2014/104

#### *i. Limitation Periods*

Before transposing Directive 2014/104, the Swedish limitation period for a claim for damages by reason of an infringement of competition law was ten years from the occurrence of harm,[14] which is generally interpreted as meaning ten years

[12] Proposal for a Directive of the European Parliament and of the Council on Certain Rules Governing Actions for Damages under National Law for Infringements of the Competition Law Provisions of the Member States and of the European Union, COM(2013) 404 final p 31 (Art 2(2)).

[13] Admittedly, the views and intentions of the EU legislator are relevant to the interpretation of EU law as shown in consistent case-law of the Court of Justice, see eg Case 26/62 *van Gend en Loos* EU:C:1963:1, 12; Case 283/81 *CILFIT* EU:C:1982:335, para 20; Case 14/83 *von Colson* EU:C:1984:153, para 26 and Case C-280/04 *Jyske Finans* EU:C:2005:753, para 32. Nevertheless, this author has been sceptical in following Recital 12 so closely, see M Strand, 'Sweden' in Monti (n 4) 309–11.

[14] Konkurrenslagen (Competition Act, 2008:579) c 3, s 25(2). Before 1 August 2005 it was five years.

from the occurrence of the harmful act or event.[15] It is of no consequence to this rule whether or not the victim has gained knowledge of the fact that there had been an infringement and that it might have caused harm. This system, where knowledge of harm is of no consequence to the limitation period for damages claims, is motivated by reasons of legal certainty and applies generally under Swedish law.[16] It should also be stressed that there are no absolute limitation periods of general application under Swedish law. Consequently, this ten-year period can be interrupted in various ways.[17] None of these would be helpful to a victim who is unaware of his or her harm, however.

Seemingly in contrast, Danish, Finnish and Norwegian law on limitation periods in respect of damages claims have all included special rules under which the limitation period (three years in all three countries) does not begin to run until the victim has become aware of having incurred harm.[18] There is nonetheless little difference if Sweden is compared to Denmark and Finland, as the latter two countries both have an absolute limitation period of ten years.[19] The difference is greater in Norway where the absolute limitation period extends to 20 years.[20]

### *ii. Interest*

Swedish courts will not award interest on a damages claim *ex officio*. Instead, it is for the claimant to claim interest and the issues of interest and its rate are at the disposal of the litigating parties. There is a Swedish Interest Act but it is, in principle, subsidiary in character and yields to special statutory provisions and to contractual agreements on interest.[21] For instance, courts will not award a higher interest amount than what the claimant requests. Consequently, a court will turn to the rules and rates in the Interest Act only to the extent that the parties disagree on the interest payable.

As mentioned above, the statutory rate of interest on damages is the interest for delay. Interest for delay is set as the so-called reference rate set twice a year (1 January and 1 July) by Riksbanken, the Swedish Central Bank, plus 8 per cent.[22] The applicable rate follows the variations of the reference rate over time, and accordingly the amount of interest payable with regard to a

[15] J Hellner and M Radetzki, *Skadeståndsrätt*, 9th edn (Stockholm, Norstedts Juridik, 2014) 401.

[16] Preskriptionslagen (Act on Limitation, 1981:130) s 2. On the reason for the rule see Hellner and Radetzki, *Skadeståndsrätt* (n 15) 401.

[17] Listed in Preskriptionslagen, s 5.

[18] Danish Lov om forældelse af fordringer (Act on Limitation of Claims, LBK nr 1238 af 09/11/2015) s 3(1–2), Finnish Laki velan vanhentumisesta (Act on Limitation of Debts, 728/2003) s 4, Norwegian Lov om foreldelse av fordringer (Act on Limitation of Claims, LOV-1979-05-18-18) s 9(1).

[19] Lov om forældelse af fordringer, s 3(3)(2); Laki velan vanhentumisesta, s 7(2).

[20] Lov om foreldelse av fordringer, s 9(2).

[21] Räntelagen (Interest Act, 1975:635) s 1.

[22] ibid, s 6.

certain damages claim may need to be calculated separately for each half-year until payment. In contrast, which is of interest in this context, the statutory rate of interest on the restitution of payments pursuant to the annulment of a contract is the so-called interest on earnings, which is set as the reference rate plus 2 per cent.[23] Neither of these rates is calculated on a compound basis, but only on a simple basis. Under Swedish law, compound interest will be available only if agreed upon.[24] It is even uncertain in Swedish law whether interest is payable on amounts of interest on debts, where the main debt has not matured but, for example, an annual amount of interest has.[25]

Under the Interest Act, interest on damages claims starts to accrue the 30th day following the claimant's presentation of the claim for damages and the evidence that can reasonably be required from the claimant under the circumstances. However, interest will not start to accrue until the defendant has been provided with the presentation of the claim and the evidence.[26] Interest will alternatively start to accrue on the date of service of an application for a payment order with Kronofogdemyndigheten, the Swedish Enforcement Authority, or a service of summons to court.[27] By way of exception, interest starts to accrue from the day on which the harm was incurred if the cause of the harm was an intentional crime.[28] However, a breach of EU or national competition law is not sanctioned as a criminal offence in Swedish law.

Interest ceases to accrue when the payment of the claim has been made. The Interest Act includes no rules on the suspension of the accrual of interest.

Generally speaking, the other Nordic countries have similar systems. For instance, statutory law on interest is at the disposal of the parties,[29] and interest payable on a damages claim is legally considered or treated as interest on a late payment.[30] As mentioned, interest rates are set in a similar way and at a

[23] ibid, s 5.

[24] See NJA 1994 s 3 (Swedish Supreme Court); and S Lindskog, *Betalning* (Stockholm, Norstedts Juridik, 2014) 510–20 (in particular 517).

[25] G Walin and J Herre, *Lagen om skuldebrev m.m.: En kommentar*, 3rd edn (Stockholm, Norstedts Juridik, 2011) 295–96; equally uncertain on this specific issue are M Mellqvist and I Persson, *Fordran & Skuld*, 9th edn (Uppsala, Iustus, 2011). The authors however agree that statutory interest cannot be calculated on compound basis in Swedish law.

[26] Räntelagen, s 4 (3).

[27] ibid, s 4(4).

[28] ibid, s 4(5). There is a statement in the Swedish *travaux préparatoires* according to which it should be possible for Swedish courts to consider interest losses that have arisen before the claim for damages is presented in their determination of the amount of harm suffered (ie the principal amount), but leading commentators are sceptical as to this view; see Walin and Herre, *Lagen om skuldebrev m.m* (n 25) section 5.4.

[29] Danish Lov om renter og andre forhold ved forsinket betaling (Act on interest and other issues concerning late payment, LBK nr 459 af 13/05/2014), s 1(3), Finnish Korkolaki (Interest Act, 633/1982) s 2, Norwegian Lov om renter ved forsinket betaling m.m. (Act Relating to Interest on Overdue Payments etc, LOV-1976-12-17-100) s 1.

[30] This is not stipulated as such but is apparent from the names of the Acts in Denmark and Norway and from the wording of the rules in Finland and Sweden.

similar level: in Denmark and Norway at a reference rate plus 8 per cent,[31] and in Finland at a reference rate plus 7 per cent.[32] It is likewise a common main rule in the Nordic countries that interest on a damages claim begins to accrue when the claim is presented to the defendant.[33]

There is nevertheless a difference, which is of some significance to the issues discussed here, between the Swedish interest regime and those in the other Nordic countries. As explained above, it is not considered possible for Swedish courts to award interest for the period at an earlier point in time (eg from the first occurrence of harm). Such a possibility is, in contrast, available under Danish statutory law[34] and according to case-law in Finland (including competition damages case-law)[35] and in Norway.[36]

## B. The New Swedish Rules

Directive 2014/104 has been transposed into Swedish law through the adoption of the Competition Damages Act which entered into force on 27 December 2016.[37] The Swedish Act will not be surveyed as such here; suffice it to say that it has been designed as a minimum transposition measure and it sticks quite closely to the Directive.

### *i. Limitation Periods*

The Competition Damages Act has brought a significant change to the Swedish rules on limitation with respect to competition damages claims. As with so many other provisions in the Directive, Article 10 has been transposed almost verbatim. Thus, under section 6 of the Competition Damages Act, the

[31] Lov om renter og andre forhold ved forsinket betaling, s 5; Lov om renter ved forsinket betaling m.m., s 3.

[32] Korkolaki, s 4.

[33] Lov om renter og andre forhold ved forsinket betaling s 3 ss 2-4, Lov om renter ved forsinket betaling m.m,. s 2; Korkolaki, ss 7 and 9 (but *cf* s 8 on damages for harm caused by an intentional criminal act).

[34] Lov om renter og andre forhold ved forsinket betaling, s 3(5).

[35] K Havu, 'Finland' in Monti (n 4) 107–12.

[36] Norwegian Ministry of Trade, Industry and Fisheries,' Høringsnotat, Forslag til endringer i konkurranseloven – gjennomføring i norsk rett av direktiv 2014/104/EU om privat håndheving av EU/EØS-konkurransereglene', available at: www.regjeringen.no/contentassets/ec9a55f8681b4262a6157c67856c45ab/horingsnotat---forlag-til-endringer-i-konkurran-l1625139.pdf, 18. See also E Hjelmeng, I B Ørstavik and E Østerud, 'Utredning av rettsspørsmål knyttet til gjennomføring i norsk rett av Parlaments- og Rådsdirektiv 2014/104/EU av 26 november 2014 om visse regler for søksmål i henhold til nasjonal rett angående erstatning for overtredelser av medlemsstatenes og Den europeiske unions konkurranserett', available at: www.regjeringen.no/contentassets/41ab189abd6340fe98e65204269c55fc/utredning-gjennomforing-av-direktivet-om-privat-handhevelse-av-konkurransereglene-i-norsk-rett.pdf, 17–18.

[37] Konkurrensskadelagen (2016:964).

limitation period has been set to five years from the point when the infringement of competition law has ceased and the victim has or can reasonably be expected to have gained knowledge (i) of the behaviour and that it constituted an infringement; (ii) of the fact that the infringement caused harm to the claimant, and (3) of the identity of the infringer. The Swedish legislator has not seized the opportunity offered in the Directive to set an absolute limitation period.

The other Nordic countries have similarly followed the Directive quite closely in this respect.[38] They have prolonged their main limitation periods from three to five years and have faithfully transposed the more precise rules on when that period begins that are laid down in Article 10 of the Directive.[39] As permitted under Recital 36 of the Directive, Denmark and Norway maintain their absolute limitation periods,[40] while Finland has opted to eliminate it. Instead Finland has introduced a special rule on interrupting the limitation period, in essence creating three alternative limitation periods that must all have elapsed before a claim is barred.[41]

### *ii. Interest*

It is striking to note that all four Nordic countries studied have, without any discussion in their *travaux préparatoires*, adopted the passage in Recital 12 of Directive 2014/104 concerning when interest should begin to accrue on a competition damages claim.[42] There are possible differences in the nuances of how this has been phrased in the respective Acts, but the intention seems to have been to follow the wording of the Recital as closely as possible. Differences are more marked when it comes to the applicable interest rates. As above, I will focus here on the Swedish Act and only offer some comparative notes on the other Nordic countries.

It has been explained above that the Swedish legislator seems to have taken the view that it was better to meet the recommendation in Recital 12 than to reject it and risk having to comply with it anyway, for example, due to a preliminary ruling on when interest should begin to accrue on a competition damages

[38] Please note that at the time of writing Norway had not yet enacted its suggested new rules for the transposition of Directive 2014/104. The process seems to have been held up by an ongoing discussion on the enforcement of competition law between the EU and the EFTA countries. References to Norwegian rules below are therefore to the Høringsnotat (n 36) containing the suggested new rules.

[39] Danish Lov nr 1541 af 13/12/2016 om behandling af erstatningssager vedrørende overtrædelser af konkurrenceretten (Act on the treatment of damages actions concerning infringements of competition law) s 15(1); Finnish Laki (1077/2016) kilpailuoikeudellisista vahingonkorvauksista (Act on Competition Law Damages) s 10, Norwegian Høringsnotat (n 36) 48–51.

[40] Lov nr 1541 s 15(3); Høringsnotat (n 36) 51.

[41] Laki (1077/2016) s 10(2).

[42] Danish Lov nr 1541, s 3(3); Finnish Laki (1077/2016) s(2); Norwegian Høringsnotat (n 36) 66 (s X-2), Swedish Competition Damages Act, c 3 s 1(2).

claim. However, this obviously entails a risk of draconian amounts of interest due to the high interest rates applicable to damages claims under Swedish law. In order to avoid that risk, the legislator chose to introduce a novelty: the interest rate applicable before the traditional starting point was set at a different, lower rate than the one applicable during the normal period of accrual. In essence, the pre-transposition rules have been maintained for the purposes of the normal period of accrual, that is, from the service of the claim until the final payment of the claim, including the main rate for damages claims. However, there will be a new and additional period of interest accrual which begins at the occurrence of harm and ends when the traditional period begins. During this period of time, interest shall accrue at the rate traditionally used for the restitution of payments pursuant to the annulment of a contract, which is set as the reference rate plus 2 per cent.[43]

A similar solution including two different interest periods has been chosen in Finland and in Norway.[44] In Denmark, however, it seems the same interest rate will apply from the occurrence of harm until the final payment of the claim.[45]

## IV. THE PRACTICAL CONSEQUENCES OF THE TRANSPOSITION

In this section it will be attempted to illustrate the very far-reaching practical consequences of the new rules in Sweden by using a simple example.[46] The example chosen will be the one mentioned in section I, which was designed for the purposes of an all-European comparative study.[47] Please recall that the example assumes that harm amounting to 100 units has been caused by cartel-inflated prices in 1993, 1998, 2006 and 2008 (in sum 400 units of harm, for simplicity presumed to have been suffered on 30 June each year). The cartel was exposed in 2009 and came to the knowledge of the claimant in that year. It will further be assumed that the defendant was served notice of the claim on 30 June 2010, that a final judgment ruling that the defendant must pay damages was delivered in 2013 and that final payment of the claim was made on 1 January 2014.

[43] The Competition Damages Act, c 3, s 1(2). This is known in Swedish law as interest on earnings, see section III.A.ii above.

[44] Finnish Laki (1077/2016) s 2 ss 2 and the *travaux préparatoires* (HE 83/2016 vp), Norwegian Høringsnotat (n 36) 18–19 which is admittedly not quite clear on this. *cf* on Norwegian law Hjelmeng, Ørstavik och Østerud (n 36) 18.

[45] Lov nr 1541, s 3(3). Danish law empowers courts to adjust the amount of interest payable if special reasons prevail, but the Supreme Court did not do that in U2005.2171H (GT-Linien) even though it must be presumed that the amount of interest in that case was extraordinarily high.

[46] Calculations in this section have been checked by an economist, for which I extend my gratitude to the Tidsskrift for Rettsvitenskap.

[47] Monti (n 4). It is not possible to present the calculations made in detail here. See instead Strand (n *) and *cf* the Monti Report for more details. A significant difference between this chapter and the Monti Report is that I have included the changes made with respect to limitation periods.

Under the pre-transposition rules in Swedish law, any claims with regard to harm incurred in 1993 and 1998 would have been barred but damages would be payable for harm incurred in 2006 and 2008 (200 units). Interest would have accrued from the date of service on 1 July 2010 until final payment on 1 January 2014. Under such circumstances, and applying the real interest rates applicable in Sweden during the interest period thus specified to calculate the interest accrued on the respective amounts of harm suffered in 2006 and 2008 respectively, the total amount of interest payable on the claim would have been 65.6 units. Add the sum principal amount of 200 units, and the total award of damages would have been 265.6 units.[48]

Under the new rules, however, no claims will be barred. Harm suffered in 1993 and 1998 can thus be included in the principal amounts claimed (sum total 400 units). The interest rate will be differentiated so that the new, lower rate applies before service of the claim and the traditional rate after that point.[49] Under this new system, the total amount of interest payable on the claim is 294.7 units. Add the sum principal amount of 400 units, and the total award of damages amounts to 665.6 units.[50]

The increase in the amount of interest alone is thus almost 250 per cent. The total amount of damages increases with over 160 per cent. As competition litigation usually concerns claims for millions of SEK or EUR, and notwithstanding that the increase of this example cannot speak for every real scenario that might occur (the percentages may be lower or higher), it is concluded that the increases of awards under the new rules, compared to the previous, will be very significant indeed.

## V. DISCUSSIONS AND CONCLUSIONS

### A. Concerning Limitation Periods and Interest per se

It can be concluded that, as a consequence of the new rules on limitation and interest, the amounts payable in competition damages awards in Sweden will increase. This will probably contribute to a greater incentive to litigate, which may in turn contribute to deterrence from infringements of competition

[48] Please find tables presenting the calculation in Strand (n *) and attached at the end of this chapter.

[49] Another complicating factor is that the reference rate was not, before 1 July 2002, necessarily changed on 1 January and 1 July (as the practice is now). This has been taken into account in my calculations.

[50] Please find tables presenting the calculation in Strand (n *) and attached at the end of this chapter.

law and thus to competition law compliance. If so, the Directive will have accomplished one of its explicit aims.[51]

From the perspective of a Swedish litigating party, however, it appears entirely arbitrary to give such preferential treatment to competition damages over similar forms of damages claims. Why should damages, for example, for an intrusion into trade secrets not be treated in the same way?[52] In both cases there is interference with the competitiveness of an undertaking in the market, an interference which is often revealed only after some time. Seen from the point of view of a company which has suffered harm by reason of an intrusion into its trade secrets it must seem unjust that limitation periods and interest rules are not as preferential to them as they would be if the obstruction of fair competition had instead taken the form of an infringement of competition law. Likewise, a company that has unwittingly taken part in a cartel must find it blatantly unfair that a competition transgression should lead to such extraordinary repercussions.

It was pointed out in section I that differentiation can be a good thing. The balance between uniformity and specialisation in law must be addressed in each individual field, and of course there should be enough flexibility to allow for courts to reach equitable solutions in particular situations. Nevertheless, this author subscribes to the view that any legislator must make an effort, particularly in our present state of multi-level law and threatening legislative elephantiasis, to keep the system of rules coherent unless there are overriding reasons for creating a special regime. For instance, in Swedish public procurement law a damages claim against the purchasing agency must be brought before the competent court within one year from the completion of the contract.[53] In that situation any claimant will be able to quickly assess the amount of harm suffered and other relevant circumstances. In essence, well-founded differences between damages regimes should be accepted, whereas random fragmentation must be avoided.

With regard in particular to the Swedish transposition of Directive 2014/104, I cannot see any reasons in legal policy that would justify a special regime of

[51] Directive 2014/104 (n 2) Recitals 1-3. For an overview of competition litigation in Stockholm City Court, see I Simonsson, 'Challenges for Swedish Courts: Will the New Directive on Antitrust Damages Actions Help?' in M Bergström, M Iacovides and M Strand (eds), *Harmonising EU Competition Litigation: The New Directive and Beyond* (Oxford, Hart Publishing, 2016) 65–80, in particular the tables at 68–70.

[52] Damages for such intrusion has not been harmonised under EU law; there is only a very general reference to the availability of civil remedies in Art 6 of Directive (EU) 2016/943 of the European Parliament and of the Council of 8 June 2016 on the protection of undisclosed know-how and business information (trade secrets) against their unlawful acquisition, use and disclosure [2016] OJ L157/1.

[53] Lagen (2016:1145) om offentlig upphandling (Public Procurement Act) c 20, s 21.

limitation and interest for competition damages that would not be equally valid for other instances where an infringement causing harm, and/or the harm itself, are revealed only after some time. I have mentioned intrusion into trade secrets as an example. Note that Danish, Finnish and Norwegian law have had special rules on limitation periods that target the problem of unknown harm since before the transposition of Directive 2014/104. Furthermore, there has been a certain amount of leeway for courts to award interest from the occurrence of harm, although their transpositions of Directive 2014/104 add some foreseeability on when this should be done. Therefore, it cannot be argued that such solutions with a broader field of application are unknown to Nordic legal tradition. On the contrary, it is submitted that they would work very well in a Swedish context. Now, the minimum transposition chosen gives the impression that the Swedish legislator only opted for a minimum solution, confining what they perceived to be overriding EU law requirements to as narrow a scope as possible. Few litigants will be happy with such an explanation. Consequently, it is submitted that the Swedish legislator should consider a broader reform concerning limitation periods and interest for any instance of unknown harm.

What has been argued here arguably applies, *mutatis mutandis*, to many aspects of the Competition Damages Act. Since it has been drafted to stay very close to the text of Directive 2014/104, certain of its provisions are phrased in a manner that is odd or even alien to the Swedish system of private law and civil procedure.[54] As a consequence, Sweden now has a special regime which is quite important as part of the rules governing the Swedish market but with a very (even unjustifiably) narrow scope. To competition litigants some of the new rules will appear strange and arbitrary. For these reasons, it is submitted that the transposition of Directive 2014/104 should have been taken as an opportunity for broader reform not only of the rules on limitation periods and interest, but of all relevant statutory law in Sweden.

This is not to say that it is too late to initiate the necessary reform. A justified differentiation of rules on limitation periods and interest could begin by making a distinction between general rules on late payments and rules on damages payments, at least with regard to non-contractual damages payments. After all, the latter category of claims has many distinctive qualities: the claim is often disputed, litigation usually involves complicated evidence assessments, and it is common that the claimant (and even the tortfeasor) have been unaware of having suffered harm for a shorter or longer period of time. With such a distinction, the Swedish legislator would be able to make room for a new approach

[54] Perhaps the most obvious example is the Competition Damages Act, c 5, s 8, transposing Art 7 of Directive 2014/104. The purpose of the rule is to protect so-called whistleblowers under the leniency programme, but from a Swedish procedural law perspective, it is completely alien to our traditional principle of free submission and assessment of evidence (Rättegångsbalken (the Code of Judicial Procedure) 1942:740, c 35, s 1).

to limitation periods and interest on such a claim that takes into account the (few) requirements in Directive 2014/104, while nevertheless avoiding unjustified fragmentation between the handling of similar damages claims. For instance, it would be possible to reconsider the interest rate for damages claims. Why not create a new, third category alongside interest for delay and interest on earnings? Why not follow the other Nordic jurisdictions in creating special rules for all instances of unknown harm? Already with these rather small adjustments many of the problems addressed above would be overcome.

### B. Being Constructive and Creative about EU Law and Private Law

As regards specialised legal regimes in general, 'fragmentation' is probably a poor choice of words to describe the phenomenon as such. It must be kept in mind that relevant differentiations in law are justified. Although it is true that like cases should be treated alike, we must not forget that the principle of formal justice continues to state that different cases should be treated differently. Consequently, although simplicity and unity in private law will serve foreseeability and legal certainty, the complexities of human society have always compelled both lawmakers and judges to find specific solutions to specific problems. Nevertheless, efforts have been made, from time to time and with varying emphasis as well as with varying success, to maintain consistency in private law and to safeguard it from arbitrary differential treatment of similar cases and from the detriments of competing and colliding jurisdictions and/or laws.[55] Indeed, there is a vast playing field between the extreme ideal types of uniform rules with a broad scope, on the one hand, and specialised rules for particular instances, on the other. What is at stake here is consequently not whether specialised rules are a good thing, generally, but how to approach the task of transposing an EU directive into national law.

Obviously, the question is not (and has never been) whether to strive for coherence or for specialisation as such. In the EU context, that is the question: whether (or, more precisely, to what extent) to suffer that new rules must be introduced in the form of an ad hoc specialised regime created solely in order

[55] Of course, this is precisely the idea driving harmonisation in EU law; to achieve coherence across the jurisdictions of the Member States. On this idea and how the striving for intra-EU coherence nonetheless gives rise to the intra-Member State confusion discussed in this chapter, see K Havu, 'Quasi-coherence by Harmonisation of EU Competition Law-related Damages Actions?' in Letto-Vanamo and Smits, *Coherence and Fragmentation in European Private Law* (n 3) 25–42. For a historical perspective on the development from pre-modern fragmentation to the codifications of modernity and on to the re-fragmentation taking place in our times, see eg Letto-Vanamo, 'Fragmentation and Coherence of Law' (n 3). As is well known, FK von Savigny was quite sceptical about the benefits of the codifications taking place in his time; see *Vom Beruf unserer Zeit für Gesetzgebung und Rechtswissenschaft* (Mohr und Zimmer, 1814) 16–24.

to transpose a certain directive,[56] or to take arms against the threat of fragmentation in order to maintain a coherent national system including the new private law rules.[57] Furthermore, EU legislation is by no means the only way in which EU private law, which becomes part of the private law of every Member State, is being created. EU primary law, ie the Treaties, the Charter and the general principles of EU law, is also a relevant source of EU private law. The obvious example is of course the rule on the nullity of anticompetitive agreements in Article 101(2) TFEU, but there are other and less direct ways in which EU primary law becomes relevant in a private law context.[58] There are seemingly endless private law consequences arising from the complexities of the interplay of EU law and national law in general, under doctrines and principles such as EU law precedence, the direct or exclusionary effect of EU law, consistent interpretation, and the principles of equivalence and effectiveness. Moreover, EU Regulations are capable of being directly applicable in private law relations, as follows from Article 288(2) TFEU. In this chapter, however, focus will be on issues related to the transposition of EU directives in the field of private law.

It is beyond the scope of this contribution to evaluate the many transposition strategies tested by national legislators in the EU, such as minimum transposition or so-called supererogatory transposition.[59] Every strategy has its risks and its benefits. Minimum transposition – which often seems to be the Swedish option in order to minimise the impact of EU legislation – is liable to create a patchwork of specialised regimes, disrupting the coherence of national private law and endangering the possibilities of drawing conclusions by analogy that have contributed so much to the success of modern law.[60] On the other hand minimum harmonisation may be a way to constrain what is perceived, by the

[56] It will be argued below that this seems to have been the approach of the Swedish legislator with regard to its transposition of Directive 2014/104.

[57] This has become the attitude of the German legislator, according to S Leible, 'The Approach to European Law in Domestic Legislation' (2003) 4 *German Law Journal* 1255–75.

[58] eg through a combination of national private law and EU law. Arbetsdomstolen (the Swedish Labour Court) has held a trade union liable in damages to compensate an employer for loss incurred by an infringement by the trade union of (now) Art 56 TFEU; AD 2009 nr 89. In the proceedings, Arbetsdomstolen made a reference for a preliminary ruling; C-341/05 *Laval un Partneri* EU:C:2007:809. In my opinion, a second reference should have been made in order to ask whether the trade union could, under EU law, be held liable in damages for the harm incurred by the employer.

[59] A term coined by Leible, 'The Approach to European Law in Domestic Legislation' (n 57) 1268, who surveys transposition methods used by the German legislator in his article. By supererogatory transposition, Leible intends that the transposing national legislation is awarded a broader scope than the EU directive transposed. Such an approach has been recommended with regard to Directive 2014/104 by M Petr, 'The Scope of the Implementation of the Damages Directive in CEE States' (2017) 10 *Yearbook of Antitrust and Regulatory Studies* 13–29.

[60] Analogies from one area of private law to another were alien to Roman law; see J Smits, 'Coherence and Fragmentation in the Law of Contract' in Letto-Vanamo and Smits (n 3) 11.

national legislator, as the adverse impact of unwanted new rules. Supererogatory transposition may be even more problematic as it leads to the problem of fragmented legal acts, where the aspects of the national act that are transposing the directive are to be interpreted and applied with the EU law method, while aspects that may fall outside the directive (or even outside the scope of EU law as such) can be interpreted and applied using the traditional national method.[61] Consequently, the act itself may become a minefield for those who try to read it as a coherent whole.

Recently it was pointed out by one of the leading private law authors in Sweden, Johnny Herre, that the Swedish legislator does not give priority to more far-reaching legislative reforms that could satisfy the need for systematic coherence. Instead, Herre submitted, legislative work is carried out on ad hoc basis in order to address what is perceived to be the most acute issues, and in particular the legislator has become too preoccupied with transposing EU legislation to give proper attention to maintaining the national system. The result, Herre argued, was 'fragmentation'.[62] Herre thus expresses the *perception of pressure* identified in section I. Nevertheless, Herre might very well agree with this author that this situation is avoidable, and ultimately hinges upon how the national legislator approaches the task of transposing an EU directive into national law.

The perception of pressure from the EU against national private law must not lead to defeatism or to settling for putting the 'blame' for fragmentation on the EU. Several commentators have argued that the problem of fragmentation should, or can only, be remedied by the EU legislator, either through more harmonisation or by creating a uniform, but optional, European civil code.[63] This author is inclined to respectfully disagree: the fragmentation of national private law cannot be blamed on the EU and other supernational or transnational 'norm bringers' only; choices made by the Member States (whether or not these choices are made consciously) play a significant role too. It is obvious, if nothing else than from the failure of the Common European Sales Law, that systematic and coherent EU private law will not fall from the *Begriffshimmel* any time soon. Instead, we need to work with what we have, where we are. To borrow a line from the sociologist Clifford Geertz, we are

[61] L Sisula-Tulokas, 'Civilrättens splittring' in Severin Blomstrand et al (eds), *Bertil Bengtsson 90 år* (Stockholm, Jure Förlag, 2016) 489.

[62] J Herre, 'Obligationsrätt i Norden – nuläge och utmaningar' (2018) 131 *Tidsskrift for Rettvitenskap* 272, 285–87.

[63] See eg Leible (n 57) 1265, and the Panel Discussion report in R Schulze and H Schulte-Nölke (eds), *European Private Law – Current Status and Perspectives* (Munich, Sellier – de Gruyter, 2011) 265–78.

today suspended in webs[64] of simultaneous and multi-layered tendencies towards coherence and fragmentation originating from several different sources of law, and we must each learn to live with it and to work with it. The EU has rightly been criticised for inconsistent terminology in private law legislation,[65] and the EU legislator must – as it has tried to do in recent years – take it upon itself to remedy this flaw. Nonetheless it is for the Member States and for each Member State alone to assume responsibility for making a whole functioning system of private law from the jigsaw puzzle of national private law and EU private law. This chapter aims to illustrate what can happen if Member States do not rise to this challenge, and offers a few pointers regarding the way forward. If the position thus advocated here is accepted, it becomes obvious that the responsibility of making a coherent whole of national law and EU law *in the process of transposing a directive* falls on the national legislators.

Consequently, EU law has broad and multi-faceted implications for national private law. Indeed, within the scope of application of EU law, it may be that we can discern a growing field of *EU private law*. As a consequence, judges and private lawyers throughout the EU must work to understand how the interplay between EU law and national law works in private law. In order for this interplay to work in a satisfactory manner, however, it is necessary that legislation transposing EU directives maintains the high standard of quality that is demanded for any act of legislation. To do that we must strive to avoid fragmentation as such, as has been argued above, but perhaps a more pressing need is to deal with the *perception of outside pressure* that lingers in private law. It is submitted that this perception itself, blaming the 'blind and blunt' EU legislator for any and all fragmentation, is the first and foremost cause for concern regarding poorer quality of legislation and law enforcement in Europe.

Insofar as lawmaking is concerned, whether prompted by the transposition of directives or by necessary adaptations to other aspects of EU law, officials in the national legislatures must, on the one hand, be intimately familiar with the principles governing interaction between EU law and national law. Familiarity, in this context, does not only denote acquaintance with the principles but also an in-depth understanding of how they have been developed, expressed and used in the case-law of the Court of Justice and how they interrelate (or seem to interrelate, for indeed this is not always easily discerned), including a capacity to identify problematic issues. On the other hand, an as intimate familiarity with the field of national law at stake is equally necessary. If the legislative process

[64] '[M]an is an animal suspended in webs of significance he himself has spun', a view that Geertz himself attributes to inspiration from Max Weber; C Geertz, *The Interpretation of Cultures* (New York, Basic Books, 1973) 5.

[65] eg by Leible (n 57) 1257 and by J Herre, 'Obligationsrätt i Norden – nuläge och utmaningar' (n 62) 284.

is based on these two fundamental conditions, then (and, it is submitted, only then) will the national legislator have the necessary tools in place to identify relevant options and to reach informed decisions. The process of transposing a directive into national law should always include a readiness to seize the opportunity to introduce a broader reform of the national sets of rules and regulations that are concerned, to the benefit of everyday legal practice.[66]

In the counselling and adjudication of legal matters, big and small, that take place every day in the Member States, we must never stop to strive for the same high quality in our interpretation and application of rules in or derived from EU law as we do with regard to purely domestic law. To that effect, it must be finally accepted that EU law is no longer outside the system, but rather inside it; private law practice in EU Member States is governed by (at least) two legal systems that operate in parallel or, sometimes, even simultaneously. In Sweden a great deal of hard work remains in order to reach that point, while for instance Denmark seems to have made greater progress.[67]

One consequence of that work will be the need to nuance the perception in private law (and other fields of national law) of *pressure coming from outside the system*. National legislators must ensure that they are able to make conscious choices of when to opt for minimum transposition and when to initiate a broader reform in order to maintain a systematically coherent body of national law – and when and how to use all the myriad of choices that lie between these extremes. Such an in-depth, constructive and creative understanding of the interrelationship between EU law and private law entails what is seemingly a paradox: EU law dictates the methods and techniques to be used for the interpretation and application of EU law, but in the Member States we are free (albeit to a varying degree) to set the legal context in which EU law norms are to be interpreted and applied. This choice of legal setting can be used in order preserve traditions, and to promote legal coherence. By remaining aware of these opportunities – this normative discretion but nonetheless normative responsibility – we can, it is submitted, acquire a nuanced attitude to the interplay of EU law and national private law that could in turn vouch for high quality in the transposition and implementation of directives. In order to avoid unwarranted fragmentation of national law we must stop *succumbing* to the transposition of directives, and rise to *managing* the integration of directives into the bigger regulatory context.

[66] *cf* Piszcz, 'Room for Manoeuvre for Member States: Issues for Decision on the Occasion of the Transposition of the Damages Directive' (2017) 1 *Market and Competition Law Review* 81–109, in particular at 106.

[67] That is, judging from the active and creative attitude to EU law displayed by Danish courts in cases such as C-94/10 *Danfoss* EU:C:2011:674 and C-441/14 *Dansk Industri* EU:C:2016:278.

**Table 1** Calculation of interest on the principal award under previous Swedish rules

| | | |
|---|---|---|
| Harm to be compensated in damages: 200 units | | |
| 1 July 2010 – 31 December 2010 | Interest rate: 8.5 % | Sum: 8.6 units |
| 1 January 2011 – 30 June 2011 | Interest rate: 9.5 % | Sum: 9.4 units |
| 1 July 2011 – 30 June 2012 | Interest rate: 10.0 % | Sum: 20.0 units |
| 1 July 2012 – 31 December 2012 | Interest rate: 9.5 % | Sum: 9.6 units |
| 1 January 2013 – 31 December 2013 | Interest rate: 9.0 % | Sum: 18.0 units |
| Sum total of interest: 65.6 units. | | |

**Table 2** Calculation of interest on the principal award under new Swedish rules

| | | |
|---|---|---|
| Harm to be compensated in damages: 100 units for 1st instance of harm | | |
| Interest before service of the claim is interest for restitution of sums paid but not due. | | |
| 1 July 1993 | Interest rate: 9.0 % | Sum: 0.0 units |
| 2 July 1993 – 7 October 1993 | Interest rate: 8.0 % | Sum: 2.1 units |
| 8 October 1993 – 3 January 1994 | Interest rate: 7.0 % | Sum: 1.7 units |
| 4 January 1994 – 3 July 1994 | Interest rate: 6.5 % | Sum: 3.2 units |
| 4 July 1994 – 3 October 1994 | Interest rate: 7.5 % | Sum: 1.9 units |
| 4 October 1994 – 3 July 1995 | Interest rate: 9.0 % | Sum: 6.7 units |
| 4 July 1995 – 5 October 1995 | Interest rate: 9.5 % | Sum: 2.4 units |
| 6 October 1995 – 2 January 1996 | Interest rate: 9.0 % | Sum: 2.2 units |
| 3 January 1996 – 1 April 1996 | Interest rate: 8.0 % | Sum: 2.0 units |
| 2 April 1996 – 1 July 1996 | Interest rate: 7.5 % | Sum: 1.8 units |
| 2 July 1996 – 1 October 1996 | Interest rate: 6.5 % | Sum: 1.6 units |
| 2 October 1996 – 2 January 1997 | Interest rate: 5.5 % | Sum: 1.4 units |
| 3 January 1997 – 30 June 1998 | Interest rate: 4.5 % | Sum: 6.7 units |
| Harm to be compensated in damages: Add 100 units for 2nd instance of harm (sum 200 units) | | |
| 1 July 1998 | Interest rate: 4.5 % | Sum: 0.0 units |
| 2 July 1998 – 4 January 1999 | Interest rate: 4.0 % | Sum: 4.1 units |
| 5 January 1999 – 5 April 1999 | Interest rate: 3.5 % | Sum: 1.7 units |
| 6 April 1999 – 3 October 1999 | Interest rate: 3.0 % | Sum: 3.0 units |
| 4 October 1999 – 3 April 2000 | Interest rate: 3,5 % | Sum: 3.5 units |
| 4 April 2000 – 30 June 2000 | Interest rate: 4.5 % | Sum: 2.2 units |
| 1 July 2000 – 2 April 2001 | Interest rate: 4.0 % | Sum: 6.0 units |
| 3 April 2001 – 2 July 2001 | Interest rate: 3.5 % | Sum: 1.7 units |

*(continued)*

**Table 2** *(Continued)*

| | | |
|---|---|---|
| 3 July 2001 – 2 January 2002 | Interest rate: 4.0 % | Sum: 4.0 units |
| 3 January 2002 – 2 April 2002 | Interest rate: 3.5 % | Sum: 1.7 units |
| 3 April 2002 – 30 June 2002 | Interest rate: 4.0 % | Sum: 2.0 units |
| 1 July 2002 – 31 December 2002 | Interest rate: 6.5 % | Sum: 6.6 units |
| 1 January 2003 – 30 June 2003 | Interest rate: 6.0 % | Sum: 6.0 units |
| 1 July 2003 – 30 June 2004 | Interest rate: 5.0 % | Sum: 10.0 units |
| 1 July 2004 – 30 June 2005 | Interest rate: 4.0 % | Sum: 8.0 units |
| 1 July 2005 – 30 June 2006 | Interest rate: 3.5 % | Sum: 7.0 units |
| Harm to be compensated in damages: Add 100 units for 3rd instance of harm (sum 300 units) | | |
| 1 July 2006 – 31 December 2006 | Interest rate: 4.5 % | Sum: 6.8 units |
| 1 January 2007 – 30 June 2007 | Interest rate: 5.0 % | Sum: 7.4 units |
| 1 July 2007 – 31 December 2007 | Interest rate: 5.5 % | Sum: 8.3 units |
| 1 January 2008 – 30 June 2008 | Interest rate: 6.0 % | Sum: 8.9 units |
| Harm to be compensated in damages: Add 100 units for 4th instance of harm (sum 400 units) | | |
| 1 July 2008 – 31 December 2008 | Interest rate: 6.5 % | Sum: 13.1 units |
| 1 January 2009 – 30 June 2009 | Interest rate: 4.0 % | Sum: 7.9 units |
| 1 July 2009 – 30 June 2010 | Interest rate: 2.5 % | Sum: 10.0 units |
| Interest after service of the claim is interest for delay. | | |
| 1 July 2010 – 31 December 2010 | Interest rate: 8.5 % | Sum: 17.1 units |
| 1 January 2011 – 30 June 2011 | Interest rate: 9.5 % | Sum: 18.8 units |
| 1 July 2011 – 30 June 2012 | Interest rate: 10.0 % | Sum: 40.0 units |
| 1 July 2012 – 31 December 2012 | Interest rate: 9.5 % | Sum: 19.2 units |
| 1 January 2013 – 31 December 2013 | Interest rate: 9.0 % | Sum: 36.0 units |
| Sum total of interest: 294.7 units. | | |

# 4

# *A First Look at the Portuguese Act 23/2018 Transposing the Private Enforcement Directive*

SOFIA OLIVEIRA PAIS*

## I. THE TRANSPOSITION PROCEDURE OF THE PRIVATE ENFORCEMENT DIRECTIVE

FOLLOWING THE ADOPTION of Directive 2014/104/EU of the European Parliament and of the Council of 26 November 2014 on certain rules governing actions for damages under national law for infringements of the competition law provisions of the Member States and of the European Union,[1] the Ministry of Economy requested that the Portuguese Competition Authority prepare a preliminary draft of a law transposing this Directive into the national legal order.

The Portuguese Competition Authority proceeded with the drafting of this proposal through an open and transparent process divided into several phases from 2015 to 2017. The first phase consisted of the drafting of a working paper and setting up a working group of external experts from the judiciary, academia and legal practice to participate in the discussions. In the second phase, the Portuguese Competition Authority sent the draft to a large number of different stakeholders, including public authorities, law firms, universities, sectoral associations, consumer associations and professional associations, inviting them to participate in a consultative workshop and, if they so wished, to present their comments on the preliminary draft.[2] After the workshop, a report was written

* Associate Professor, Universidade Católica Portuguesa, Jean Monnet Chair.

[1] Directive 2014/104/EU on certain rules governing actions for damages under national law for infringements of the competition law provisions of the Member States and of the European Union [2014] OJ L 349/1.

[2] See MJ Melícias, 'The Art of Consistency between Public and Private Enforcement: Practical Challenges in Implementing the Damages Directive in Portugal' (2016) 26 *Revista de Concorrência e Regulação* 37, 39.

with the aim of presenting, in a succinct way, the different perspectives that were suggested by the participants, 'for future memory and as a potential working tool'.[3] In the third phase, the Portuguese Competition Authority promoted a public consultation process on the first draft proposal for the transposition of the Directive, which ran from 26 April to 27 May 2016, and was published through the Portuguese Competition Authority's website. The main strategic goal of this public debate, according to the Portuguese Competition Authority, was to engage stakeholders 'so that they might regard the new private enforcement regime as their own, and thus be actually encouraged to field-test it once implemented'.[4]

Curiously, the Portuguese Competition Authority's proposal was only submitted to the Parliament a year later. After being criticised by some of the left-wing parties, the Government presented a new proposal for transposition (Proposal 101/XIII), which, with some minor exceptions, included the main solutions of the Portuguese Competition Authority's proposal. On 5 June 2018, the Act 23/2018 (Portuguese Act), establishing the new legal framework on action for damages for the infringements of competition law, was finally published.[5]

## II. THE SCOPE OF THE PORTUGUESE ACT

The majority of the provisions adopted in the Portuguese Act followed the Directive. The scope of Act 23/2018 is wide. It applies to stand-alone and to follow-on actions and includes infringements of Articles 101 and 102 of the Treaty on the Functioning of the European Union, infringements of Articles 9.º, 11.º and 12.º of the Law 19/2012 as well as infringements of similar legal rules of other Member States. The aim of this solution, according to the Portuguese Competition Authority, is to ensure the creation of a unitary frame of reference as well as a non-discriminatory system for those causing damages by infringing EU or national competition laws and to promote, therefore, a higher level of legal certainty, fulfilling at the same time the principle of equivalence.[6]

Damages caused by infringements of state aid or mergers rules are not, however, addressed by the Portuguese Act,[7] which might be explained by the fact

[3] M Sousa Ferro, 'Workshop consultivo sobre o anteprojeto de transposição da Diretiva 2014/104/UE – relatório síntese' (2016) 26 *Revista de Concorrência e Regulação* 51, 51–52.

[4] ibid, 40. See also Autoridade da Concorrência, *Proposta de Anteprojeto de Transposição da Diretiva Private Enforcement* (Lisboa, 22 de junho de 2016), available at: www.concorrencia.pt/vPT/Noticias_Eventos/ConsultasPublicas/Documents/Private%20Enforcement/Proposta%20de%20Anteprojeto.pdf.

[5] Diário da República, 1ª série, N.º 107, 5 de junho de 2018, p. 2368.

[6] Autoridade da Concorrência, 'Exposição de motivos' (2016) 26 *Revista de Concorrência e Regulação* 103.

[7] Act 23/2018, Art 2, l).

that actions for damages are almost exclusively related to cartels.[8] In fact, recent studies have reviewed the judgments issued by national courts on damages caused by the infringement of competition rules and concluded, on the one hand, that the situation has changed significantly in the last few years and that the level of uncertainty surrounding private enforcement issues has diminished as the national courts have provided many insights in their decisions. Moreover, the studies also confirm that the majority of claims are still related to cartels.[9]

On the other hand, concerns regarding the fact that the transposition procedure and the solutions adopted would inevitably undermine the internal systematic consistency of Portuguese legislation were also referred to in the workshops (organised by the Portuguese Competition Authority) and during public consultation.[10] For instance, the presumption of cartel damages and the solution established in the Portuguese Proposal, concerning the sharing of responsibilities between co-infringers according to their market shares, might be difficult to reconcile with certain rules of the Portuguese legal order. Nevertheless, those solutions were adopted in Act 23/2018.

## III. EXCLUSIVE COMPETENCE OF THE SPECIALISED PORTUGUESE COURT FOR COMPETITION REGULATION AND SUPERVISION

A novelty in the Portuguese Act that goes beyond the Directive is to grant exclusive jurisdiction for this kind of action to the already existing Portuguese Specialised Court of First Instance, the *Tribunal da Concorrência Regulação e Supervisão* (TCRS). In other words, it is for the Specialised Court – the Portuguese Court for Competition Regulation and Supervision (TCRS) – to decide not only cases of public enforcement (it already reviews the antitrust and merger decisions from the Portuguese Competition Authority) but also actions for damages based solely on the infringement of competition law. So the Portuguese Court will hear those actions as well as actions for the exercising of

[8] See the survey conducted by M Kuijpers, S Tuinenga, E Whiteford and TB Paul, 'Actions for Damages in the Netherlands, the United Kingdom, and Germany' (2017) 8 *Journal of European Competition Law & Practice* 65. For an analysis of the situation of private enforcement in Spain, see R Alonso Soto, 'La aplicación privada del derecho de la competencia' (2015) 22 *Revista de Concorrência e Regulação* 94, 96, and the excellent article by A Robles Martín-Laborda, 'La directive 2014/104 sobre daños antitrust y la configuración del derecho español de danos' (2015) 22 *Revista de Concorrência e Regulação* 107.

[9] J-F Laborde, 'Cartel Damages Claims in Europe: How Courts have Assessed Overcharges (2017 ed.)' (2017) 4 *Concurrences* 1, 1–2. In this survey, updated and extended in the summer 2017, 98 cartel damages claims were identified, and the cases come from 12 countries: 'Germany (38 cases), France (27 cases), Hungary (7 cases), Italy (6 cases), the Netherlands (4 cases), Austria, Denmark and Finland (3 cases each), Belgium, Poland and Spain (2 cases each), and Greece (1 case)'; and of the 98 cases only 4 were stand-alone actions.

[10] Published in Diário da Assembleia da República, Series II-A, No 18, 24/10/2017, 4–18. See also Autoridade da Concorrência, 'Exposição de motivos' (n 6) 103.

the right of contribution between co-infringers, and the requests for access to evidence relating to such actions.[11]

This solution, according to the Portuguese Competition Authority, would take advantage of specialisation (avoiding civil judges who lack experience of these issues) and would avoid contradictory judicial decisions.[12] Furthermore, the exclusive competence of the TCRS will only apply after the entry into force of the law and the pending actions before the civil courts will not be transferred to that court (Article 24.°, n.° 2, Act 23/2018).

Finally, to monitor private enforcement the Portuguese Act sets up an information system according to which national courts must notify the Portuguese Competition Authority of their actions involving the application of antitrust rules as well as a request for the disclosure of evidence.[13]

It is important to mention that the solution adopted by the Portuguese Act, regarding the granting of jurisdiction to a specialised court, is not consensual.[14] The main problem highlighted was that there would be few actions based *solely* on the infringement of competition law. In fact, as Maria José Costeira has already mentioned 'notwithstanding the fact that there will be a single specialised court (…) there is still a large number of cases, perhaps the majority, which stay away from the specialisation'. In fact, 'all the cases in which the cause of action is not uniquely the competition law infringement, as well as the ones in which the competition law is invoked in the defendant pleading, [that is to say] most of the pending cases in our courts, are excluded from the TCRS' competence'; in addition, 'there are still a considerable number of cases that will remain in the administrative courts where the private enforcement actions have been increasing'.[15] These meaningful insights are also supported by a study published by the Centre for Research in European, Economic, Financial and Tax Law, which anticipates that the majority of the cases will be heard in other courts of first instance and the specialised court will only cover fewer than 8 per cent of the cases.[16]

In conclusion, although the reasons for granting exclusive jurisdiction to TCRS remain valid, the interest and effectiveness of that solution might be, for the reasons already mentioned, very limited in practice.

[11] Art 22 of Act 23/2018 modifies Art 112 of Law 62/2013, 26 August.

[12] Taking the opposite view, others have argued that this reform might promote the rethinking of the fairness of the solutions of the general regime. See Melícias, 'The Art of Consistency between Public and Private Enforcement' (n 2) 47.

[13] Art 21 of the Act 23/2018 modifies the Law 19/2012 adding the new Art 94-A.

[14] See the relevant arguments presented by MJ Costeira, 'The Transposition of the Private Enforcement Directive: a Critical Perspective' (2017) 3 *UNIO – EU Law Journal* 148, 155–56.

[15] ibid, 155–56.

[16] See the Study of the Centre for Research in European, Economic, Financial and Tax Law, available at: www.cideeff.pt/xms/files/Projeto_4_grupo_III/Jurisprudencia_de_Private_Enforcement.pdf.

## IV. SUBSTANTIVE SOLUTIONS

The Portuguese Act has mainly adopted the solutions of the Directive but gone beyond it regarding certain specific issues.

### A. The Concepts of Undertaking, Parent Company and Joint Liability

With the aim of providing legal certainty, the Portuguese Act defines an undertaking in accordance with the case-law of the Court of Justice and mentions that it will be liable for the infringement of competition law;[17] in other words, it will have to fully compensate those injured by the damages resulting from such an infringement.

The 'parent company' will also be liable if it has exerted decisive influence over the undertaking's business under Article 36, paragraph 3, of Law no 19/2012, of 8 May, and a decisive influence is presumed to exist (rebuttable presumption) when the parent company holds 90 per cent or more of the share capital of the subsidiary and exercises decisive influence over its business. With this solution, the Portuguese Competition Authority argued that the consistency between public and private enforcement would be improved.[18]

It should be highlighted, however, that these solutions are still not consensual in Portugal as well as in other legal orders. In Portugal, it has been argued that the Act should use legal language consistent with our traditions, namely the Commercial Company Code.

In other Member States,[19] there is literature arguing that a parent company should only be held responsible for its own wrongdoing or if it has infringed the duty to supervise its subsidiaries, calling into the equation the constitutional principles of assessing legal responsibility according to individual guilt and *nulla poena sine lege*.[20] In addition, with the *Kone* judgment[21] it has also been

[17] Case C-41/90 *Höfner and Elser* EU:C:1991:161. This definition of undertaking was already inserted in Art 3 of the Portuguese Competition Act.

[18] Melícias (n 2) 42.

[19] See eg Maria José Costeira stressing that 'neither the companies include a plurality of legal persons nor the infractions committed by a company are imputable to other. Companies are or might be in group relations or domain. On the other hand, it is not the imputation that is transmitted. What may be transmitted is the responsibility/liability resulting from the infringing action'; Costeira, 'The Transposition of the Private Enforcement Directive' (n 14) 151–52.

[20] F Janka, 'National and International Developments Parent Company Liability in German and EU Competition Law: Two Worlds Apart?' (2016) 7 *Journal of European Competition Law & Practice* 616. However, in June 2017, the German Competition Act was amended and parental liability was aligned with EU rules; in other words, the amendment extends liability to all companies constituting a 'single economic entity. For a brief description of the German law, see B Burkhardt, *The New German Competition Law in a Nutshell*, available at: www.lexology.com/library/detail.aspx?g=535d2bda-4598-413d-86c6-05b592b1c7b5.

[21] Case C-557/12 *Kone AG and others against ÖBB-Infrastruktur AG* EU:C:2014:1317.

argued that the application of the concept of 'single entity' to civil responsibility is a decision for the Member States.[22] In fact, in this judgment, the Court of Justice held that in the absence of EU rules, and as along as the principles of equivalence and effectiveness are fulfilled, 'it is for the domestic legal system of each Member State to lay down the detailed rules governing the exercise of the right to claim compensation for the harm resulting from an agreement or practice prohibited under Article 101 TFEU'.[23]

Finally, if the infringement of competition law results from the joint conduct of two or more undertakings, they are jointly liable.[24] This means that each of those undertakings has to compensate for the harm in full, and the injured party has the right to require full compensation from any of them. Joint liability has been established in the Directive as a general rule and only the derogations provided for in its text are allowed, namely an immunity recipient,[25] small and medium-sized enterprises, provided that certain conditions are met,[26] and the situation where the injured party has reached a consensual settlement with one of the co-infringers.

Concerning the right of contribution between co-infringers, the Portuguese Act goes beyond the Directive. It establishes in Article 5, n.º 5, a rebuttable presumption that the extent of the liability of each undertaking is 'presumed to be equivalent to the average of their market shares in the affected markets during their participation in the infringement, unless proven otherwise'. In other words, the capability of the undertakings to restrict competition, measured through their market shares, will be taken into account to apportion liability for the assessed damages. In addition, this solution would be 'in line with public enforcement'.[27] The general rule of Portuguese civil law, establishing

[22] S Thomas and S Legner, 'Die wirtschaftliche Einheit im Kartellzivilrecht' (2016) *Neue Zeitschrift für Kartellrech* 155, 156; P Stauber and H Schaper, 'Die Kartellschadensersatzrichtlinie – Handlungsbedarf für den deutschen Gesetzgeber?' (2014) *Neue Zeitschrift für Kartellrecht* 346, 357 and Janka, 'National and International Developments Parent Company Liability in German and EU Competition Law' (n 20) 616.

[23] *Kone* (n 21) para 24.

[24] The Portuguese Act adopts the solution provided in Art11 of the Directive.

[25] That is to say a person that has been granted immunity from fines by a competition authority under a leniency programme. It will only be liable to its direct or indirect purchasers or providers, and to other injured parties where full compensation cannot be obtained from the other undertakings that were involved in the same infringement and the amount of its contribution shall also not exceed the amount of the harm it caused to its own direct or indirect purchasers or providers. See Art 11(4)–(5) and Art 2(19) of the Directive.

[26] Small or medium-sized enterprises (SMEs), as defined in Commission Recommendation 2003/361/EC of 6 May 2003 concerning the definition of micro, small and medium-sized enterprises, OJ [2003] L 124/36, are only liable for their own direct and indirect purchasers if their market share in the relevant market was below 5% at any time during the infringement and the application of the normal rules of joint and several liability would irretrievably jeopardise their economic viability and cause their assets to lose all their value. The exception, however, does not apply if the SME has led the infringement or has coerced other undertakings to participate therein, or if the SME has previously been found to have infringed competition law.

[27] Melicias (n 2) 43.

a presumption of equal responsibility (based on fault, which is presumed equal), was, therefore, put aside.

## B. Disclosure of Evidence

Bringing actions for damages for infringement of competition law is only possible if courts are also able to order that evidence relevant to damages claims be disclosed by third parties, including public authorities. In fact, given the information asymmetry in competition law litigation, it is necessary to ensure that claimants are afforded the right to obtain the disclosure of evidence relevant to their claim, namely, from national or European competition authorities. Concerning the relationship between national courts and the European Commission, the courts can order disclosure of evidence, following the principle in Article 4(3) TEU of sincere cooperation between the Union and the Member States and Article 15(1) of Regulation (EC) No 1/2003. On the other hand, the Directive underlines that the principle of proportionality provides that disclosure can be ordered only where a claimant has made a plausible assertion; in other words, the claimant presents reasonably available facts in the reasoned justification.

Furthermore, the disclosure of evidence must also take into account the effectiveness of the leniency programme, which is labelled as an essential tool to combat secret cartels effectively.[28] In order to achieve an equilibrium between these conflicting interests, the Directive establishes that 'Member States shall ensure that, for the purpose of actions for damages, national courts cannot at any time order a party or a third party to disclose any of the following categories of evidence: (a) leniency statements; and (b) settlement submissions' (Article 6, no 6).[29] With this solution, the Directive apparently clarifies the doubts arising from the *Pfleiderer* and *Donau* case-law holding that national courts must decide on a case-by-case basis whether or not disclosure is possible, weighing the interests of effective application of antitrust rules and the right of the claimant to full compensation.[30] With the Directive, this case-law will no longer apply to leniency statements and settlement submissions and that is why some authors have argued that EU policy makers are restricting the principle of effective redress.[31]

[28] As Wils explains, *cf* WPJ Wils, 'Private Enforcement of EU Antitrust Law and Its Relationship with Public Enforcement: Past, Present and Future' (2017) 40 World Competition 3, 33, 'denying damages claimants access to leniency statements appears fully justified', as leniency statements and settlements submissions would not have existed without the cartel participant's voluntary act of making a leniency application.

[29] F Laina and A Bogdanov, 'The EU Cartel Settlement Procedure: Latest Developments' (2016) 7 *Journal of European Competition Law & Practice* 72.

[30] Case C-360/09 *Pfleiderer AG v Bundeskartellamt* EU:C:2011:389; Case C-536/11 *Bundeswettbewerbsbehörde. v Donau Chemie AG* EU:C:2013:366.

[31] S Peyer, 'Access to Competition Authorities' Files in Private Antitrust Litigation' (2015) 3 *Journal of Antitrust Enforcement* 58.

These statements must, however, take into account Article 7 of the same Directive, which provides that:

> Member States shall ensure that evidence in the categories listed in Article 6(6) which is obtained by a natural or legal person solely through access to the file of a competition authority is either deemed to be inadmissible in actions for damages or is otherwise protected under the applicable national rules to ensure the full effect of the limits on the disclosure of evidence set out in Article 6.

The word '*solely*' used in this Article has raised certain doubts, namely whether the protection only extends to leniency documents obtained through the file of a competition authority and whether pre-existing documents should be disclosed. If the prohibition of disclosure only applies to documents in the possession of a competition authority, this would mean that leniency material in the possession of co-infringers is not blacklisted. The problem, as already pointed out, is that 'the omission of the possibility that leniency statements may be held by a co-infringer is an unfortunate oversight that, if left unamended, might seem to leave a loophole that private litigants could use to obtain access to corporate statements'.[32]

On the other hand, although the Directive allows the disclosure of infringement decisions of the competition authorities, the *Pergan* and *Pilkington* cases might make it difficult.[33] A possible solution would be to follow the experience of the High Court in the UK, which provides access to such documents, based on the views expressed by the EU Commission in correspondence exchanged with other players. In the context of the Damages Directive, if this example is followed, the scope of disclosure might be extended.[34]

In the Portuguese context, the Act 23/2018 did not lead, in general, to wider disclosure of evidence than is provided for in the Directive. Nevertheless, it introduced certain specific solutions.

First, in order to assure pre-trial discovery, it allowed the alleged injured party to request the court to order immediate and effective provisional measures to preserve evidence of the infringement, in cases where there are strong

[32] P van Osch, 'Disclosure of Leniency Documents: Did the Dutch Highest Administrative Court Open Pandora's Box?' (2016) 7 *Journal of European Competition Law & Practice* 682, 685. The problem is that certain national courts, such as the Dutch court in the *CBb* case, had already ordered the disclosure of leniency transcripts, even if there were specific circumstances that could explain the decision.

[33] In the first case, Case T-474/04 *Pergan v Commission* EU:T:2007:306, the General Court refused the disclosure of a non-confidential version of a Commission's infringement decision in a cartel case arguing that it contained several prejudicial references to the applicant which were not addressed in the decision. In the second decision, Case T-462/12R *Pilkington Group Limited v Commission*, upheld in Case C-278/13 *Commission v Pilkington* EU:C:2013:558, the Court also refused the disclosure of the decision as it would cause irreparable harm to Pilkington.

[34] A Howard, 'Disclosure of Infringement Decisions in Competition Damages Proceedings: How the UK Courts Are Leading the Way Ahead of the Damages Directive' (2015) 6 *Journal of European Competition Law & Practice* 256.

indications that it took place. Interim measures to preserve evidence are, therefore, a solution provided in Article 17 of the Portuguese Act.

Second, in order to deter behaviour, such as the destruction of relevant evidence and failure or refusal to comply with a court disclosure order, the Portuguese Act establishes penalty payments (compulsory sanctions) for delays in delivering evidence and fines (Article 18).[35]

Finally, concerning settlement talks, while the Directive allows for the disclosure of withdrawn settlement submissions after the conclusion of the procedures, the Portuguese Act blacklists settlement talks that fail (ineffective submissions). In other words, Article 14(4)(c) of the Portuguese Act allows the disclosure of withdrawn settlement proposals after the close of the proceedings. Its Article 20.º modifies the Portuguese Competition Act and provides that settlement talks that fail (called ineffective because the undertaking that proposed the settlement did not accept the Portuguese Competition Authority's proposal, but did not withdraw its proposal either) cannot be used as proof against those involved in the settlement procedure.

### C. Effects of National Decisions

Since the *Masterfoods* case,[36] codified later in Article 16 of the Regulation 1/2003, it has been well known that Commission decisions are binding on national courts. The Court of Justice held that this solution did not violate Article 47 of the Charter of Fundamental Rights providing a right to an effective remedy and to a fair trial.[37]

Following these solutions, Article 9 of the Directive provides that 'Member States shall ensure that an infringement of competition law found by a final decision of a national competition authority or by a review court is deemed to be irrefutably established for the purposes of an action for damages brought before their national courts under Article 101 or 102 TFEU or under national competition law', while equivalent decisions taken in another Member State should be considered at least 'prima facie evidence'.

Recital 34 of the Directive explains that the binding effect in follow-on actions for damages covers 'only the nature of the infringement and its material,

[35] Law n.º 114/2017, 29 December, Art 178.

[36] Case C-344/98 *Masterfoods and HB* EU:C:2000:689, paras 48–52. See also Case C-302/13 *FlyLAL-Lithuanian Airlines* EU:C:2014:2319, in which the Court of Justice allows the recognition and enforcement of rulings on antitrust damages from other Member States. On this topic, *cf* P Fruhlin and J Delarue, 'FlyLAL-Lithuanian Airlines: EU Rules on Jurisdiction Cover Antitrust Damages' (2015) 6 *Journal of European Competition Law & Practice* 493.

[37] Case C-199/11 *Europese* EU:C:2012:684. Notice that following this case-law the national court is required to accept a European Commission decision on an infringement of competition rules but the existence of a loss and the direct causal link between the loss and the agreement or practice in question remains a matter to be assessed by the national court (see para 65).

personal, temporal and territorial scope as determined by the competition authority or review court in the exercise of its jurisdiction' and Article 17(2) of the Directive provides a rebuttable presumption that cartel infringements cause harm.

The Portuguese Act transposes this disposition correctly and establishes, in Article 7, the irrefutable presumption of the existence of the infringement once there is a final decision of the Portuguese Competition Authority or of the Court of Appeal as to the existence, nature and material, subjective, temporal and territorial scope of the infringement. In addition, there is the rebuttable presumption of infringement (this solution goes beyond the need to establish prima facie evidence) of the equivalent final decisions adopted by the competition authorities of other Member States or by the Court of Appeal of other Member States of the European Union.[38]

The problem of the probative value of infringement decisions, described above, is that, in the Portuguese legal order, courts are usually only bound by the decision of other courts in the context of a procedure of appeal and not by administrative decisions (especially because Article 206 of the Portuguese Constitution establishes that courts are independent and only have to respect the law).[39]

Nevertheless, taking into account the case-law of the Court of Justice, the legal solutions provided in the previous EU Regulations, and the fact that administrative decisions are subject to judicial scrutiny, and that all the bodies of the Member States have to respect the principles of due process, effective judicial protection and the right to a fair trial, the solution described in the Directive and adopted by the Portuguese Act should not raise concerns.

### D. Limitation Periods, Quantifying Damages and Passing-on Defence

In line with the Directive, under Article 6 of the Portuguese Act, Member States shall ensure that the limitation periods for bringing actions for damages are at least five years and that limitation periods shall not begin to run before the

> infringement of competition law has ceased and the claimant knows, or can reasonably be expected to know (a) of the behaviour and the fact that it constitutes

[38] The initial draft of the Portuguese Proposal also established a non-rebuttable presumption for the decisions of antitrust authorities of other Member States. However, given the negative reactions of the stakeholders during the workshop and public consultation, that solution was replaced by a rebuttbale presumption.

[39] A similar issue was discussed in the Italian legal order. See C Massa, 'The Effects of Decisions Adopted by Competition Authorities in the Frameworkof Directive 2014/104/EU: Criticalities and Future Prospects' in R Mastroiani and A Amadeo (eds), *60 Years of EU Competition Law: Stocktaking and future Prospects* I Quaderni del Corso di Perfezionamento in Diritto Dell'Unione Europea Dell'Universitá di Napoli 'Federico II' 4 (Napoli, Editorial Scientifica, 2017) 113.

an infringement of competition law; (b) the identity of the infringer; (c) the fact that the infringement of competition law caused harm to it, even if it was not aware of the full extent thereof.

With this solution, the Portuguese general rule (Article 498, Civil Code), establishing the limit of three years for liability for tort, is set aside and effectiveness of the action is promoted. On the other hand, the Directive and the Portuguese Act do not explain the situations where the claimant knew or could be expected to know the relevant facts. However, certain literature and case-law hold that this should be the moment where a competition authority publishes an infringement decision.[40] Doubts remain, nevertheless, regarding situations without public enforcement decisions.

Concerning the quantification of damages, under Article 4 of the Portuguese Act, the obligation to pay damages shall include actual loss and loss of profits calculated from the time when the harm occurred and updated under Article 566(2) of the Civil Code. In addition, Article 9 (3) of the Portuguese Act, establishes that 'it shall be presumed that cartels cause harm' and if it is 'impossible or excessively difficult to quantify the total harm' the Portuguese courts shall decide on the grounds of 'approximate best estimate assessments'; and the Portuguese Competition Authority shall assist the court in the quantification of damages upon request (unless the Portuguese Competition Authority requests, with due justification, to be excused). With this solution, the Portuguese legislator took into account the concerns of the Portuguese courts to fulfil this task, especially given the shortage of resources of the Portuguese courts.

Finally, in order to avoid overcompensation, the Portuguese Act follows the Directive and presumes, in certain circumstances, the passing on of the overcharges (Article 8).

## V. AMENDMENTS BEYOND THE IMPLEMENTATION OF THE DIRECTIVE: COLLECTIVE REDRESS

Although the Directive does not deal with matters such as collective redress (which were dealt with under the Recommendation on common principles for injunctive and compensatory collective redress mechanisms in the Member States concerning violations of rights granted under Union Law), the Portuguese Act, in order to ensure full right to the full reparation of the injured parties, decided on the applicability of the 'Popular Action' regime, under Law 83/95, 31 August (Popular Action Act), and Decree-Law no 214-G / 2015, 2 October.

[40] See the cases *Arcadia Group Brands Ltd v Visa Inc* [2014] EWHC 3561 (Comm); *Arcadia Group Brands Ltd v Visa Inc* [2015] EWCA Civ 883 mentioned in K Havu, 'Limitation Periods in Damages Claims: Notes on a Finnish Supreme Court Precedent in the Context of the European Landscape' (2016) 7 *Journal of European Competition Law & Practice* 402.

The European Commission favours the opt-in model (even if experience shows that it is not very effective) because it is compatible with the legal traditions of the Member States, respects the freedom of potential claimants to decide whether to take part in the litigation or not, and avoids abuses, such as overcompensating class representatives. On the other hand, opt-out group actions seem to be most useful where individual claims are difficult to prove or when the value of such claims is too low to motivate consumers to participate, reducing, in addition, transaction and information costs.[41]

Portugal is one of the EU Member States that has an opt-out collective redress model called '*Ação Popular*' (Popular Action) and it has been considered 'the most extensive form of collective action based on the "opt-out model" available in the EU'.[42]

Article 52(3) of the Portuguese Constitution provides that:

> Everyone shall be granted the right of popular actions, to include the right to apply for the adequate compensation for an aggrieved party or parties, in such cases and under such terms as the law may determine either personally or via associations that purport to defend the interests in question. That right shall be exercised namely to (…) promote the prevention, cessation or judicial prosecution of offences against public health, consumer rights, the quality of life or the preservation for environment and the cultural heritage.

This constitutional right was implemented through Law 83/95 of 31 August and has a broad scope.

Among the substantive issues, the concepts of legal standing, quantification of damages and payment of compensation are probably the most controversial issues and are mentioned in the Portuguese Act, Article 19.

A Popular Action may be granted to: (i) any citizen; (ii) a legally constituted association or foundation (as long as it is a legal entity); and (iii) the public prosecutor's office, which may replace the claimants if the contested behaviour endangers the interests involved (Articles 2 and 3, Popular Action Act). In addition, Article 19 of the Portuguese Act adds: 'a) Associations and foundations whose aim is to protect consumers; and b) Associations of undertakings whose associates are injured by the infringement of antitrust rules'. Furthermore, under Article 19 'if the injured parties are not identified individually, the court shall set an overall amount of damages', which might have to be shared among them in proportion to the harm they have each suffered. Moreover, under Article 19, the judgment 'will identify the entity responsible for receiving,

[41] See SO Pais and A Piszcz, 'Package on Actions for Damages Based on Breaches of EU Competition Rules: Can One Size Fit All?' (2014) 7 *Yearbook of Antitrust and Regulatory Studies* 210.

[42] C Leskinen, 'Collective Actions: Rethinking Funding and National Cost Rules' (2011) 8 *The Competition Law Review* 91, who mentions, besides Portugal, the existence of opt-out collective actions in the Netherlands and Denmark. For a detailed analysis of Popular Action, see Pais and Piszcz, 'Package on Actions for Damages Based on Breaches of EU Competition Rules' (n 41) 209.

managing and paying the damages due to the injured parties not identified individually' and damages not paid will revert to the Ministry of Justice.

To sum up, with this solution the Portuguese Act aims to enhance consumer protection and encourage individuals and SMEs to use this mechanism and obtain compensation in an effective way.[43]

## VI. CONCLUSION

The Portuguese transposition procedure was transparent, inclusive and provided certainty and confidence. The Act 23/2018 adopted the solutions in the Directive, even if in certain specific areas it went beyond the existing ones with the aim of enhancing consumer protection. Although certain solutions might not be completely effective, as already mentioned, the final assessment is positive and the Portuguese Act managed to strike the right balance between private and public enforcement.

[43] Melícias (n 2) 46.

# Part II

# Balancing Public and Private Enforcement

# 5

# *Private Enforcement of Public Law – An Inconsistent Approach to Remedies?*

LARS HENRIKSSON*

## I. PRIVATE ENFORCEMENT IN GENERAL

PRIVATE ENFORCEMENT OF competition law in Sweden cannot be presumed to pursue the same objectives as public enforcement, at least not from the perspective of undertakings. In the view of the legislator, both public and private enforcement contribute to the realisation of the objectives of EU competition law and its national counterparts. As such, they contribute to making undertakings steer clear of market behaviour or agreements and practices that may prevented by the prohibitions enshrined in Article 101 and 102 TFEU.

The private enforcement of competition law is in most cases limited to actions related to the nullity of an agreement in part or in its entirety, or actions for damages, whereby an aggrieved party is compensated for antitrust wrongdoings. Swedish law also allows for the adjustment of contracts under section 36 of the Contracts Act, although case-law is scarce in relation to its application in connection with competition law.

Nonetheless, it plays an important role in filling the gaps in the legal consequences amongst parties to a contract in cases of abuses of dominance because there is no counterpart to Article 101(2) TFEU in Article 102 TFEU. Under Swedish law, it has been considered that the nullity of contracts may follow as a civil consequence under section 36 of the Contracts Act when an agreement is an expression of a violation of a legal prohibition, such as the prohibition against the abuse of a dominant position.[1] In many cases, undertakings affected

* Professor of law at Stockholm School of Economics, LL.D., M.Sc. Econ & BA.

[1] See *SAS v Luftfartsverket*, Norrköping District Court, case T 2746-96, Göta Court of Appeal, case T 33/00. The Supreme Court did not grant leave to appeal, decision of 11 November 2002,

by infringements may simply have an interest in bringing anticompetitive behaviour or abuses swiftly to an end. The question that subsequently arises is what enforcement instruments are at the disposal of the Competition Authority and others in addition to actions for administrative fines?

The Swedish Competition Authority (SCA) is empowered to issue injunctions against an infringer of EU and Swedish competition law. Under Chapter 3, section 1 of the Swedish Competition Act (CA) (SFS 2008:569), the SCA may order an undertaking to terminate an infringement of any of the prohibitions laid down in Chapter 2, section 1 or 7 or Article 101 or 102 TFEU. Essentially, this implies that the SCA is primarily entrusted to issue injunctions in the first instance by means of the Swedish national instrument that resembles, for example, a cease and desist order (Sw. *ålägga ett företag att upphöra med överträdelser*).

An injunction takes effect immediately, unless other provisions are established by the SCA. All injunctions pursuant to Chapter 3, sections 1–3 of the CA may also be subject to conditional fines under Chapter 6, section 1 of the CA.

Already in 1993, when the first EEA-based Competition Act was introduced into Swedish law, the possibility of imposing injunctions was included. In addition, and in case the SCA decided not to pursue injunctions against a purported infringer, the legislation allowed for any undertaking *affected by the infringement*[2] to bring an action for such an injunction before the Stockholm District Court. This is commonly known in Swedish law as the *subsidiary claim for an injunction* (Sw. *subsidiär talan*) or the special right to litigate (Sw. *särskilda talerätten*).[3] There has been, and still is, no counterpart to this special right to litigate in EU law, although (in Sweden) it has been part of Swedish competition law since the 1950s despite the fundamental changes to the antitrust rules in Sweden during the 1990s.

In this chapter, I will examine whether this special right to litigate entrusted to undertakings is an adequate tool. I will give a critical overview of whether the original justifications still hold and if it is likely to generate unexpected or undesirable side effects that may undermine the enforcement system.

case T 2137-01. For commentary, see U Bernitz, 'Missbruk av dominerande ställning i form av prisdiskriminering – restitution och betalningsbefrielse' (2003) 2 *Europarättstidskrift* 382.

[2] Undertakings 'affected' means competitors of the alleged infringer, but also undertakings up or downstream in the distribution chain that are directly affected by the alleged infringement. Normally, an undertaking that has submitted a complaint to the SCA relies on this right, subsequent to which the SCA decides not to proceed. See K Carlsson and M Bergman, 'Commentary to c 3, s 2 of the CA' in *Konkurrenslagen*, available through the online database Zeteo.

[3] The rule itself fills a gap in the enforcement of competition law. A decision by the SCA to impose an injunction may be appealed under c 7, s 1 of the CA, to the Patent and Market Court. However, a decision not to issue an order/injunction may not be appealed. This is why there is a subsidiary right to litigate. Parties relying on that right must, however, bring such actions directly before the Patent and Market Court according to c 8, s 1 of the CA.

## II. BEHAVIOURAL REMEDIES IN SWEDISH COMPETITION LAW

The possibility to impose an injunction/order corresponds to the European Commission's (Commission) powers under Article 7 of Regulation 1/2003,[4] whereby the Commission may by decision require the undertakings and associations of undertakings concerned to bring such infringement to an end. The Commission is assigned to impose on them any behavioural or structural remedies, which are proportionate to the infringement committed and necessary to bring the infringement effectively to an end. Structural remedies can only be imposed either where there is no equally effective behavioural remedy or where any equally effective behavioural remedy would be more burdensome for the undertaking concerned than the structural remedy. There are no corresponding rights for the SCA to impose structural remedies under Swedish law. What instead remains is the behavioural remedy.

Already in 1993, the possibility of imposing injunctions was an important instrument of public enforcement. It has never been explicitly regulated what an injunction may entail or, more specifically, how it should be designed. Instead, in accordance with well-established principles of Swedish law regarding sources in law, one has to seek further guidance in the preparatory works. The Government was initially quite unclear on this issue and acknowledged that the wording of the statute permitted the selection of the 'most appropriate order necessary', but underlined that injunctions, as a general rule, must nevertheless be proportionate. Regarding the subject matter of the injunction, the Government held that it could be in the form of ceasing to apply a certain agreement, condition or other prohibited practice. Bearing in mind the circumstances of any particular case, it could also be in the form of a duty to supply, rectify certain behaviour or practice, or order to apply a certain price. In all cases, however, an injunction may only serve the purpose of furthering competition as a direct consequence of the prohibitions in the CA and may never be used to promote business policy in general.[5]

The preparatory works of the current CA from 2008 draw on the same line of reasoning as the first Competition Act from 1993. According to these, an injunction under Swedish law may be imposed in the form of an order to cease to apply a certain agreement, condition or other prohibited practice. Other forms of infringements may necessitate an undertaking being ordered to supply another undertaking certain goods or services or other utilities on terms and conditions that are offered to other undertakings. Another example of injunctions may be that the undertaking in question is ordered to not exceed or undercut a certain price.[6] In essence, therefore, the injunctions are designed to force infringers to

[4] Council Regulation (EC) No 1/2003 of 16 December 2002 on the implementation of the rules on competition laid down in Articles 81 and 82 of the Treaty (Regulation 1/2003) [2003] OJ L1/1.

[5] Government Bill, 1992/93:56, 90.

[6] Government Bill 2007/08:135, 74.

discontinue the antitrust wrongdoing, be it in the form of abstaining from a practice or undertaking an activity of some kind.

There are some nuances that have developed since the inception of EEA/EU-based competition law in Sweden, especially regarding measures related to pricing practices. Previously, government intervention comprised using the different price regulations as a macroeconomic instrument. In the 1970s and 1980s, most recently by means of the Price Regulation Act (SFS 1989:978), such intervention was a common feature of economic policy. Proven essentially unsuccessful to combat underlying structural challenges, the Government later abandoned attempts to control market behaviour through such interventions, which coincided with the accession to the EEA Agreement and the enactment of the 1993 Competition Act.[7] Now, the examples provided in the preparatory works appear to be more closely linked to prohibitions in the CA and EU competition law.

A decision of the SCA may be appealed to the Patent and Market Court, which is a specialised court within the Stockholm District Court. In turn, the court's ruling may be appealed to the Patent and Market Court of Appeal.[8]

According to Chapter 3, section 3 of the CA, the SCA also has the option, if *special reasons* exist, to impose interim measures, pursuant to Chapter 3, section 1 of the CA, for the period until a final decision is made on the matter, ie until the court has ruled on an appeal regarding an injunction, which otherwise does not come into effect until the matter has entered into legal force. For subsidiary claims for injunctions, the court may only impose such an obligation following the commencement of legal proceedings.

It appears obvious that the imposition of interim measures is an important complementary tool to the possibility of imposing injunctions. The general idea is, naturally, to promptly bring infringements to an end and combat ongoing threats against the functioning of the competition structure. If injunctions are appealed and do not take effect until the cases have been finally decided by the courts, there is a clear risk that protracted proceedings – and the absence of the possibility of imposing interim measures – could undermine the very purpose of injunctions.

[7] For a general overview of the market interventions conducted in the 1970s and 1980s, see the Commission of Inquiry *Ransonering och prisreglering i krig och fred*, SOU 2009:3, *En ny ransonerings och prisregleringslag*, SOU 2009:69, *Prisreglering mot inflation?*, SOU 1981:40, Ministry Publication *Ny Prisregleringslag*, Ds Fi 1987:5 and Government Bill 1989/90:21.

[8] Before the reform of the Market Court system in Sweden in 2016, when the Patent and Market Court was introduced, the subsidiary right to litigate was initially subject to a two-instance procedure whereby the claim was first handled by the Stockholm District Court and could be appealed to the Market Court. Then, in 1998, this was changed, and subsidiary claims were brought directly before the Market Court as the first and final instance. Now, the two-instance procedure has returned following the winding-up of the Market Court and the establishment of the Patent and Market Court and the Patent and Market Court of Appeal, see Act (SFS 2016:188) on Patent and Market Courts. See also H Andersson and E Legnerfält, 'Skadestånd vid brott mot konkurrensreglerna – ligger svensk lagstiftning i framkant?' (2009) 2 *Europarättstidskrift* 300.

The rules on interim measures mirror Article 8 of Regulation 1/2003, according to which, in cases of urgency due to the risk of serious and irreparable damage to competition, the Commission, acting on its own initiative, may by decision, on the basis of a prima facie finding of infringement, order interim measures. A temporal consideration is outlined in Article 8(2), whereby such a decision shall apply for a specified period of time and may be renewed insofar as this is necessary and appropriate.

The Swedish corresponding rule does not provide for anything similar in substance related to what interests must be in jeopardy in order to prompt the application of interim measures other than that there should exist 'special reasons'. Guidance must be sought in the preparatory works in order to clarify under which circumstances interim measures are warranted under Swedish law. According to legal doctrine, an interim measure is warranted provided that (i) it is plausible that a serious infringement exists ('prima facie infringement'); (ii) the delays in acting against the infringement may cause severe and irreparable damage pending a final decision; (iii) the interest of protecting competition outweighs the negative effects that may arise for the undertaking; and (iv) the measure is proportionate.[9] However, interim measures are in practice a rarity in Swedish competition law.[10]

Originally, the requirement for imposing interim measures was that there should exist *extraordinary* reasons. The Government held the view, however, that this threshold was set too high and lowered the requirement in 1998 in order to make it easier for the SCA (and others) to be able combat infringements of competition law swiftly.[11]

Paradoxically, this change in legislation has not led to any increase in the use of interim measures. The reasons for this are unclear, but the SCA appears to favour and prioritise cases involving clear infringements that will lead to administrative fines. Bringing such actions against undertakings will no doubt also have a chilling effect on infringements because if the undertaking does not discontinue the behaviour or actions under scrutiny, this may exacerbate the infringement and be regarded as an aggravating factor in the setting of fines.

## III. SUBSIDIARY CLAIMS IN SWEDISH LAW

### A. The History of the Subsidiary Right to Litigate

The special right to litigate stems from rules in the 1953 Act on Anticompetitive Practices (konkurrensbegränsningslagen, SFS 1953:603), which underpinned

[9] See 'Commentary to c 3, s 3 of the CA' in Carlsson and Bergman, *Konkurrenslagen* (n 2).

[10] See eg MD 2010:7, *Interim measures against Ekfors Kraft*, confirmed by the Market Court; MD 2010:5, *Interim measure against Swedish Civil Air Administration (Luftfartsverket)* (regarding taxi lanes at Arlanda airport), confirmed by the Market Court.

[11] Government Bill 1997/98:130, 36–37.

principles that were very different from the current legislation. Competition law in the Nordic countries during the 1950s and 1960s deviated considerably from the EEC rules. There were no equivalent legal prohibitions and the ex post assessment was based on a general clause, whereby practices that were deemed harmful from a public point of view could be prohibited.

According to section 2 of the 1982 Competition Act (repealed), the Market Court could decide on measures in order to prevent restrictions of competition having a detrimental effect within Sweden. Such a measure could be directed against a trader who caused such a harmful effect. Harmfulness was defined slightly differently under that legislation. Harm could essentially arise in relation to the practice in question, which detrimentally affected price formation, inhibiting business efficiency or obstructed or impeded another undertaking's business practice.

Measures under the 1982 Act comprised:

- a *prohibition* to apply a certain agreement, contractual terms or other anticompetitive procedures or to apply substantially the same procedure as the prohibited one;
- a *sales order*, ie an order to provide another trader with particular goods, service or other utilities on terms equivalent to what he offered to other traders (sales order); or
- a *corrective order*, ie an order to rectify any anticompetitive procedure applied by him, to comply with a particular condition or to provide certain information or to take other action contrary to the procedure.

An undertaking could also be subject to a *price order* by means of a price cap for a maximum of three years, insofar as the detrimental effect on competition entailed that a price, bearing in mind the cost structure and other circumstances, was obviously too high and that the matter was of 'greater importance'.

These measures were to be imposed by the Market Court. However, in cases of 'lesser importance', the Competition Ombudsman (Sw. Näringsfrihetsombudsmannen, NO), who headed the Competition Authority could impose prohibitions, sales and corrective orders subject to conditional fines, although such measures could not be imposed by the Ombudsman unless the undertaking on the receiving end of such measures did not approve. A lack of consent implied that the Market Court had to decide on the matter.

Therefore, the old Competition Acts from 1953 and 1982 entailed a rather different approach to the handling of restrictive practices and relied heavily on the Ombudsman taking an active part in *negotiations* with undertakings to ad hoc or *in casu* endeavour to correct or persuade the undertakings to act differently in a less harmful way from a competition point of view. In fact, negotiations were mandatory before any measures could be ordered against the undertaking under scrutiny.

Therefore, measures taken under the older competition rules presupposed an unsuccessful outcome of the negotiations, after which the Ombudsman had to decide whether to pursue the matter with actions before the Market Court. In cases where the Ombudsman decided not to go ahead with any such actions, such a claim could be brought before the Market Court by an association of consumers, salaried persons or undertakings, or by an individual undertaking affected by the restriction of competition.[12] The circle of persons entitled to bring such actions was indeed wide. Also, the special right to litigate arose essentially only after two circumstances were fulfilled: the unsuccessful negotiations and the decision by the Ombudsman/Competition Authority not to proceed.

The uncertainty ex ante of what exact market practices were unlawful under the older competition rules and the flexibility enshrined in the negotiation procedure and ad hoc outcome did not trigger any major concerns in relation to legal certainty, although at some level such considerations may also have been called into question.[13] At that time, the sanctions were indeed quite low and could be avoided altogether if the undertaking which the measure was directed against simply complied with the order. If not, it could also be questioned whether the conditional fines were high enough to have a true deterrent effect on infringers.

Already in the 1950s there were concerns about the organisation and handling of competition matters. The Government acknowledged that the issue of the restriction of competition was a concern for many stakeholders in society at large: competitors, consumers, the government, workers and local communities. Therefore, the question of who should be entitled to bring actions or conduct negotiations needed to be resolved. In the end, it was decided that the Ombudsman should have the primary right to conduct negotiations and bring matters before a settlement body (a body which was later upgraded to and succeeded by the Market Court). It was also deemed undesirable to entrust any and all parties with the primary right to call for negotiations or bring actions, because this would otherwise have opened the door to potential harassment amongst competitors and might have been misused by querists. Consequently, it was decided that the circle of persons with the right to litigate should be constrained and that the right to litigate itself should be made not primary, but subsidiary, to actions taken by the Ombudsman.[14]

## B. The Origin of the Subsidiary Right to Litigate in Swedish Criminal Law

The subsidiary right to litigate was modelled after the rule in Chapter 20, section 8 of the Swedish Code of Judicial Procedure, namely the subsidiary right

[12] See 1982 Competition Act, s 17, para 2.

[13] There were, however, some important prohibitions to steer clear from, namely the criminalised behaviour related to resale price maintenance and bidding cartels, 1982 Competition Act, ss 13–16.

[14] See Government Bill 1953 No 103, 263–64.

for the injured party to bring a private prosecution when the public prosecutor has decided not to prosecute for criminal acts subject to public prosecution.[15]

In criminal law, there are several reasons as to why an injured party does not have a primary right to prosecute. Most importantly, the public prosecutor is almost without exception the person or authority best suited to bring actions. The thoroughness and robustness of the investigation and the adequate presentation of the subject matter conducted by the public prosecutor offer far better guarantees for an acceptable level of justice than if individuals were to prosecute on their own. The subsidiary right to prosecute strikes a balance between different interests. Firstly, there is the state's special interest in taking measures against actions that according to the legislator warrant public prosecution. Secondly, you need to consider whether the abolition of the right for the injured party to bring subsidiary prosecution complies with the general conception of justice. This is why the legislator chose to allow individuals to prosecute, but only subsidiary to the public prosecutor's decision not to go ahead with prosecution.[16]

The sense of justice amongst injured parties is essentially built up by the *redress* and *control function*. Anyone who has suffered a violation of law should be granted the possibility of obtaining restitution through a procedure before the courts. As such, the workings of prosecutions brought by individuals appear to be rooted in the aggrieved party's ancient right to claim retribution for an injustice, hence the redress function. The control function, on the other hand, serves the purpose of controlling that the public prosecutors do not unduly or without due cause refrain from bringing prosecutions before the courts, which, according to the preparatory works, could be of particular importance in times of political unrest or when the justice system is under pressure.[17]

Nonetheless, the subsidiary right to prosecute is indeed not undisputed in criminal law and a public inquiry proposed four decades ago the abolition of this right, although the Government later disagreed with the report and the special right to prosecute still remains under Swedish law.[18] To date, there are currently no initiatives to repeal this right under criminal law.

From a competition law point of view, this is of particular interest, because the motives behind the legal instruments differ substantially. The interest in satisfying the need for retribution or ideal justice in general appears less important in competition law in relation to economic indemnification. Although justice in general is important for both natural and legal persons, it seems dubious to argue that that very sense of being violated or desecrated is common amongst undertakings and companies in general. The control function may still

[15] ibid, 277.

[16] See the preparatory works NJA II 1943, 263 and P Fitger et al, 'Commentary to c 20, s 8 of the Swedish Code on Judicial Procedure' in *Rättegångsbalken*, available through online database Zeteo.

[17] ibid. See also Public Inquiry SOU 1976:47, 32, 333.

[18] ibid, 331 and Government Bill 1981/82:41, 13. See also L Heuman, 'Reformfrågor rörande målsäganderätten' (1977) *Svensk Juristtidning* 241.

have some merits but its raison d'être within competition law appears to me essentially dependent on how competent and efficient the SCA is in bringing infringements to an effective end.

### C. Subsidiary Claims for Injunctions in Swedish Market Law

The special right to litigate must also be viewed in the enforcement context of years gone by. As already mentioned, the ways of ridding the marketplace of unwanted and restrictive behaviour differed substantially from today's principles. Also, competition law was (and to a large extent, still is) part of the wider area of market law, comprising areas such as marketing law, unfair business practices and unfair contract terms.

In the preparatory works to the 1982 Competition Act, the Government highlighted that when the Ombudsman was unable to find sufficient reasons to take action against an undertaking, there might still be a residual interest from the business community at large to bring that practice before the court for scrutiny. In that process, the rules on competition were deemed *parallel* [sic] to rules in the Marketing Act (SFS 1975:1418) and the Act on the Prohibition against Unfair Contract Terms (SFS 1971:112).[19] This complementary function was therefore equated with what applied under the Marketing Act.

This complete enforcement parallelism between marketing and competition law no longer exists, although both areas of legislation serve inter alia the purpose of protecting the function of the market.[20] While the enforcement principles have changed, the legislator has let these subsidiary instruments remain without having addressed how to handle the shift in enforcement principles.

Following the changes to Regulation 1/2003,[21] the 1993 Competition Act was modernised in 2004 to better align the national Swedish rules with the procedures of the European Commission. In relation to the special right to litigate, the rules on the suspension or termination of proceedings in Article 13 of Regulation 1/2003 attracted the Government's attention. According to that Article, where the competition authorities of two or more Member States have received a complaint or are acting on their own initiative under Article 101 or 102 TFEU against the same agreement, decision of an association or practice, the fact that one authority is dealing with the case shall be sufficient grounds for

[19] Government Bill 1981/82:165, 213.

[20] *cf* s 47 of the Marketing Act (SFS 2008:486), which states that injunctions may be brought by the Consumer Ombudsman, any undertaking affected by the marketing or an association of consumers, undertakings or salaried employees (primary right to litigate). Subsidiary claims for administrative fines under s 48 of the Marketing Act can be brought before the Patent and Market Court by an undertaking affected by a marketing practice. This differs considerably from the CA. One should bear in mind that the administrative fines are double capped (maximum MSEK 10 and never higher than 10% of the annual turnover, s 31 of the Marketing Act).

[21] Reg 1/2003 (n 4).

the others to suspend the proceedings before them or to reject the complaint. The Commission may likewise reject a complaint on the grounds that a competition authority of a Member State is dealing with the case. Also, where a competition authority of a Member State or the Commission has received a complaint against an agreement, decision of an association or practice, which has already been dealt with by another competition authority, it may reject it.

A decision to suspend or terminate under this Article is somewhat different compared to when the SCA decides to terminate an investigation for other reasons. Article 13 presupposes that the investigation is not permanently terminated. Instead, the decision by the SCA not to pursue a case is based on the circumstance that the practice or agreement is being pursued by another competent authority. The handling of cross-border practices of this kind that restrict competition is dealt with within the framework of the European Competition Network (ECN).[22]

The changes are relevant to the special right to litigate. Already in 1994, the SCA was empowered to apply EC competition rules. However, the modernisation in 2004 highlighted a possible problem with injunctions based on EC rules in connection with Article 13. In 1994, the imposition of injunctions based on EC rules had already been extended to the subsidiary right to litigate. Between 1994 and 2004 there were no formal limitations regarding the subsidiary right to litigate within the meaning that it could be motivated by any practice that infringed EC competition law.

Following the enactment of Regulation 1/2003, this did, however, create a potential challenge of parallel application by different courts and authorities, which Article 13 was designed to counteract. Therefore, the subsidiary right to litigate was constrained not to apply when the SCA decided to not pursue injunctions based on an Article 13 decision.[23] Notwithstanding this limitation, parallel application cannot be ruled out if, for example, timing factors lead to a certain practice being dealt with within the ECN and enforcement is commenced in Sweden, subsequent to which another competent authority takes measures in another Member State. Sweden, therefore, stands out within the EU insofar as the subsidiary right to impose injunctions may counteract the objectives of Article 13.

## D. Voluntary Commitments by an Undertaking and the Special Right to Litigate

When examining the special right to litigate it is also relevant to consider the rules on voluntary undertakings under Chapter 3, section 4 of the CA. It follows

[22] See Commission Notice on cooperation within the Network of Competition Authorities [2004] OJ C 101/43.

[23] See Government Bill 2003/04:80, 132.

from that section that a commitment by an undertaking may give the SCA a reason not to intervene. The Authority's decision to accept the commitment may pertain to a determined period of time, during which *the Authority*, in respect of matters covered by the commitment, is prevented from issuing any order pursuant to Chapter 3, sections 1–3 of the CA. The legal effect of accepting a commitment is essentially that during its binding period, an injunction cannot be imposed for the same practice. Also, it implies immunity against administrative fines under Chapter 3, section 7 of the CA. The acceptance of a voluntary commitment may only be revoked under certain circumstances after which proceedings may be reopened.[24]

Notwithstanding the preclusion and immunity that normally follows on from a voluntary commitment, a subsidiary claim for injunction may still be brought in parallel to the decision to accept a commitment.[25] Indeed, acceptance decisions do not entail an enunciation of the true breadth of the infringement, but the motivation behind the rule is naturally to complement other instruments and ensure swift compliance. Even though commitments normally preclude injunctions in parallel, this applies only to public enforcement, whereas claims for injunctions can still be brought by private parties. Inconsistent as this may seem, the preclusion seems to be motivated by the fact that the public interest is satisfied by the commitment decision and what then remains is the residual individual interest of the affected undertaking. Paradoxically, injunctions are not primarily designed to uphold that interest – or are they?

## E. A Self-constraining Inherent Mechanism?

Imposing injunctions presupposes a finding of an infringement. It should be noted that the competition rules – both the EU rules and the corresponding national rules – are legal prohibitions subject to severe penalties and grave consequences for infringers. This needs to be borne in mind and affects both the burden of proof and the standard of proof in competition cases in Sweden.

The Government held that successful litigation by an undertaking that brings a subsidiary claim for damages must naturally be able to produce sufficient material or evidence to support its claim. Also, the Government held it reasonable to assume that undertakings generally could not justify the cost of

[24] *cf* Art 9(2) of Reg 1/2003 (n 4). Where there has been a material change in any of the facts on which the decision was based, where the undertakings concerned act contrary to their commitments, or where the decision was based on incomplete, incorrect or misleading information provided by the parties.

[25] This does not follow explicitly from the legislation but becomes apparent from a closer reading of the CA, which does not preclude subsidiary claims. See J Karlsson and M Östman, *Konkurrensrätt – En handbok*, 5th ed (Stockholm, Karnov Group, 2014) 1201. See also 'Commentary to c 3, s 4 of the CA' in Carlsson and Bergman (n 2).

the investigation that court proceedings would require other than in cases with a closer connection to the Swedish market. Therefore, the Government failed to see any need to limit the subsidiary right to litigate when the practice covers international practices.[26]

This statement is hard to comprehend and the logic behind it is obscure. Undertakings are entrusted with a far-reaching right – albeit subsidiary – to claim imposition of injunctions based on Articles 101 and 102 TFEU in Sweden without limitation (apart from Article 13 cases) and this right, which requires considerable resources, will seldom – if ever – be used. Underlying legal requirements on the standard of proof will therefore act as a self-constraining mechanism. This appears to be a strong argument in favour of repealing or constraining the measure rather than keeping or expanding it.

## F. Damages or Injunction – Which Instrument Best Serves Private Interests?

The current CA from 2008 essentially inherited the substance of the older rules. The Government acknowledged that the CA is designed to protect the interests of the public and the individual. The public interest regarding a well-functioning market is primarily ensured through public enforcement in the form of injunctions and actions for administrative fines. In addition, the SCA also applies the rules on the control of concentration. Private or individual interests are *primarily* upheld by the rules on *damages*. Already in 2008, the circle of persons entitled to damages as a result of infringements of Swedish and EU competition law was widened. At the same time, it was considered whether to widen the circle of persons entrusted to bring subsidiary claims for injunctions. The Government, however, found that only undertakings affected by an alleged infringement should be entitled to such a special right to litigate. The Government thereby explicitly disagreed with the Swedish Consumer Ombudsman, who advocated making the subsidiary right more aligned with what applies within the field of marketing law, essentially reinstating the order that applied under the older competition rules. In disagreeing with this, the Government acknowledged that one consultation body had suggested repealing the subsidiary right altogether. However, the Government succinctly held that this question had not been examined by the inquiry and could therefore not present any changes to that effect.[27]

It is clear that the Government viewed the right to damages as the primary measure to protect the interest of the individual. On the matter of the interplay between public and private enforcement, the Antitrust Damages Directive states that 'to ensure effective private enforcement actions under civil law and effective

[26] Government Bill 2003/04:80, 133.
[27] Government Bill 2007/08:135, 216.

public enforcement by competition authorities, both tools are required to interact to ensure maximum effectiveness of the competition rules'.[28]

Therefore, the EU legislator has underlined the necessity of regulating the coordination of those two forms of enforcement in a coherent manner. In that process, it has also emphasised the interest of avoiding a divergence of applicable rules, which could jeopardise the proper functioning of the internal market. Apart from Sweden, the matter of private subsidiary enforcement of the prohibitions has not been addressed in EU law.

Article 35(1) of Regulation 1/2003 clearly states that Member States shall designate the *competition authority* or *authorities* responsible for the application of Articles 101 and 102 TFEU in such a way that the provisions of this Regulation are effectively complied with. Such designated authorities *may include courts*. The Regulation remains silent on the matter of *who* shall be entitled to bring actions before the designated competition authority. Regardless, there may be an element of confusion insofar as it appears clear that the application of EU competition rules is to be undertaken by these designated authorities or courts. There is no indication that private parties should be entrusted with the public enforcement of competition law, although the Swedish subsidiary claims for injunctions cannot be deemed as illicit in relation to EU law per se. Nonetheless, entrusting undertakings or individuals with the primary right to bring actions for injunctions or fines or to fulfil a complementary function in (not *to*) public enforcement has never been discussed.

## IV. THE EFFECTS OF THE SUBSIDIARY RIGHT TO LITIGATE

Bearing in mind the above-mentioned discussion, it appears that the subsidiary right to bring actions of injunctions is today only warranted by the control function, ie to serve as a safety valve when the SCA fails or decides not to pursue an injunction, presumably for the wrong reasons. Naturally, one cannot rule out that the instrument serves the purpose of supporting individual interests, although that has never been claimed explicitly by the legislator or in the preparatory works. If one were to grant the control interest merit and assume that this measure were adequate, certain doubts would still remain as to the effectiveness of the measure and the legal effects it may produce. Broadly, there are some areas that need to be addressed:

1. Is a successful subsidiary claim for injunctions tantamount to an expression that the SCA was wrong in not pursuing an injunction?

[28] Directive 2014/104/EU of the European Parliament and of the Council of 26 November 2014 on certain rules governing actions for damages under national law for infringements of the competition law provisions of the Member States and of the European Union [2014] OJ L 349/1 (the Damages Directive) Recital 6.

2. Is the SCA obligated to, or perhaps indirectly induced to take follow-on actions for administrative fines based on a positive finding of an infringement?
3. Do follow-on actions for administrative fines trigger concerns related to *ne bis in idem*?
4. Are there any procedural differences between privately enforcing the public rules and public enforcement in general?
5. What does a successful subsidiary claim entail with regard to evidential value and binding effects for follow-on cases?[29]

The first two questions appear clear. The fact that the SCA abstains from pursuing a case by means of injunctions can neither be regarded as an acceptance of the behaviour under scrutiny, nor is it a negative clearance. The current state of law does not require the SCA to issue injunctions whenever warranted, viewed objectively. The second question should also be answered in the negative. A successful subsidiary claim for an injunction is, on the one hand, a finding of infringement which could perhaps give rise to a renewed investigation by the SCA. However, on the other, the SCA and the court may have different views on the infringement issue and caution seems necessary when drawing inferences in such cases.

The remaining three questions have been dealt with in Swedish case-law, at least in part in 2014 and 2016 in the *Swedavia* cases.[30] The third question was explicitly dealt with in case MD 2015:4, where the Market Court held that although Chapter 3, section 7 of the CA is designed to prevent collisions of applications between administrative fines and injunctions, injunctions subject to conditional fines are not criminal sanctions per se. There is, in the view of the Market Court, nothing that prevents the imposition of injunctions subject to conditional fines for future behaviour and to impose fines for past behaviour – these are two different instruments essentially designed to address different situations and thereby not causing any *ne bis in idem* concerns.[31]

The fourth question is arguably the most problematic one. The imposition of injunctions – be it by private or public enforcement – is essentially a *public law instrument*, where the procedural rules on cases not amenable to settlement in court (Sw. *indispositivt tvistemål*) apply. An imposition of an injunction hinges on the existence of an infringement of EU or Swedish competition law, whereby

[29] I have dealt with these issues in greater detail elswhere; see L Henriksson, 'Indispositiva tvistemål – handläggningsregler för tillämpning av konkurrenslagen' in P Carlson et al (eds), *Amici Curiae Marknadsdomstolen 1971–2016* (Stockholm, Jure, 2017) 287–312.

[30] See MD 2011:28 and the subsequent ruling by the Stockholm District Court in case T-9131-13, where the SCA claimed administrative fines based on the Market Court's ruling; decision of 13 January 2013 on the claim not being dismissed because of *ne bis in idem* (appealed, case MD 2015:4; unsuccessful) and the ruling of 9 June 2016. The SCA did not appeal the decision of the Stockholm District Court, which therefore entered into legal force.

[31] Case MD 2015:4, *Swedavia v SCA*.

the finding of an infringement – regardless of who brings such actions – is integral to the SCA or the court's decision to impose an injunction.

The procedure of establishing the existence of an infringement itself is therefore subject to official review (Sw. *officialprövning*), which in Sweden entails that the court in such cases has the possibility of *ex officio* collecting evidence that confessions of infringements are not binding for the court and that default judgment will not follow during court proceedings due to a party in absentia.[32]

For competition law cases involving injunctions, the examination of relevant facts and circumstances must be *robust* so that the court is able to rule on the matter. This deviates inter alia from the standard of proof and procedures in civil law cases and implies a higher standard of proof. Although an official review was originally subject to a more inquisitorial approach by the court, and because in almost all cases there are two parties involved, with one being an authority, today it is more of a two-party approach and the court is not at all as active as the impression created by the rules.[33]

In cases involving injunctions, the party positions are equated with cases involving administrative fines. Essentially, this means that the examination or process material presented by the SCA to the court in injunction cases does not differ just because the remedy sought after is another one. The question remains whether this changes in subsidiary claims for damages. In such cases, the SCA is not party to the process, and two private parties face each other before the Patent and Market Court. The question is not explicitly regulated, but the Market Court has held that the party bringing such an action assumes the *same* [sic] burden as the SCA in relation to the completeness of the investigation and the standard of proof regarding the infringement.[34]

Therefore, there appears to be no alleviation in the standard of proof for undertakings bringing subsidiary claims for injunctions in relation to how robust or complete the process material needs to be and what level of proof needs to be satisfied.

It is possible to argue that there is no public interest in subsidiary claims for injunctions and that this should be taken into consideration when setting the standard of proof at an appropriate level. That would, however, fall short of the legal requirements that follow on from the obvious fact that this is a public law instrument in essence designed to uphold a public interest – not a private one.[35]

All in all, this brings about the obvious procedural shortcoming that the private party bringing a subsidiary action for injunctions is subject to the same

[32] See Government Bill 1992/93:56, 116.

[33] See Government Bill 2015/17:57, 203, Government Bill 1995/96:22, 77, Government Bill 1995/96:115, 87 and U von Essen, 'Förvaltningsdomstols utredningsansvar' (2012) 1 *Förvaltningsrättslig Tidning* 31.

[34] See MD 2007:26. *cf* also Art 2 of Reg 1/2003 (n 4).

[35] See MD 2015:4, para 49, where the Market Court clearly states that the *character of the claim* does not change depending on *who* brings an action for injunction regardless of the sentiments of the claimant.

procedural requirements in terms of what to demonstrate before the court in support of a finding of an infringement. At the same time, that party has no investigatory instruments at its disposal and does not nearly possess the same prospects of obtaining evidence in comparison to the SCA.

Lowering the standard of proof for private litigants appears inappropriate because this would imply double standards of proof depending on who brings the same type of action. If that were to be accepted, a finding of an infringement would be much less reliable in follow-on cases for administrative fines,[36] yet clearer in other private follow-on cases, for example, for damages.[37]

## V. CONCLUDING REMARKS

A subsidiary claim for injunctions is largely an enforcement instrument in law that was designed to satisfy the objectives of an entirely different system than the current one within competition law. As such, it is a relic that is burdened with severe legal challenges. It is remarkably unclear why the current competition law enforcement system inherited the instrument and the legislator has neither explicitly justified why it should remain nor stated what true purpose it fulfils within the current competition law enforcement system.

Essentially, only one of the original justifications for the introduction of the instrument appears to remain, namely the control function. Naturally, there is also an interest *in casu* for an individual undertaking to protect its commercial interests, but that interest alone does not seem to justify any alleged wronged party to take on the role of a competition authority.

The existence of the instrument therefore seems dependent on the objective necessity of controlling the SCA's decisional practice, which indirectly presupposes that it would be necessary for purported aggrieved parties to have a 'second bite' of any undue leftovers from the enforcement of behaviour under scrutiny. There is, however, no empirical evidence or experience from the case-law that would indicate that the SCA would be overly unwilling, unfit or lacking

[36] This problem was addressed by the Stockholm District Court in case T-9131-13 *Swedavia*, in a follow-on action for administrative fines, based on a positive finding of an infringement in a case before the Market Court for a subsidiary claim for injunction (n 31). The Stockholm District Court held that the analysis undertaken by the Market Court was 'not particularly detailed' as to whether the behaviour under scrutiny was objectively justified and that the succinct reasoning by the Market Court negatively influenced the possibility of relying on the finding of infringement. As a result, there was no binding effect of the Market Court's ruling in substance.

[37] Under c 5, s 9 of the Antitrust Damages Act (SFS 2016:964), there is a binding effect of a finding of infringement based on subsidiary claims for injunctions in cases where a litigant seeks antitrust damages. This appears essentially unproblematic, as the standard of proof is considerably lower in cases involving damages. Whether the legislator has acknowledged the clear risk of the double standards this causes, remains unclear. The preparatory works indicate that this rule is motivated by requirements in Art 9(1) of the Damages Directive (n 28), although the added complication of double standards for infringements are addressed in particular. See Government Bill 2016/17:9, 91.

in competence to uphold the interest of bringing infringements to a swift end. In addition, there is nothing thus far that suggests that the SCA has systematically prioritised wrongly or that it has made erroneous assessments in substance in relation to infringements and their timeliness, gravity and effects that would justify another body to replace the SCA and its duties. Naturally, one can always ask for more intervention, but this residual right still needs in my opinion to be properly and objectively justified.

Nonetheless, to act as a true control function for upholding the general interests of competition, any party acting in this subsidiary capacity should reasonably be entrusted with all the necessary legal tools to fulfil such a task. Alternatively, and although remaining shrouded in obscurity, it may, as mentioned above, serve the more limited interest of the individual undertaking in addition to, for example, damages.

One obvious way of dealing with shortcomings in terms of powers to investigate and the gathering of evidence is to lower the standard of proof. Steps in that direction, however, create double standards for findings of infringements, which are subject to official review. According to the case-law, the evidential value of the finding in follow-on cases involving administrative fines is limited. For follow-on cases on damages, the binding effect is, on the contrary, mandatory and for follow-on cases on, for example, the nullity of agreements, the binding effect is – at best – uncertain.

*In summary*, it is questionable whether the legal instrument has any true remaining merits within the current competition law enforcement system. Admittedly, repealing the right may, in the absence of adequate resources within the SCA, lead to a reduction of enforcement.[38] Therefore, it is essential that any changes leading to possible gaps in enforcement are properly addressed by the legislator.

[38] The matter of adequate resources may, however, be resolved by the Commission's ECN+ initiative. See the Commission's proposal for a directive to empower the competition authorities of the Member States to be more effective enforcers and to ensure the proper functioning of the internal market, Brussels, 22.3.2017 COM(2017) 142 final, 2017/0063 (COD).

# 6

# *The Binding Effects of Decisions and Judgments under EU Competition Law*

TORBJÖRN ANDERSSON*

## I. INTRODUCTION

AS A PROCEDURALIST one must maintain shallow knowledge of different areas of substantive law. For me, and this has been so for a considerable period now, the area of competition law has turned out to be particularly interesting.

One reason for this is that the area includes both administrative and civil procedure due to the fact that competition law regulates both public law relations and private legal relations.

A second reason is that competition law is construed on a peculiar paradox: the free, independent behaviour of undertakings in economic markets is safeguarded through public prohibitions and public intervention. One of the consequences of this is that the principle of party autonomy in civil procedure does not fully apply in private litigation over competition law matters.

A third reason is the strong link between competition law and EU law and the difficult procedural issues which emerge when substantive EU law is applied by national courts, and particularly in view of the possibility that the same case may be decided in subsequent proceedings at the EU level and national level, in administrative and civil proceedings and also before arbitration tribunals.

Over the years, the concept of effective enforcement of EU competition law has been a matter of concern and ambivalence for the European Commission (Commission). On the one hand, it has become clear that the Commission

* Torbjörn Andersson is Professor of civil and criminal procedural law at Uppsala University. His research is primarily concerned with the fields of Swedish and international civil and criminal procedural law, EU law in general and EU competition law.

is not fit to be the exclusive body to apply competition law. This realisation may be understood as one of the reasons for a number of developments in respect of its enforcement: the attribution of direct effect to the rules in the early 1970s, the decentralisation policy in the early 1990s, the new enforcement Regulation 1/2003[1] and the recent Damages Directive[2] and Recommendation on collective redress.[3]

On the other hand, it is also clear that the Commission wishes to maintain its position as the central power in the field. This can be seen from how the 'system' of antitrust law is structured within the EU. One indication is the fact that decisions by the Commission (and to some extent by national competent authorities) are binding in subsequent private proceedings regarding the same subject matter. This is hard to understand from a procedural perspective: ultimately administrative proceedings concern whether or not particular undertakings should be subject to sanctions, like fines, whereas private proceedings concern legal relations between individuals.

Another indication of the special position afforded to the Commission is that the Court of Justice, in cases where there are subsequent administrative proceedings concerning the same subject matter, has interpreted the concept of *ne bis in idem* in a much narrower way in comparison to the understanding of the concept in the EU Charter of Fundamental Rights (the Charter) and in the European Convention of Human Rights (ECHR). It is highly questionable whether it will be possible to maintain this view, as it is difficult to understand why competition law should contain a more restricted protection of human rights. Nevertheless, it is a clear indication that the effectiveness of administrative enforcement is important from an EU perspective.

This is the backdrop against which the rest of this chapter should be understood. I will examine the binding and occasionally evidentiary effects of decisions and judgments made by the administrative and judicial bodies entrusted with the task of applying EU competition law. Although the new Damages Directive contributes with some elements necessary for such an examination, the subject of this chapter is not limited to the effects of the Directive and thus its focus is a bit wider.

For the purpose of this chapter, the following bodies may be identified and separated: *the Commission* (on appeal the General Court and the Court of Justice), *the national competition authorities* (CA) (on appeal domestic

[1] Council Regulation 1/2003/EC of 16 December 2002 on the implementation of the rules on competition laid down in Articles 81 and 82 of the Treaty [2003] OJ L 1/1.

[2] Directive 2014/104/EU of the European Parliament and of the Council of 26 November 2014 on certain rules governing actions for damages under national law for infringements of the competition law provisions of the Member States and of the European Union [2014] OJ L 349/1.

[3] Commission Recommendation of 11 June 2013 on common principles for injunctive and compensatory collective redress mechanisms in the Member States concerning violations of rights granted under Union Law [2013] OJ L 201/60.

appeal bodies, like review courts) and *national courts dealing with civil litigation*. When I refer to 'courts' below, I mean courts in the latter meaning, not, for example, administrative courts reviewing administrative decisions. When examining how parallel and subsequent proceedings should be handled within the EU system, I not only distinguish between these different types of bodies, I also make a distinction between intra-state and cross-border situations. This means that I will not deal with the application of competition law before arbitration tribunals nor with parallel proceedings in third states, like for example, Switzerland. Dealing only with these three kinds of decision-making bodies in an EU context is a broad enough subject for this limited space; the purpose and disposition of the examination is bound to give the chapter an inventory-like (and quite frankly a slightly tedious) enough character as it is, without including even more in its catalogue of headings. Still, I have found that it is justifiable to undertake this cumbersome journey to provide something of a basis for future analysis; not everything that may be of use, has to be fun and exciting.

I will briefly describe the effects of judgments and decisions under EU law in the order below and make a brief comparison and some few critical remarks at the end. I will use examples from EU competition law to illustrate the points this chapter wants to make.

## II. COURT JUDGMENTS IN SUBSEQUENT DOMESTIC COURT PROCEEDINGS

A judgment will generally have a binding effect in subsequent proceedings within the same state when the new proceedings concern the same cause of action/subject matter between the same parties.

The ways in which the *idem* (cause of action) is defined varies between jurisdictions, but that is merely with regard to the details. At least in Continental and Nordic Member States, the *idem* is understood in more or less the same way.

When the criteria are fulfilled, a new action on the same *idem* will be refused due to *res judicata*. In a second case concerning another but interrelated matter, the findings of the court in the first case will be binding.

Example 1: A cartel member makes a claim for declaratory judgment that its agreement with purchaser X is valid. After the judgment becomes final, a new action on the validity of the contract will be dismissed due to *res judicata*. In new proceedings between the same parties on, for example, damages due to breach of contract, the earlier findings on the validity of the contract will be binding and that particular question cannot be tried again.

Where some of the criteria are not met, the judgment will not have a binding effect but may still have some impact as evidence.

Example 2: A claimant/purchaser brings an action for damages against a cartel member A due to an alleged infringement of Article 101 TFEU and eventually the judgment becomes final. When the claimant brings another action against cartel member B, the earlier findings in respect of whether there has been a cartel infringement may be used as evidence but will not relieve the court from making a fresh assessment of the question. This also applies to situations where other purchasers sue cartel member A or B. Generally, the evidentiary weight attributed to a previous judgment depends on how similar the cases are (how many of the disputed facts are relevant in both cases), but also on the second court's assessment of the previous court's evaluation of the evidence and legal reasoning.

The binding and evidentiary effects of a judgment in subsequent proceedings serve a number of purposes. Without binding effects in the form of *res judicata*, you would risk *irreconcilable judgments*, putting parties in impossible legal relations. This risk is imminent since, generally, the principle of party autonomy applies in civil procedure, that is, it is up to the parties to determine the frame of proceedings by the formulation of their claims.

Without binding effects in related matters, you would risk allowing openings for inconsistent regulation of private legal relations. Furthermore, when one of the parties has chosen to single out one issue as the main subject of litigation, it would not be in line with procedural economy to try to do so again when it appears as a preliminary question in another dispute.

Without the evidentiary effect, there will be a risk of an inconsistent application of law and in the long run a risk of a lack of public trust in the administration of justice. As regards an individual case, however, should a court make an assessment which deviates from an earlier assessment of the same question by another court it will not place the parties in an impossible situation.

It should be observed that the structure of binding effects is symmetrical in the sense that it does not matter whether an earlier judgment is positive or negative (upholds or rejects the claim) and that it is indifferent to the hierarchical position of the courts involved.

## III. COURT JUDGMENTS IN CROSS-BORDER SITUATIONS

The Brussels I Regulation[4] contains no rules on binding effect or *res judicata*, but on *lis pendens*, in Article 29. Due to Article 45(d), a foreign judgment may not be recognised if it is irreconcilable with an earlier judgment given in another Member State. The consequence of this will be that binding effects are attributed to judgments in subsequent proceedings involving (i) the same cause of action/subject matter; (ii) the same parties; and (iii) where the requirements for recognition in the Member State of enforcement are met.

[4] Regulation (EU) 1215/2012 of 12 December 2012 on jurisdiction and the recognition and enforcement of judgments in civil and commercial matters (recast) [2012] OJ L 351/1.

Furthermore, according to the Court of Justice, the principle of mutual trust requires courts to respect judgments from another Member State.[5]

The examples given above will also work the same way in situations where the first judgment is delivered in one Member State and subsequent proceedings take place in another Member State. As to the evidentiary effects, it should be noted that under Article 30 of the Brussels I Regulation, a court may *stay* proceedings, where related actions are pending in courts in another Member State and furthermore, there is a possibility to decline jurisdiction if the court first seized has jurisdiction and its laws permit a joinder of claims. These measures are laid down to mitigate inconsistent judgments and although the question of the evidentiary value of judgments in cross-border situations is not mentioned, it is clear that such an assumption underlies the possibility to stay proceedings.

## IV. JUDGMENTS IN SUBSEQUENT ADMINISTRATIVE PROCEEDINGS

The question of whether a judgment by a court in a civil litigation on, for example, the validity of a contract contested with reference to competition law, should be binding in subsequent proceedings before an administrative authority, is not addressed by EU legislation. It is safe to assume that a court's finding of a contract being invalid due to breach of Article 101 TFEU, cannot be binding in subsequent administrative proceedings concerning sanctions based on the same contract. At least under purely domestic Swedish law, the binding effects of a judgment or a decision do not exceed the limits of the procedural order from which the court's jurisdiction is conferred. Thus, where the same legal relation has been tried by a court as a basis for a claim for damages, it must be tried again in administrative proceedings when it is relevant as a possible basis for an administrative sanction.

However, a previous judgment in private litigation may have *evidentiary value*, and particularly so when the objects of the two sets of proceedings are more or less identical. For example, this may be the case where a court has dealt with the question of an infringement of Article 101 TFEU when determining the validity of an agreement or provisional measures and that is followed by administrative proceedings concerning the same alleged infringement.

It is important to remember, however, that administrative proceedings which may end in conferring fines on undertakings are considered to be of a quasi-criminal nature. Therefore it is likely that the *standard of evidence* required will not be the same in private and administrative proceedings (the *burden of proof* is legally regulated in Regulation 1/2003 and placed on any party claiming

[5] See eg Case C-157/12 *Salzgitter Mannesmann Handel* EU:C:2013:597, paras 31–36.

that there has been an infringement of competition). Furthermore, since the ultimate claims in administrative and civil litigation are different – fines and, for example, damages respectively – even if they concern the same alleged infringement, it is difficult to say that the objects of both sets of proceedings are the same. Accordingly, there will be no risk of putting parties in impossible situations due to different assessments of the question of infringement; like OJ Simpson you may have to live with being acquitted and still being liable to damages.

## V. CA DECISIONS IN SUBSEQUENT ADMINISTRATIVE PROCEEDINGS

In Article 13(1) of Regulation 1/2003, there is a *lis pendens* rule providing that where the same matter is dealt with by another CA, there shall be sufficient grounds for the suspension of proceedings or rejection of a complaint. According to Article 13(2), where the same matter has been dealt with by another CA, a CA may reject the complaint.

From the Regulation you cannot conclude that decisions contain a *res judicata* effect or are binding in some other way; Article 13 seems to be there as a means to prevent inconsistent decisions (and possibly also for reasons of procedural economy).

Still, since administrative competition law proceedings qualify as criminal proceedings under the ECHR and the Charter, the *ne bis in idem* rule in Article 4 of Protocol 7 of the ECHR as well as Article 50 of the Charter are triggered. The former rule applies only when there are subsequent proceedings in the same state, but the latter applies whenever substantive EU law is applied.

The concept of *idem* has come to be interpreted identically by the Luxembourg and Strasbourg courts – 'a set of factual circumstances inextricably linked together in time and space'[6] and the distinction of an *idem* must not be made by using legal qualifications or legal interests, but only by assessing whether the relevant facts in two subsequent cases, if not the same, form an inextricable unit.

However, in competition cases, the Court of Justice of the EU (the CJEU) has laid down a different formula: two cases are thought to concern the same matter where the facts are the same, the offender is the same as is the legal interest protected. In the *Toshiba* case, the CJEU used this narrower understanding of *idem* when it determined whether the two cases concerned the same matter.[7]

[6] See eg Case C-436/04 *Van Esbroeck* EU:C:2006:165 and the European Court of Human Rights case *Zolotukhin v Russia*, 10 February 2009 A 14939/03.

[7] See Case C-17/10 *Toshiba et al* EU:C:2012:72, paras 96–103.

This is difficult to reconcile with the general formula laid down by the CJEU and the European Court of Human Rights. Since it is hard to justify a deviation peculiar to competition cases, hopefully there will be some converging precedent to come from the CJEU on this point.

Still, whether or not the *Toshiba* criteria or the general criteria apply, subsequent proceedings will be subject to limitations under Article 50 of the Charter and Article 4 Protocol 7 of the ECHR.

## VI. CA DECISIONS IN SUBSEQUENT PROCEEDINGS BEFORE DOMESTIC COURTS

Under Article 9 of the Damages Directive, a final decision shall be deemed to have been irrefutably established for the purposes of an action for damages. Therefore, within the same state a final positive decision by a CA will be binding in subsequent court proceedings.

The binding effect attributed under this rule is both interesting and problematic from the traditional way of understanding the binding effects of authoritative decisions in civil procedures. Under Article 9, the binding effect attributed to decisions is asymmetrical in several ways:

i. the binding effect only goes one way;
ii. the binding effect is not attributed to decisions resulting in no finding of infringements; and
iii. the binding effect covers only actions for damages, not restitution, validity of contract or injunctions, since the Directive only concerns damages.

From a civil procedural perspective, it is difficult to justify the binding effect attributed to CA decisions. By any applicable criteria, administrative proceedings and civil proceedings concern different subject matters/areas (see also above), because different matters are at stake. Even if a private action and administrative proceedings may share a common set of facts (a particular potential infringement of competition), the former concerns the question of whether damages should be awarded and the latter concerns whether an undertaking should be fined. As discussed above, different assessments of the question of infringement will not place the parties in impossible situations.

However, admittedly the binding effect will contribute to the effectiveness of the private enforcement of competition law, since bringing a claim for damages will be easier where a claimant does not have to prove the relevant facts or make the legal arguments in respect of the question of infringement. On the other hand, this will only apply where there has been *a positive decision* by a CA of *the same state* as the court. In the conclusion, I will address the question of whether this does not in practice make private litigation dependent on previous decisions by CA and the Commission, and saves the Council and CJEU from developing the law, for example, in respect of evidence, in order to facilitate independent private litigation.

## VII. CA DECISIONS BEFORE COURTS IN CROSS-BORDER SITUATIONS

In contrast to intra-state situations, decisions do not have binding effects in cross-border situations. However, Article 9(2) of the Damages Directive provides that a final decision from another Member State may be presented at least as prima facie evidence that an infringement of competition law has occurred and may be assessed along with any other evidence adduced by the parties.

In a way, this rule seems to be superfluous. In all the jurisdictions I am familiar with, the parties may present whatever they want under the principles of the free presentation and evaluation of evidence. Thus, also in subsequent actions for breach of contract, injunctions and so on, a relevant administrative decision may be presented as evidence and must be considered by the court.

As discussed earlier, the evidentiary value of a decision must be determined in view of its relevance to the case before the court, the evidence which the decision is based on, but also in view of the accuracy of the evaluation of evidence and legal reasoning. It would be difficult to apply the requirement that an administrative decision should be afforded status as prima facie evidence, without taking into account the relevance of the decision to the case before the court.

## VIII. COMMISSION DECISIONS IN SUBSEQUENT PROCEEDINGS BEFORE COURTS

Under Article 16(1) of Regulation 1/2003, national courts cannot make rulings running counter to decisions by the Commission and must avoid giving judgments that would conflict with a decision contemplated by the Commission in proceedings it has initiated (and may therefore assess a stay in the national proceedings).

The binding effects of a Commission decision do not seem to be limited to actions in damages, nor to positive decisions. And there are no explicit limitations such as to the parties involved or the *idem*, but a reasonable interpretation would be that the binding effect is restricted to the actual cases the Commission has decided, the parties involved and to situations where concrete elements of such cases emerge in subsequent civil litigation.

The same critical remarks may be brought forward in respect of the binding effects of Commission decisions as well as of CA decisions, except that the cross-border differentiation is irrelevant and the binding effect is not restricted to subsequent actions for damages.

## IX. COMMISSION DECISIONS IN SUBSEQUENT PROCEEDINGS BEFORE CA

Under Article 16(2) of Regulation 1/2003, a CA cannot make decisions running counter to decisions by the Commission. Furthermore, there cannot even be a second set of proceedings because of Article 50 of the Charter, where the proceedings concern the same subject matter. This goes both ways and therefore I do not cover the effects of CA decisions in subsequent Commission proceedings separately. No matter whether the *Toshiba*-criteria or the *Zolotukhin*-criteria[8] are used to apply Article 50, outside the scope of that Article, a CA cannot reassess findings made by the Commission; whereas the Commission will probably not be bound by findings by a CA.

## X. CONCLUDING REMARKS

From the traditional view of civil procedure, the asymmetry in the structure of effects of decisions by the Commission in respect of subsequent court proceedings is not aesthetical and lacks reciprocity. The binding effects depend on which body has made the decision and also on whether the decision has been positive or negative; as to the binding effects of decisions by a CA it also matters what the claim in subsequent civil proceedings is and whether subsequent proceedings are brought before a court of the same Member State as the CA. This order is not ideal, and over time it will be difficult to grasp for the actors concerned. In fact, the reasons and objectives for public normative regulation of this sort are in many respects incomprehensible. For example, it is unclear from that normative perspective why CA decisions are not binding in cross-border situations, why they are not binding in civil litigation on the validity of contracts, why administrative competition proceedings are exempted from the ordinary understanding of the Charter while, for example, criminal proceedings on suspected terrorists are not and, finally, if positive Commission decisions are binding in subsequent proceedings, why the administrative procedure is not designed in such a way that negative decisions have the same effects.

One possible way to understand the binding effects attributed to decisions by the Commission and to some extent by CAs, would be to see them as a means to extend administrative competence to the very threshold of their attributed powers. In this sense, the order sets the Commission but also the CAs in unique power positions in the application of EU competition law, which cannot be explained by ordinary justifications of mitigating irreconcilable decisions or preserving the uniform application of the law. If decisions by CAs and the Commission did not possess binding effects, these negative repercussions would

[8] See section V above.

still not exist. Parallel proceedings in the field of competition law cannot lead to irreconcilable decisions since the ultimate claims differ and there are mechanisms, like preliminary rulings under Article 267 TFEU, and possible dialogue with the Commission, to safeguard the uniform application.

Thus, it seems that the only possible grounds for the order that has been set up, would be to keep a centralised system of enforcement in the field of competition law, which is paradoxical in a field of law protecting individual initiative, party autonomy and deregulated markets. The price that the EU has agreed to pay for that is not only disincentives to private initiative, but also providing a procedural device that suffers from a lack of essential elements that traditionally have been considered necessary for procedural design: foreseeability, comprehensibility and reasonability.

Still, one may say that the system, with its asymmetrical defects, is necessary for making the enforcement of competition law effective; without the binding effects of administrative decisions, undertakings would have to cope with too great obstacles when bringing private actions. For instance, they would have to suffer the burden of proof for facts that are notoriously difficult to prove.

On the other hand, you may argue that the consequence of this asymmetric system will be that *only* those potential distortions of the markets that have been subject to positive administrative decisions will be followed by subsequent private proceedings. Thus, if you view the enforcement of competition law as a market, private initiatives would in practice be totally dependent on public governance.

An alternative way of designing private enforcement would be to revise the rules on the burden of proof and evidence; it is hard to justify the rules on the burden of proof in Regulation 1/2003, if you want to enhance private enforcement. Furthermore, you could develop new rules and principles in respect of private law sanctions, allowing treble damages, and abolish the old idea that every individual harmed by an infringement should be compensated fully for the harm suffered. In order to facilitate group actions, you could apply an opt-out rule instead of an opt-in rule, which the Commission has proposed in its recommendation on collective redress.

Developments of that kind would probably contribute to independent private actions as a means of effective enforcement. However, in order to enhance private initiatives, such a development will most probably need to be supplemented with a removal of binding effects attributed to administrative decisions in subsequent proceedings. Before the introduction of Regulation 1/2003, very few civil cases were brought. Furthermore, undertakings and competition lawyers were little involved in genuine competition law assessments, since all proceedings were administrative and started by way of an application for exemption or negative clearance or a complaint. The order of that time created the procedural behaviour of individual actors. The Damages Directive does not fundamentally change that, since individual initiatives will be dependent on administrative decisions, except that the scope of private enforcement is somewhat greater.

# 7

# *Facilitating Follow-on Actions? Public and Private Enforcement of EU Competition Law After Directive 2014/104*

KATHARINA VOSS*

## I. INTRODUCTION

When the Commission proposed Directive 2014/104/EU (the Directive), two explicit aims were to optimise the interaction of public and private enforcement as well as ensuring that those who have suffered damages as a result of competition law infringements can receive full compensation.[1] As is well known, infringements of competition law are difficult to discover and difficult to prove in court, even for competition authorities with extensive investigation rights.[2] Therefore, many damages claims brought by private parties are so-called 'follow-on actions', that is to say damages actions brought once a competition law infringement has been established by the relevant competition authority.[3] As much as private claimants depend on public enforcement by competition authorities, it has also been acknowledged that private enforcement is complementary to public enforcement and should

* Doctoral Candidate of EU Law at Stockholm University. Email: katharina.voss@juridicum.su.se.

[1] Proposal for a Directive of the European Parliament and the Council on certain rules governing actions for damages under national law for infringements of the competition law provisions of the Member States and of the European Union, COM(2013) 404 final 3.

[2] Directive 2014/104/EU of the European Parliament and of the Council of 26 November 2014 on certain rules governing actions for damages under national law for infringements of the competition law provisions of the Member States and of the European Union [2014] OJ L 349/1, para 26.

[3] European Commission, 'Impact Assessment Report: Damages Actions for Breach of the EU Antitrust Rules' [2013] SWD(2013) 203 final, para 180.

as such be encouraged by competition authorities.[4] This raises the question of whether the enforcement policy presently pursued by the Commission actually facilitates follow-on actions or whether it instead hampers such actions? The Directive is aimed at procedural rules in the Member States rather than the Commission's enforcement of Articles 101 and 102 TFEU. However, the enforcement carried out by the Commission may still be subject to private follow-on actions in Member States, whereby the national rules implementing the Directive will become applicable.

The remainder of this chapter is structured as follows: Section II gives a short summary of the tasks of public and private enforcement. Section III discusses the Commission's case resolution mechanisms and their impact on private enforcement. The case resolution mechanism chosen by the Commission may be more or less conducive to follow-on actions. Section IV assesses whether the payment of damages could be facilitated by the reduction of fines or be included in remedies imposed on undertakings. Section V concludes.

## II. THE TASKS OF PUBLIC AND PRIVATE ENFORCEMENT

Public and private enforcement are interdependent, but have separate tasks. Not only the tasks but also the interests that govern public and private enforcement differ. *Public enforcement* is driven by the general interest of preventing anti-competitive behaviour. On the one hand, the state shall guarantee freedom of business. On the other hand, this freedom shall not go so far as to allow undertakings to restrict each other's freedom of business in the form of competition law violations.[5] In this respect, the public enforcer is tasked with prioritising its scarce resources so that the most important cases are pursued. 'Most important' may, for example, refer to the value of fines that could be imposed or novel conduct that should be investigated and possibly prohibited.[6] *Private enforcement,* in contrast, is driven by injured parties' interest in the damages that can be achieved, rather than bringing important cases from a policy point of view. Private parties are also limited in the cases they *can* take to court, as they must have standing to bring such a case.[7] Thus, already from the outset, public and private enforcement have different starting points. Their respective tasks are outlined further below.

[4] ibid, para 22; B Lasserre, 'Integrating Public and Private Enforcement of Competition Law: Implications for Courts and Agencies' in P Lowe and M Marquis (eds), *European Competition Law Annual 2011: Integrating Public and Private Enforcement of Competition Law: Implications for Courts and Agencies* (Oxford, Hart, 2014) 318–19.

[5] DJ Gerber, *Law and Competition in Twentieth Century Europe: Protecting Prometheus* (Oxford, Clarendon, 1998) 245–48.

[6] Council Regulation 1/2003/EC of 16 December 2002 on the implementation of the rules on competition laid down in Articles 81 and 82 of the Treaty [2003] OJ L1/1, Recitals 2–3.

[7] In this regard, the Directive gives a wide mandate: Directive (n 2) Art 3.

### A. Public Enforcement

Article 103 TFEU, which is the legal basis for Regulation 1/2003, holds that implementing legislation should 'ensure compliance with the prohibitions laid down in Article 101(1) and in Article 102 by making provision for fines and periodic penalty payments'.[8] The Treaty thus envisages a system of enforcement which stops and prevents infringements of Articles 101 and 102 through the imposition of a monetary punishment. For this purpose, Article 7 of Regulation 1/2003 allows the Commission to impose remedies designed to bring the infringement in question to an end. Article 23 of Regulation 1/2003 allows the Commission to impose fines. The Court of Justice elaborates in *ENI* that the aim of competition law enforcement is 'penalising conduct contrary to the competition rules … and to prevent its repetition'.[9] And in *Archer Daniels*, the General Court held that,

> it should be recalled that it is for the Commission both (i) to pursue a general policy designed to apply, in competition matters, the principles laid down by the Treaty and to *guide the conduct of undertakings* in the light of those principles and (ii) to investigate and *punish* individual infringements[10]

and

> for the purpose of fixing the amount of the fine, the Commission must take into consideration not only the particular circumstances of the case but also the context in which the infringement occurs and must ensure that its action has the necessary *deterrent effect*.[11]

Public enforcement thus has a clear role in pursuing the goals of the Treaty through its enforcement, ensuring inter alia that the economy is not distorted by infringements of competition law. In particular, the Commission, through its enforcement shall (i) bring infringements to an end; (ii) guide the conduct of undertakings; (iii) punish infringements of competition law; and (iv) also achieve a deterrent effect that shall prevent further infringements of competition law.

### B. Private Enforcement

Private enforcement has the main goal of making good damages caused by competition law infringements in the past. The Directive contains several

[8] Treaty on the Functioning of the European Union (TFEU) [2010] OJ C 83/47, Art 103(2)a.

[9] Case C-508/11 P *ENI SpA v European Commission* EU:C:2013:289, para 50. See also Case T-69/91 *Georgios Peroulakis v Commission* EU:T:1993:16, para 191; Case C-510/06 P *Archer Daniels Midland Co v Commission* EU:C:2009:166, para 149; and Case T-329/01 *Archer Daniels Midland Co v Commission* EU:T:2006:268, para 275.

[10] Case T-329/01 *Archer Daniels* (n 9) para 275 (emphasis added).

[11] ibid, para 176 (emphasis added).

rules as regards the damages that can be awarded to claimants. Importantly, Article 3 states that

> Member States shall ensure that any natural or legal person who has suffered harm caused by an infringement of competition law is able to claim and to obtain full compensation for that harm …
>
> Full compensation under this Directive shall not lead to overcompensation, whether by means of punitive, multiple or other types of damages.

In marked contrast to private enforcement in the USA, treble damages are not available under EU law. The role of private enforcement is thus to *compensate* damaged parties, rather than to *punish* offenders. Besides rules of pre-trial discovery, the lack of treble damages is the most important reason why private enforcement in the EU has not reached the same prominence as in the USA.[12] During the long discussions before the adoption of the Directive, US-style private enforcement was considered undesirable for a number of reasons, amongst others because it may set perverse incentives for damages claimants.[13] The Directive rather aims to facilitate private enforcement and ensure its smooth coordination with public enforcement.[14] Therefore, private enforcement before national courts in the EU has mostly taken the form of follow-on actions, where damages are claimed in cases where a public authority has already found an infringement of competition law. In relation to public enforcement, this means that private enforcement mostly plays a strengthening role. However, it also means that private enforcement in the EU is much more dependent on public enforcement than it is in the USA. Without public enforcement, there is less private enforcement.

The strengthening role of private enforcement for public enforcement should not be underestimated, as many observers comment that public enforcement carried out by the Commission does not achieve a sufficiently deterring effect.[15] However, more immediately, private enforcement can be perceived as a hindrance to public enforcement. This was forcefully illustrated in the *Pfleiderer* case.[16] In that case, a national competition authority did not want to give a potentially injured party access to the leniency submission of an undertaking found guilty of an infringement of competition law for fear of reduced

[12] OECD Secretariat, 'Relationship between Public and Private Antitrust Enforcement' (2015) DAF/COMP/WP3(2015)14, para 4.

[13] WPJ Wils, 'The Relationship between Public Antitrust Enforcement and Private Actions for Damages' (2009) 32 *World Competition* 3, 8–9.

[14] Directive (n 2) Recital 6.

[15] F Smuda, 'Cartel Overcharges and the Deterrent Effect of EU Competition Law' [2014] ZEW Discussion Paper No 12-050, available at: ftp.zew.de/pub/zew-docs/dp/dp12050.pdf; M Motta, 'On Cartel Deterrence and Fines in the European Union' (2008) 29 *European Competition Law Review* 209.

[16] Case C-360/09 *Pfleiderer AG v Bundeskartellamt* EU:C:2011:389.

effectiveness of the leniency programme.[17] The Court of Justice's weighing approach with regard to access to competition authorities' files laid down in the *Pfleiderer* case was visibly one of the reasons why the Commission finally submitted the proposal that led to the adoption of the Directive.[18] Thus, on the one hand, private enforcement can complement and strengthen public enforcement. But, on the other hand, private enforcement may also hinder effective public enforcement, for example by resulting in fewer leniency applications, which are crucial for the discovery of many competition law infringements.[19] Therefore, the relationship between public and private enforcement is not only characterised by different aims, but also by certain conflicts of interest where private enforcement can facilitate, but also hinder the aims of public enforcement.

## III. ENCOURAGING PRIVATE ACTION BY PUBLIC ACTION

As demonstrated above, private enforcement in the EU is partly dependent on public enforcement. Thus, how the Commission carries out its enforcement has a large impact on private claimants. More precisely, what type of case resolution mechanism the Commission utilises in its enforcement has an impact on the possibilities to pursue private follow-on action. Below, it is considered if and how the different case resolution mechanisms result in Commission decisions that can be used for the purposes of private enforcement.

### A. Article 7 Decisions

A prohibition decision according to Article 7(1) of Regulation 1/2003 (an Article 7 decision) requires the termination of an infringement of Article 101 or 102 TFEU. Where the Commission finds an infringement, it can impose behavioural or structural remedies to ensure that the infringement is brought to an end.[20] Therefore, these remedies are not meant to be a punishment for the undertaking in question, but merely a measure that removes the infringement as well as its effects and thereby restores competition.[21] It is sometimes argued that remedies should not only restore the competitive process, but also the situation that would have existed 'but for' the infringement. However, this may require

[17] ibid, paras 25–27.

[18] Proposal for a Directive of the European Parliament and the Council on certain rules governing actions for damages under national law for infringements of the competition law provisions of the Member States and of the European Union (n 1) 3.

[19] European Commission, 'Report on Competition Policy 2017' COM(2018) 482 final, 3.

[20] Reg 1/2003 (n 6) Art 7.

[21] Case C-49/92 P *Commission v Anic Partecipazioni SpA* EU:C:1999:356, para 81.

compensation for competitors for losses sustained in the past.[22] For now, this aim is left to private damages claimants who can pursue follow-on claims.[23]

Claimants can use the Commission's Decision, naming the involved undertakings and describing their behaviour in detail, as a basis for their damages claims. The Article 7 decisions taken by the Commission are binding on national courts, so that the claimants do not need to re-establish the competition law infringement in question, often the most difficult part for private claimants without the investigative powers of public authorities.[24] Beyond that, claimants will also need documents from the Commission's file to further substantiate their claim. The Directive restricts severely the documents that can be received from the Commission, especially as regards leniency and settlement submissions. However, there are also a number of documents that can be received from the Commission.[25]

Thus, substantively, an Article 7 decision provides a good basis for private claimants aiming to receive damages from infringers of competition law. The procedural disadvantage is that the Commission often takes a long time to adopt Article 7 decisions and these are then followed by appeals to the General Court and the Court of Justice, further delaying the finalisation of the decision.

## B. Consensual Article 7 Decisions

Article 7 decisions against infringements of Article 101 TFEU may also be taken in the form of cartel settlements according to Article 10a of Regulation 773/2004. These settlements are essentially a modified form of Article 7 decisions that require cooperation by the undertaking(s) in question.[26] The basic procedure is outlined in Article 10a of Regulation 773/2004 and further detailed in the settlement notice.[27] In rough terms, the undertaking in question must admit the infringement as described by the Commission in return for the 10 per cent reduction of the fine granted within the framework of the Article 7 decision and

[22] F Wenzel Bulst, 'Wiederherstellung von Wettbewerb' (2014) 2 *Neue Zeitschrift für Kartellrecht* 245, 245–46.

[23] P Hellström, F Maier-Rigaud and F Wenzel Bulst, 'Remedies in European Antitrust Law' (2009) 76 *Antitrust Law Journal* 43, 61.

[24] Directive (n 2) Recital 47.

[25] ibid, Arts 5–7.

[26] Commission Notice on the conduct of settlement procedures in view of the adoption of Decisions pursuant to Article 7 and Article 23 of Council Regulation (EC) No 1/2003 in cartel cases (Settlement Notice) [2008] OJ C167/1, para 32.

[27] Commission Regulation 773/2004/EC of 7 April 2004 relating to the conduct of proceedings by the Commission pursuant to Articles 81 and 82 of the EC Treaty [2004] OJ L123/18, Art 10a; Settlement Notice (n 26).

subsequently adopted by the Commission.[28] This is mainly meant to simplify the procedure carried out by the Commission resulting in shorter time for the processing of each individual case.[29] For the Commission, the fact that the undertaking in question admits the prohibited conduct means that Article 7 decisions made as settlements are seldom appealed to the General Court, saving resources otherwise needed for lengthy court proceedings.[30]

For private claimants, settlements provide Article 7 decisions more quickly than under the usual circumstances allowing them to pursue damages claims sooner. However, settlement decisions, though formally Article 7 decisions, are often shorter and less detailed than 'ordinary' Article 7 decisions, making them less valuable as evidence before a national court.[31]

It can also be noted that the Commission seems to have added another variant of Article 7 decisions to its case resolution mechanisms in its decision in *ARA*. ARA was found to have abused its dominant position, but received a 30 per cent discount on the fine because

> ARA acknowledged the infringement as set out in this Decision as well as the need for a structural remedy, which it accordingly proposed. The proposed structural remedy further ensures that the legal gap as to the legal obligation to grant shared use is removed. The acknowledgment and the accompanying waiver also allowed for administrative efficiencies.[32]

As regards private enforcement, this type of settlement, if the Commission uses it more often, would have the same effect as the settlements according to Article 10a of Regulation 77/2004 discussed above. It is likely that they will be shorter, but also determined in a shorter period of time. If one sees shorter decisions as a major disadvantage to settlements, there is a danger that this disadvantage is further increased if this new settlement type leads to more consensual decisions overall.[33] However, another possibility is that some of the cases that have so far been closed by commitments will now be concluded by this new mechanism. As we will see below, settlements, still producing an Article 7 decision, are more advantageous for private claimants than Article 9 decisions.

[28] ibid, Art 10a(3).

[29] Settlement Notice (n 26) para 1.

[30] There are two cases concerning different aspects of the settlement procedure. Case C-411/15 P *Timab Industries and CFPR v Commission* EU:C:2017:11 as regards the calculation of fines where the procedure is reverted to an 'ordinary' Art 7 procedure and Case T-95/15 *Printeos, SA and Others v Commission* EU:T:2016:722 as regards the Commission's duty to state reasons. However, neither of these cases is relevant for the present chapter.

[31] K Hüschelrath and U Laitenberger, 'The Settlement Procedure in the European Commission's Cartel Cases: An Early Evaluation' (2017) 5 *Journal of Antitrust Enforcement* 458, 479–80.

[32] *ARA Foreclosure* (Case AT.39759) Commission Decision C(2016) 5586 [2016] OJ C 432/6, para 162.

[33] See also Asus (Case AT.40465) Commission Decision C(2018) 4773 final [2018] OJ C 338/13.

### C. Article 9 Decisions

A decision according to Article 9 of Regulation 1/2003 (an Article 9 decision) accepting commitments is a form of consensual case resolution. Article 9 provides that the Commission may accept commitments in cases where it intends to adopt a decision according to Article 7 of Regulation 1/2003. Commitments can be behavioural or structural remedies that dispel the concerns of the Commission in a particular case. These remedies are intended to stop the potential infringement in a targeted manner. By making commitments binding for an undertaking with an Article 9 decision, the Commission finds that there is no further ground for action in that case. However, an Article 9 decision does not formally find an infringement of EU competition law, nor does it find that no infringement has taken place.[34]

Commitment decisions and their increased use are not beneficial to private claimants as such decisions do not establish an infringement that can be used as evidence in court.[35] Conversely, the commitments themselves are often aimed at restoring competition in the market concerned, so that injured parties at least do not continue to suffer from anti-competitive behaviour. Nevertheless, from the point of view of parties wishing to claim damages, commitment decisions are quite useless for the purposes of a follow-on damages action.

## IV. DAMAGES AS PART OF PUBLIC ENFORCEMENT

Depending on the case resolution mechanism, it may be difficult for private claimants to base damages actions on Commission decisions. Since a follow-on action may be difficult to base on a Commission decision, depending on the case resolution mechanism used, the Commission could facilitate private actions within its own case resolution, for example, through fines or remedies.

### A. The Calculation of Fines in the Presence of Private Enforcement

Fines shall punish undertakings and deter future infringements, both by the infringing undertaking and by third parties. This deterrent effect is increased by damages paid by undertakings, as the total cost of a competition law infringement rises. This means that the total sum paid could reach the level where such an infringement becomes 'too expensive' or over-deterrent, leading

[34] European Commission, 'Antitrust Manual of Procedures: Internal DG Competition Working Documents on Procedures for the Application of Articles 101 and 102 TFEU' (2012) 178–79, available at: ec.europa.eu/competition/antitrust/antitrust_manproc_3_2012_en.pdf.

[35] M Mariniello, 'Commitments or Prohibition? The EU Antitrust Dilemma' Bruegel Policy Brief Issue 2014/1, available at: www.bruegel.org/download/parent/809-commitments-or-prohibition-the-eu-antitrust-dilemma/file/1701-commitments-or-prohibition-the-eu-antitrust-dilemma.

to a chilling effect on the economy. This could be a reason for competition authorities to grant fine rebates where damages have been paid.

Article 18(3) of the Directive holds that national competition authorities may reduce fines if the undertaking concerned has paid damages to a private party. Though not a national competition authority within the meaning of the Directive, the Commission has on two occasions granted such a rebate, in *Nintendo* (2003) and in *Pre-insulated pipes* (1993).[36] Since then, the Commission has not granted any such rebate, nor is it obliged to do so.[37] What is more, fine reductions can no longer be granted by the time follow-on actions are brought. Admittedly, the Commission could encourage compensation by granting fine rebates to undertakings who offer to pay compensation to victims while the procedure before the Commission is ongoing, such as in the *Nintendo* case. In that case, the Nintendo fine was reduced by EUR 300,000 in exchange for the compensation that it had offered and then paid to a number of third parties identified as harmed parties by the Commission.[38] Unfortunately, this option would put an extra burden on the Commission, for example, with regard to the identification of potentially harmed parties and the monitoring of damages paid.

Besides timing, there are both conceptual and practical problems attached to fine reductions. Fines and damages serve different aims. Damages for infringements of competition law shall not be punitive, like fines, but rather compensatory. As the Directive clearly states, punitive damages cannot be obtained under EU law.[39] Thus, mixing up fines and damages, as the Directive conversely also suggests, does not appear to be a suitable measure. Moreover, in practice, deterrent fines are notoriously difficult to calculate and taking an additional factor into consideration would not make it easier for competition authorities to calculate fines. And, as already noted, currently it does not appear that fines imposed by the Commission are reaching deterrent levels, making private enforcement a welcome addition to public enforcement with regard to the 'cost' of infringing competition law.[40]

## B. Damages as a Remedy

Unlike fines, which aim to punish and deter, remedies aim to stop the infringement and restore competition. Given that most private actions take the form

[36] *Pre-insulated pipes* (Case No IV/35.691/E-4) Commission Decision C(1998) 3117 [1999] OJ L 24/1, para 172; *Nintendo* (Cases COMP/35.587, COMP/35.706 and COMP/36.321) Commission Decision C(2002) 4072 [2003] OJ L 255/33, paras 440–41.

[37] Case T-59/02 *Archer Daniels Midland Co v Commission* EU:T:2006:272, paras 349–55.

[38] *Nintendo* (n 36) para 440.

[39] Directive (n 2) Recital 13.

[40] Smuda, 'Cartel Overcharges and the Deterrent Effect of EU Competition Law' (n 15); Motta, 'On Cartel Deterrence and Fines in the European Union' (n 15).

of follow-on actions, the question is whether the Commission could, within its own enforcement, encourage or even order compensation to private parties. Such an action could save considerable litigation costs for both the infringer and the injured parties.[41] Facilitating private claims through remedies is systematically the more logical choice as compared to the reduction of fines. Remedies are designed to restore competition and compensating victims of infringements is one way of restoring competition. However, this does not mean that the payment of damages could be integrated in remedies without any problems. Depending on the decision in question, the Commission is limited as regards the remedies that it may impose. Even if it could include the compensation of third parties in remedies, problems as regards the design of the remedy and the role of the Commission surface. In the following assessment, it is necessary to distinguish between cases closed by an ordinary Article 7 decision and cases concluded by a consensual case resolution mechanism.

*i. Article 7 Decisions*

Article 7(1) of Regulation 1/2003 empowers the Commission to impose behavioural and structural remedies that are proportionate to ending an infringement. It is clear from the wording of that provision that the remedies imposed by the Commission must have the *purpose* of bringing the infringement to an end. Going beyond ending an infringement, in *Akzo*, the Court of Justice considers that a behavioural remedy imposed by the Commission may *also* 'prevent repetition of the infringement and … eliminate its consequences'.[42] Further, that particular remedy allowed Akzo's competitor 'to re-establish the situation that existed before the dispute'.[43] According to the Court, remedies may thus aim to re-establish the situation that existed before the infringement. Conversely, damages may 'cover the right to compensation for actual loss and for loss of profit, plus the payment of interest'.[44] Damages thus not only target the situation before the infringement was committed, but also the situation that would have existed 'but for' the infringement. But, considering the available case-law, it appears that the Commission's powers do not permit the imposition of a remedy that contains the duty to pay damages, since such a remedy would aim to re-establish the situation but for the infringement.

Adding to the above interpretation of Article 7 of Regulation 1/2003, the Court has made it clear that the Commission may not restrict the freedom of contract of an undertaking arbitrarily. Even if the Commission could aim

[41] OECD Secretariat, 'Relationship between Public and Private Antitrust Enforcement' (n 12) para 70.
[42] Case C-62/86 *AKZO Chemie BV v Commission* EU:C:1991:286, para 155.
[43] ibid, para 157.
[44] Directive (n 2) Art 3(2).

to restore the situation that would have existed but for the infringement, it is likely that the specificity of a requirement to pay damages would make such a remedy impossible to impose. First, with regard to remedying an infringement of Article 101 TFEU, the General Court held in *Automec* that

> there cannot be held to be any justification for such a restriction on freedom of contract where several remedies exist for bringing an infringement to an end … Consequently, the Commission undoubtedly has the power to find that an infringement exists and to order the parties concerned to bring it to an end, but it is not for the Commission to impose upon the parties its own choice from among all the various potential courses of action which are in conformity with the Treaty.[45]

Further, in *Magill*, a case regarding an infringement of Article 102 TFEU, the Court of Justice held that 'the imposition of that obligation with the possibility of making authorisation of publication dependent on certain conditions, including payment of royalties *was the only way of bringing the infringement to an end*'.[46]

The Court thus clarifies that the Commission cannot impose one specific remedy where several remedies exist to end an infringement. Specifically, imposing remedies that require contractual relations may violate the freedom of contract. If, however, such a remedy is the only way to bring the infringement to an end (as in *Magill*), it is within the Commission's powers to order that remedy. Fortunately, not all types of remedies intrude on the freedom of business of undertakings. One step towards facilitating private actions could be information.[47] The Commission has previously required undertakings to inform customers about infringements, for example, in *Schöller*.[48] This case concerned an infringement of Article 102 TFEU, but there is no reason to think that such a remedy would not be permissible for infringements of Article 101 TFEU.

Lastly, a practical point that can be made is that the imposition of a compensation scheme by the Commission may meet considerable practical difficulties. Such a scheme would need to contain details as regards the parties entitled to compensation, the calculation of the compensation as well as the supervision of the compensation scheme. As regards the appointment of monitoring trustees, the Commission is only empowered to appoint trustees with limited powers.[49] It is thus questionable whether an out-of-court compensation scheme that constitutes a 'once-and-for-all' settlement could be practically arranged by the Commission under the constraints of Article 7 of Regulation 1/2003.

[45] Case T-24/90 *Automec Srl v Commission* EU:T:1992:97, para 52.

[46] Joined Cases C-241/91 P and C-242/91 P *Radio Telefis Eireann (RTE) and Independent Television Publications Ltd (ITP) v Commission ('Magill')* EU:C:1995:98, para 91 (emphasis added).

[47] OECD Secretariat (n 12) para 80.

[48] Case T-9/93 *Schöller Lebensmittel GmbH & Co KG v Commission* EU:T:1995:99, para 158.

[49] *Microsoft (Decision regarding trustees)* (Case COMP/37.792) Commission Decision of 4 March 2009.

### *ii. Consensual Case Resolution Mechanisms*

Contrary to the situation in Article 7 decisions, the Commission is freer where it is using a consensual case resolution mechanism to end a potential infringement, or 'meet the Commission's concerns' as is the official terminology of Article 9 of Regulation 1/2003. There are two different case resolution mechanisms to be discussed: Article 9 decisions and consensual Article 7 decisions, such as the one concluded in the *ARA* case.[50] Settlements according to Article 10a of Regulation 773/2004 are not relevant, since they do not differ from 'ordinary' Article 7 decisions with regard to remedies.

Firstly, whether the Commission could impose the payment of remedies as part of an Article 9 decision shall be discussed. As already mentioned, the Commission has great freedom when accepting remedies considered suitable to 'meet its concerns'. Therefore, it is likely that a voluntary compensation scheme could be made binding by the Commission as part of an Article 9 decision. Nevertheless, undertakings may be reluctant to agree to such a remedy, as this could be seen as an admission of guilt, spurring further private actions beyond the scope of a voluntary scheme (should this not constitute a 'once-and-for-all' settlement).[51] Interestingly, there is indeed one example of a compensatory remedy within an Article 9 decision. In *Deutsche Bahn I/II*, an infringement of Article 102 TFEU in the railway power supply market was at issue. Deutsche Bahn agreed to compensate all direct customers of railway power supply. The compensation was calculated based on the previous year's bill.[52] This remedy suffers from the problem of having compensated only direct customers and thus not all parties that might have been entitled to compensation according to the Directive.[53] The practical problem of designing a compensatory remedy is thus easily illustrated in this case. Even if the options for the Commission, also with regards to monitoring trustees, are broader in Article 9 decisions than in Article 7 decisions, the design of such a remedy remains difficult.

Yet a different situation surfaces in a consensual Article 7 decision, such as *ARA*. As explained above, the *ARA* case was closed by an Article 7 decision, but with a considerable reduction of the fine in exchange for, inter alia, the suggestion of a remedy. It can be assumed that, as is the case with the Article 9 procedure, there was a dialogue between the Commission and the undertaking in question to discuss a suitable remedy. In that kind of process, it is not impossible that an undertaking would agree to compensate injured parties in exchange

[50] *ARA Foreclosure* (n 32).

[51] More recent case-law from France indicates that Art 9 decisions may be seen as prima facie evidence in any case, so agreeing to a voluntary compensation scheme may not make any difference in this context. See A Duron, 'Private Damages Actions in the Wake of a Commitment Decision: New Risks after the Judgment of the Paris Commercial Court in Eco-Emballages?' (2016) 7 *Journal of European Competition Law & Practice* 125.

[52] *Deutsche Bahn I/II* (Cases AT.39678 and AT.39731) Commission Decision C(2013) 9194 final [2013] OJ C 86/4.

[53] Directive (n 2) Art 3.

for a reduction of the fine for its cooperation. A question that arises is whether it is possible for the Commission to impose remedies that go beyond remedies that might ordinarily have been imposed under Article 7 if they are suggested by the undertaking? The Court of Justice held already in *ICI* that the Commission may require an undertaking to suggest a remedy.[54] In *ARA*, the undertaking suggested a structural remedy and also confirmed that it considered the remedy proportionate and necessary. Consequently, it appears likely that the Court would have considered that remedy legal.[55] Unfortunately, cases such as *ARA* are unlikely to reach the Court. Until there is case-law on this issue, the question above will not receive a final answer. There is thus considerable uncertainty as regards the ability of the Commission to impose a remedy that includes the duty to pay damages in a consensual Article 7 decision.

## V. CONCLUDING DISCUSSION

The goal of this chapter was to assess how private follow-on actions can be encouraged by the Commission's own public enforcement. First, it must be observed that public and private enforcement have different aims, but that private enforcement, in the EU, is heavily dependent on public enforcement. The Commission also has an interest in encouraging private enforcement as this will strengthen the deterrent effect of public enforcement. Yet, strong private enforcement may hamper public enforcement, for example by reducing leniency applications. This chapter has examined two relevant factors for the encouragement of follow-on actions, namely the case resolution mechanisms used by the Commission and the accommodation of private enforcement in fines and remedies.

Examining the Commission's present enforcement, it must be observed that the Commission increasingly uses consensual case resolution mechanisms to close cases. These case resolution mechanisms, albeit of a differing nature, are not ideal for the purposes of private enforcement since they do not contain the same amount of evidence as 'ordinary' Article 7 decisions. In particular, Article 9 decisions do not even find an infringement, which may be a serious problem for a private claimant aiming to prove a case in court. At the same time, Article 7 decisions are burdensome for the Commission to adopt and often result in appeals, thus consuming large resources.

The suggestion that the Commission could encourage compensation through reductions of fines is not ideal for several reasons. As regards timing, such reductions are difficult to make where follow-on actions are the main mode of private

[54] Joined Cases 6/73 and 7/73 *Istituto Chemioterapico Italiano S.pA and Commercial Solvents Corporation v Commission* EU:C:1974:18, para 45.

[55] *ARA Foreclosure* (n 32) para 162.

enforcement. Fine reductions would further complicate the calculation of fines and would confuse the conceptual difference between fines and damages. After all, fines are supposed to be punitive, while damages are merely compensatory. With regards to compensation schemes being included in remedies, it is likely that such remedies cannot be imposed in Article 7 decisions. Negotiated case resolutions could include compensatory remedies, but these still suffer from practical problems as regards their design.

Finally, it can be concluded that the best way to encourage private follow-on actions would be for the Commission to close more cases through Article 7 decisions, something that is also in line with the general criticism against the Commission's enforcement.[56] However, besides the higher workload imposed on the Commission with the adoption of Article 7 decisions, the Commission may actually be more interested in protecting its immediate interest, effective public enforcement. The improved deterrent effect achieved by private enforcement will only show itself within the years and decades to come, considering the speed at which competition law infringements are discovered and enforced. Even then, the deterrent effect of the combined interventions of public and private enforcement will be difficult to measure. Whether public enforcement can be carried out will, at least to the Commission, be more obvious on an immediate basis, for example if leniency applications decline or are of a lesser quality regarding the evidence provided.

Considering the number of tasks to be carried out by a public enforcer such as the Commission, one can even question how much regard public enforcement authorities *should* take of private enforcement? After all, private enforcement serves just that, private interest, rather than the public interest. Where the public and the private interest overlap, or where the Commission is presented with an opportunity to facilitate private enforcement, the Commission should do so.

Given that the Commission also has an interest in concluding a certain number of cases by ordinary Article 7 decisions, for example to establish precedent, such decisions can be used for follow-on actions. Likewise, in cases such as *Deutsche Bahn I/II*, though not a flawless example, the Commission may take the opportunity to facilitate private interest if it considers suitable.

[56] F Wagner-von Papp, 'Best and Even Better Practices in Commitment Procedures after Alrosa: The Dangers of Abandoning the "Struggle for Competition Law"' (2012) 49 *Common Market Law Review* 929; N Petit and MPL Rato, 'From Hard to Soft Enforcement of EC Competition Law – A Bestiary of "Sunshine" Enforcement Instruments' (2008), available at: ssrn.com/abstract=1270109.

# 8

# *The Practical and Legal Effects of National Decisions in Subsequent Damages Actions*

PER KARLSSON*

IN THIS CHAPTER, I share some of my thoughts and reflections on Article 9 of the Directive on Competition Damages Actions[1] (the Directive) and the Article's implementation from a Swedish perspective. I will try to cover both legal and practical aspects of the Article. My experience after several years in private practice tells me that these two aspects often merge and that the law in itself is not interesting before it has been applied in practice.

## I. ARTICLE 9 OF THE DIRECTIVE

Let me start by taking you through Article 9 of the Directive and the relevant provisions in the Preamble to see what we can learn from these texts. The first relevant provision in the Preamble is Recital 34 (i) and it reads as follows:

> To enhance legal certainty, to avoid inconsistency in the application of Articles 101 and 102 TFEU, to increase the effectiveness and procedural efficiency of actions for damages and to foster the functioning of the internal market for undertakings and consumers, the finding of an infringement of Article 101 or 102 TFEU in a final decision by a national competition authority or a review court should not be relitigated in subsequent actions for damages.

Here, we can see the motives behind Article 9. The first motive is to enhance legal certainty. Legal certainty has to do with the use of powers and predictability.

* This chapter was written while the author was Chief Legal Officer at the Swedish Competition Authority. All opinions expressed herein are strictly personal and do not represent the position of the Swedish Competition Authority.

[1] Directive 2014/104/EU of the European Parliament and of the Council of 26 November 2014 on certain rules governing actions for damages under national law for infringements of the competition law provisions of the Member States and of the European Union [2014] OJ L349/1.

It should be possible to foresee the consequences of possible action. Therefore, legal certainty is an obvious motive also in the context of damages. The second motive is effectiveness. Legal certainty is often a countervailing factor to effectiveness and these two have to be balanced.

The third motive is to avoid inconsistencies. That means that Article 9 on the binding effect of decisions is there to promote consistencies to turn the wording around. This applies to the interpretation and application of Articles 101 and 102 TFEU and, presumably, although this is not specifically mentioned, the material provisions on damages. The application should not differ and be diversified within the European Union (EU).

The fourth is close to the second motive, but it is expressed as procedural effectiveness. There should be effective ways of taking action against companies that have been found to have violated the competition rules. The fifth motive is to foster the functioning of the internal market, and it is clear that this refers to undertakings and consumers.

The way to achieve these five motives is through prohibiting the possibilities of relitigating the matter of a public enforcement case in subsequent actions for damages. This is expressly described in Recital 34 (ii).

> Therefore, such a finding should be deemed to be irrefutably established in actions for damages brought in the same Member State of the national competition authority or review court relating to that infringement. The effect of the finding should, however, cover only the nature of the infringement and its material, personal, temporal and territorial scope as determined by the competition authority or review court in the exercise of its jurisdiction. Where a decision has found that provisions of national competition law are infringed in cases where Union and national competition law are applied in the same case and in parallel, that infringement should also be deemed to be irrefutably established.

The next recital of interest here is the subsequent one, Recital 35, which deals with the situation where there is a finalised public enforcement decision made either by a court or by a national authority in another Member State. During the negotiations of the Directive, it was suggested that a decision by a national court or national authority should bind damages actions in the whole EU. However, that was not the end result of the political negotiations, and the Directive was not ultimately worded in that way.

Recital 35 provides that it should be possible to present the finding in a final decision made by the national competition authority or the review court to a national court as at least prima facie evidence of the fact that an infringement of competition law has occurred. The finding can be assessed as appropriate, along with any other evidence adduced by the parties.

Let us now look at the specific Directive provision dealing with the effects of a national decision. This matter is regulated in Article 9, which reads as follows:

> 1. Member States shall ensure that an infringement of competition law found by a final decision of a national competition authority or by a review court is deemed

to be irrefutably established for the purposes of an action for damages brought before their national courts under Article 101 or 102 TFEU or under national competition law.

2. Member States shall ensure that where a final decision referred to in paragraph 1 is taken in another Member State, that final decision may, in accordance with national law, be presented before their national courts as at least prima facie evidence that an infringement of competition law has occurred and, as appropriate, may be assessed along with any other evidence adduced by the parties.
3. This Article is without prejudice to the rights and obligations of national courts under Article 267 TFEU.

The formula that needs to be implemented by the Member States is that a finding of a national competition authority or by a review court is binding. The rule here is that a final decision is deemed to be irrefutably established for the purposes of an action for damages brought before a national court under Articles 101 or 102 TFEU or under national competition law. This means that it cannot be challenged effectively by the defendant in a damages action and the court in a damages action case will be bound by the earlier final judgment. I will return to the interpretation of that later in this chapter.

## II. THE TRANSPOSITION OF ARTICLE 9 IN SWEDISH LAW

Let me now continue with the Directive's transposition process in Sweden. Article 9 has been transposed into Swedish law through a specific provision in the new Competition Damages Act (SFS 2016:964), namely Chapter 5, section 9 of the Act. I will not go further into the wording of the provision here.

In the preparatory works, comparisons were made to labour law and criminal law. In Sweden, as in many other countries, an earlier judgment only has evidentiary value in another proceedings when applying another material provision to the same facts. However, as stated in the preparatory works,[2] using the same standards as in labour law and criminal law did not suffice. The effect of a decision had to be extended in order to transpose the Directive in a proper manner. Therefore, a provision was introduced in Sweden stating that the legal effect of a decision is irrefutable.

What effect is irrefutable? A finding of a violation has many parameters. It deals with the nature of the infringement – this means the material scope, the type of infringement. It also has to do with the duration of the violation. As I understand it, that is the temporal scope. In addition, it is the territorial scope in the final decision. The Swedish preparatory works explicitly state that any further clarification cannot be made and it should be left open to the courts, and ultimately to the Court of Justice of the EU, to interpret this provision.

[2] Government Bill 2016/17:9 Konkurrensskadelagen.

What decisions and laws are meant to be included? To begin with, in the Swedish context, decisions at least cover court judgments by either the Patent and Market Court or the Patent and Market Court of Appeal, and the Supreme Court, in the extraordinary situation where the Patent and Market Court of Appeal has opened up the possibility for an appeal and the Supreme Court has granted leave of appeal. What laws should it apply to? Violations of Articles 101 and 102 TFEU and the equivalent provisions under national law (Chapter 2, sections 1, 2 or 7 of the Swedish Competition Act), applied either alone or in parallel.

Another interesting observation is the following. It is probably not self-evident, but according to the Swedish preparatory works, 'fine orders' imposed by the Swedish Competition Authority (SCA) are also covered. A fine order in Swedish competition law is something other than a 'fine decision'. Instead of instituting proceedings regarding an administrative fine, the SCA may order an undertaking to pay such a fine (fine order). Such an order may only be issued if the SCA considers that the material circumstances regarding the infringement are clear. According to government officials, including fine orders in the decisions with binding effect was a last minute amendment and their inclusion is not, I believe, obvious to all practitioners. There was no comment on this, according to my knowledge, when the earlier proposals from the Swedish Ministry were sent out for public consultation.

New timing aspects on follow-on actions are also of importance. The new Directive entails a new timing aspect compared to the situation in Sweden before the transposition of the Directive. This has to do with the limitation period, which was five years from 1993 until 2005, when it was extended to ten (years). The important change here is that the Directive, under certain circumstances, seems to fully open up for the claimants to await the public enforcement proceedings in a way that was not possible before the transposition.

Under the new regime, there is more leeway for the claimant to await and word its claims depending on the outcome of the fine case and to subsequently set the scope of its damages action at a later stage than before and use the full effect of the binding final judgment. Before the transposition of the Directive, a claimant often had to set the scope for the damages proceedings by filing a suit before the fine case was finally decided, due to limitation risks. This occurred in, for example follow-on actions against Telia in the ADSL margin squeeze cases and against construction companies such as Skanska and NCC originating from the fines proceedings in the asphalt cartel cases.

There are also important practical issues regarding temporal and geographical scope. The period of a violation, or a certain conduct can be evaluated differently in a fine case than in a damages case. So, for example, the temporal scope could be shortened substantially in a fine case, due to the higher standard of proof that the court applies to its findings. As I will explain in my observations below, the courts will not, without an explicit provision like the one in

Article 9 of the Directive, follow earlier judgments even if they only hold evidential value. This was the case in the follow-on actions against Telia in the ADSL margin squeeze cases. Thus, the outcome has been quite surprising for those who thought that the standard of proof was higher in a fine case compared to a damages case, which is of civil character. If you thought it would be easier to win a damages case against a dominant undertaking than a fine case, we now know that it is simply not that straightforward.

Will Article 9 of the Directive greatly help the claimant? Overall and in general terms the new rule ought to be helpful and should be less burdensome as regards taking legal action. However, there must be a link between the damages action and the binding effect of the final earlier decision, which will depend on a number of issues. The standard of proof may be different in court proceedings regarding the imposition of a fine and a damages case, where the standard of proof may be less strict than in the former. In other words, the violation of the prohibitions may to a certain extent be harder to establish in a fine case than in a damages case, which has a civil character. This is illustrated by the surprising outcome of some recent damages cases before the Swedish courts, to which I will now turn.

## III. ANALYSIS OF ARTICLE 9: A SWEDISH EXAMPLE OF INCONSISTENCIES

In the margin squeeze case *The Swedish Competition Authority v Telia*, the background was the following: at the end of the 1990s and the beginning of the 2000s, a growing number of Swedish end users of internet services moved from dial-up internet connections with low transmission speeds to various types of broadband connection with considerably higher transmission speeds. At that time, the most widespread form of broadband connection was that achieved by asymmetric digital subscriber line (ADSL). Those connections used a telephone network, a cable television network, or a local area network.

Historically, Telia had been the Swedish landline telephone network operator, the holder of exclusive rights in the past. It had long been the owner of a local metallic access network to which almost all Swedish households were connected. In particular, Telia owned the local loop, in other words the part of the copper pairs' telephone network that connects the telephone operator's exchange to the subscriber's telephone.

Telia offered access to the local loop to other operators in two ways. On the one hand, it offered unbundled access, in accordance with its obligations under certain regulations.[3] On the other (hand), without being legally obliged to do so, Telia offered to operators an ADSL product intended for wholesale users. That product enabled the operators concerned to supply their broadband connection

[3] Regulation (EC) No 2887/2000 of the European Parliament and of the Council of 18 December 2000 on unbundled access to the local loop [2000] OJ L 336/4.

services to end users. At the same time, Telia offered broadband connection services directly to end users.

In the opinion of the SCA, between April 2000 and January 2003, Telia abused its dominant position to the extent that it applied a pricing policy under which the spread between the sales price of ADSL products intended for wholesale users and the sales price of services offered to end users was not sufficient to cover the costs which Telia itself had to incur in order to distribute those services to the end users concerned. For that reason, the SCA brought an action before the Stockholm District Court requesting that the court order Telia to pay an administrative fine for infringements of competition rules, from April 2000 until January 2003.

Apart from the above-mentioned administrative fine court proceedings, there have also been two damages court proceedings brought as follow-on actions. Altogether there have been three cases on almost the same substantive matters. There are in total six Swedish court judgments from three different Swedish courts. They have come to different conclusions based on almost the same facts and law regarding Telia's pricing policy on the wholesale and consumer markets during a period of approximately three years (2000–03). An illustration of the results of these six cases is given below, in Table 1.

## A. The First Court Judgment on Telia's Margin Squeeze – The SCA I

The first court judgment was in the fine proceedings that the SCA initiated in 2004 before the Stockholm District Court claiming for a fine of SEK 144 million for an alleged abuse of dominance consisting of margin squeeze during the above-mentioned period. The Stockholm District Court referred the case to the ECJ for a preliminary ruling.[4]

The ECJ ruled that in the absence of any objective justification, the fact that a vertically integrated undertaking, holding a dominant position on the wholesale market in asymmetric digital subscriber line input services, applied a pricing practice of such a kind that the spread between the prices applied on that market and those applied in the retail market for broadband connection services to end users was not sufficient to cover the specific costs which that undertaking had to incur in order to gain access to that retail market might constitute an abuse within the meaning of Article 102 TFEU.

When assessing whether such a practice is abusive, all of the circumstances of each individual case should be taken into consideration. In particular, as a general rule, (primarily) the prices and costs of the undertaking concerned on the retail services market should be taken into consideration. Only where it is not possible, in particular circumstances, to refer to those prices and costs

[4] Case C-52/09 *Konkurrensverket v TeliaSonera Sverige AB* EU:C:2011:83.

**Table 1** Telia's Margin Squeeze Abuse of Dominance – Overview of Fines Proceedings and Follow-on Actions (damages)

<table>
<tr><th></th><th colspan="4">Fines proceedings<br>Claim MSEK 144</th><th colspan="2">Damages case Yarps<br>Claim MSEK 369<br>(+ extensive interest)</th><th colspan="2">Damages case Tele 2<br>Claim MSEK 708<br>(+extensive interest)</th></tr>
<tr><td>Court</td><td colspan="2">Stockholm District Court</td><td colspan="2">Market Court</td><td>Stockholm District Court</td><td>Svea Court of Appeals</td><td>Stockholm District Court</td><td>Svea Court of Appeals</td></tr>
<tr><td>Date of judgment</td><td colspan="2">2 Dec 2011</td><td colspan="2">12 March 2013</td><td>7 March 2013</td><td>29 July 2017</td><td>26 May 2016</td><td>21 Dec 2017</td></tr>
<tr><td>Dominance</td><td colspan="2">April 2000–Jan 2003</td><td colspan="2">July 2001–Jan 2003</td><td>July 2001–Jan 2003</td><td>April 2000–Jan 2003</td><td>July 2001–Jan 2003</td><td>Yes</td></tr>
<tr><td>Abuse – Margin squeeze (vis-à-vis Single Customers[X] Or Group Customers[Y])</td><td>Yarps<br>Feb–March 2002[X]<br>Feb 2002–Jan 2003[Y]</td><td>Tele2<br>March–April 2001[X]<br>May 2002–Jan 2003[Y]</td><td>Yarps<br>18 Feb 2002–Jan 2003</td><td>Tele2<br>23 May 2002–Jan 2003</td><td>18 Feb 2002–Jan 2003</td><td>No</td><td>3 July 2001–Jan 2003</td><td>26 March 2001–Jan 2003</td></tr>
<tr><td>Effect/Damage</td><td>Feb–March 2002[X]<br>Feb 2002–Jan 2003[Y]</td><td>March–April 2001[X]<br>May 2002–Jan 2003[Y]</td><td>18 Feb 2002–Jan 2003</td><td>23 May 2002–Jan 2003</td><td>18 Feb 2002–Jan 2003</td><td>No</td><td>3 July 2001–Jan 2003</td><td>Not proven</td></tr>
<tr><td>Fee/Damages</td><td colspan="2">144 MSEK</td><td colspan="2">35 MSEK</td><td>65 MSEK</td><td>0</td><td>240 MSEK</td><td>0</td></tr>
</table>

should those of competitors on the same market be examined. Moreover, it is necessary to demonstrate that, taking particular account of whether the wholesale product is indispensable, that practice produces an anti-competitive effect, at least potentially, on the retail market, and that the practice is not in any way economically justified.

Some factors were found not to be relevant to such an assessment such as inter alia:

- the absence of any regulatory obligation on the undertaking concerned to supply asymmetric digital subscriber line input services on the wholesale market in which it holds a dominant position;
- the degree of dominance held by that undertaking in that market; and
- the fact that that undertaking does not also hold a dominant position in the retail market for broadband connection services to end users.[5]

The case in the Stockholm District Court was heard in October 2011. In December 2011, the Stockholm District Court ruled in the SCA's favour. The court found that Telia was dominant during the entire period. The court found that Telia had abused its dominant position by squeezing the margin vis-à-vis Yarps (Spray) in both February and March 2002 (single customers) and between February 2002 and January 2003 (group customers) and vis-à-vis Tele 2 in both March and April 2001 (single customers) and between May 2002 and January 2003 (group customers).[6]

The court found that the margin squeeze had an effect during the same period of time and was therefore unlawful. Thus, the court imposed a fine on Telia that amounted to SEK 144 million.

## B. The Second Court Judgment on Telia's Margin Squeeze – The SCA II

Telia appealed to the Market Court. The Market Court came to partly different conclusions concerning the market definition and on dominance in that market. Telia was not dominant before July 2001, according to the Market Court.

According to the ECJ, in the present case, there would be such a margin squeeze if, inter alia, the spread between the wholesale prices for ADSL input services and the retail prices for broadband connection services to end users were either negative or insufficient to cover the specific costs of the ADSL input services which Telia had to incur in order to supply its own retail services to end users, so that that spread did not allow a competitor which was as efficient as the undertaking in question to compete for the supply of those services to end users.[7]

[5] ibid, para 115.
[6] Case T 31862-04 *Konkurrensverket v TeliaSonera Sverige AB*.
[7] Case C-52/09 *TeliaSonera* (n 4) para 32.

The Market Court found, based on new evidence and a new expert witness, that the specific costs of the ADSL input services which Telia had to incur in order to supply its own retail services to end users should be determined differently than the Stockholm District Court had done. According to the court, the Swedish Competition Authority did not have sufficiently solid evidence to prove that the specific costs were as high as was alleged. Therefore, Telia's behaviour was not abusive other than during a more limited period of time compared to the time established by the Stockholm District Court. The costs were not considered substantially lower (around SEK 30 per customer) and the margin squeeze test resulted in a more favourable outcome for Telia. The court found that Telia had abused its dominant position by squeezing the margin vis-à-vis Yarps (Spray) between 18 February 2002 and January 2003, and Tele 2 between 23 May 2002 and January 2003.[8]

The Market Court judgment gained legal force[9] and the administrative fine case was once and for all finally resolved after an investigation and very long court proceedings spanning two national instances and a reference for a preliminary ruling to the ECJ that of course extended the court proceedings in the court of the first instance.

## C. The Third Court Judgment on Telia's Margin Squeeze – Yarps I

Let us now turn to the damages cases and have a look at the conclusions that were drawn. The first case is the Yarps case before the Stockholm District Court. Yarps (formerly Spray), a company under liquidation, brought a damages action against Telia with a claim of in total SEK 369 million plus interest. Yarps claimed that the abusive behaviour of Telia did not only consist of a margin squeeze but also of discrimination and the denial of supply.

Full-scale court proceedings took place through which the questions (facts and law) were to a large extent relitigated. Based on a fully independent finding regarding the administrative case referred to above, the court found that Telia was dominant during exactly the same period of time as established in the administrative fine case by the Market Court. This period was from 1 July 2001 to the end of January 2003, when Telia was the only company to offer the wholesale product and therefore had a de facto monopoly, according to the court.[10]

However, as regards the costs, the court made a different evaluation that was more plaintiff-friendly than in the fine case. That is reasonable, since you could argue that a civil case does not have the same requirement regarding the standard of proof as an administrative fine case, which has similarities with a criminal case. After a fair and moderate evaluation, the court found that Telia's costs

[8] The other competitors that were subjected to a margin squeeze by Telia are not mentioned here.
[9] Case MD:2013:5 *TeliaSonera v Konkurrensverket*.
[10] Case T 15382-06 *Yarps v Telia*, p 115.

could be deemed to have been at a certain level (around SEK 61 per customer). From that, the court calculated when the margin was not enough for an efficient competitor and found that the margin squeeze had taken place against Yarps between 18 February 2002 until the end of January 2003.[11]

The court found that Telia had caused Yarps harm due to lost profit from missed potential customers and lost income from incumbent customers during the same period of time.[12] The court declared that Yarps had a right to damages. The damages were set at SEK 65 million. Both parties appealed to the Svea Court of Appeal.

## D. The Fourth Court Judgment on Telia's Margin Squeeze Yarps II

The Svea Court of Appeal defined the relevant market differently and found that customers switched only one way from dial-up to broadband and not vice versa and that Telia had previously offered an ADSL wholesale product. Therefore, the court came to the conclusion that Telia was dominant already from April 2000 until the end of January 2003.[13]

However, the Svea Court of Appeal evaluated the evidence on Telia's additional costs for providing customer services differently. The evidence was not solid enough to establish that the costs were as high as the Stockholm District Court had found. Instead, it came to the same conclusion in that respect as the Market Court had done in the administrative fine case. Again, the additional costs were considered substantially lower (approximately SEK 30 per customer) and again the margin squeeze test resulted in a more favourable outcome for Telia.[14]

In addition, the Svea Court of Appeal found that the wholesale ADSL product was not indispensable.[15] Regarding the abuse, the court found that Telia had only subjected Yarps to a margin squeeze during a period of 11 months for one-fifth of the end consumer market.[16] That did not point strongly enough at an effect of the behaviour. The court found no exclusionary strategy proven.

To summarise, the court did not find sufficient evidence of any effects of Telia's pricing. It was thus not proven that Telia had abused its dominant position.[17] The claim for damages was therefore dismissed.

[11] ibid, p 129.
[12] ibid, p 141.
[13] Case T 2673-16 *Yarps v Telia*, p 18.
[14] ibid, p 28.
[15] ibid, p 33.
[16] ibid, p 37.
[17] ibid, p 46.

## E. The Fifth Court Judgment on Telia's Margin Squeeze – Tele 2 I

The second damages case was the Tele 2 damages case also before the Stockholm District Court. Tele 2 brought a damages action with a claim of in total SEK 708 million plus interest. Tele 2 claimed that the abusive behaviour of Telia consisted of a margin squeeze and that the company had suffered damages to the extent that the company claimed compensation for.

Again, full-scale court proceedings took place through which the questions (facts and law) were to a large extent relitigated for a third time in addition to the fines case and the Yarps case. Based on a new subsequent and fully independent finding regarding the administrative fine case referred to above and the Yarps case, the court found that Telia was dominant during the exact same period of time as that established in the administrative fine case. This period was from 1 July 2001 to the end of January 2003, when Telia was the only company to offer the wholesale product and therefore had de facto a monopoly, according to the court.[18]

On the issue of costs, the Stockholm District Court made a plaintiff-friendly evaluation especially with regard to the fine case, but also one that was close to the evaluation in the Yarps case. After an evaluation, the court found that Telia's additional costs should be deemed to have been around SEK 62 per customer.[19]

The court found that Telia had subjected Tele 2 to a margin squeeze between 3 July 2001 until the end of January 2003.[20] The court found that Telia had caused Tele 2 harm from lost profit during the same period. The court calculated the damages to SEK 240 million, lost income of SEK 4 000 and 60 000 lost customers, all caused by the abuse.[21]

## F. The Sixth Court Judgment on Telia's Margin Squeeze – Tele 2 II

Both sides appealed just as in the Yarps case. The Svea Court of Appeal did not clearly define the period of dominance, but my interpretation is that the court came to the conclusion that Telia was dominant already from April 2000 until the end of January 2003.[22]

The court found that Tele2 was subjected to a margin squeeze by Telia from 26 March 2001 until the end of January 2003. The costs were found to be established at a much higher level (SEK 62–70 per customer) than the Svea Court of Appeal had previously found in the Yarps case (SEK 30 per customer).[23]

[18] Case T 10956-05 *Tele 2 v Telia*, p 121.
[19] ibid, p 134.
[20] ibid, p 141.
[21] ibid, p 159.
[22] Case T 5365-16 *Tele 2 v Telia*, p 29.
[23] ibid, p 41.

The court found that the margin squeeze had a potential effect and that it constituted an abuse of Telia's dominant position during the same period of time.[24]

However, the Svea Court of Appeal came to a different conclusion compared to the Stockholm District Court on another matter. It found that the alleged damages could not adequately be explained by Telia's margin squeeze. Therefore, it had not been established that the lost market position in the broadband market was linked to the proven abuse. The claim for damages was therefore dismissed.

## IV. CONCLUSIONS

This is an illustrative example of inconsistencies by the Swedish courts based on almost the same facts and law. In my opinion, the inconsistencies are troublesome. It is surprising that the courts regarding the Telia ADSL took so little notice of other courts' findings, although to a certain extent that could be explained by the independence of the courts.

It remains to be seen whether Article 9 of the Directive will make a marked difference or not, through the prohibition of relitigation. It cannot be excluded that a court might find that an earlier judgment really is refutable, despite Article 9. There may be possible loopholes for parties and judges that are not willing to accept an earlier judgment concerning a fine. However, that would contradict the intention behind Article 9 in the Directive. It will be interesting to follow the application in the future.

[24] ibid, p 47.

# 9

# *The Quest for Evidence – Still an Uphill Battle for Cartel Victims?*

HELENE ANDERSSON*

## I. INTRODUCTION

NEARLY TWO DECADES have passed since the Court of Justice of the European Union (the Court or the ECJ) established that victims of competition law infringements should be able to seek damages and be entitled to compensation in full for any loss suffered.[1] However, the Court's rulings in the now seminal cases of *Courage* and *Manfredi* did not reflect the reality at the time. Surveys conducted by the Commission in the wake of the rulings revealed that most victims rarely obtained any compensation at all.[2] As a response, the Commission later presented a proposal for a Directive on antitrust damages actions. Following certain modifications, Directive 2014/104/EU (the Directive) was adopted in November 2014,[3] introducing a framework designed to ensure an effective private enforcement system throughout the Union.

The Directive identifies and addresses a number of obstacles to the realisation of such system, one being the difficulties that cartel victims encounter when they seek to obtain evidence of the damage sustained. It goes without saying that access to evidence is key to ensuring effective private enforcement. Actions for damages in this type of case typically require a complex factual and legal analysis, and the evidence required is often held exclusively by the opposing party, third parties or the competition authority investigating the case.[4]

* Post-doctoral researcher at Stockholm University.

[1] Case C-453/99 *Courage Ltd v Bernard Crehan and Bernard Crehan v Courage Ltd and Others* EU:C:2001:465 and Case C-295/04 *Manfredi* EU:C:2006:461.

[2] European Commission, Green Paper – Damages actions for breach of the EC antitrust rules SEC(2005) 1732.

[3] Directive 2014/104/EU on certain rules governing actions for damages under national law for infringements of the competition law provisions of the Member States and of the European Union [2014] OJ L 349/1.

[4] ibid, Recitals 14 and 15.

In its initial proposal, the Commission declared that it was widely recognised that in many Member States, the difficulty a claimant encountered in obtaining all necessary evidence constituted one of the key obstacles to damages actions in competition cases.[5]

In order to remove this hurdle, the Directive introduces a number of provisions on disclosure, requiring Member States to ensure that national courts are able to order disclosure of the evidence necessary for the applicants to prove their claim. However, disclosure is not mandatory and there are a number of conditions governing its application. The question is therefore whether the rules, as they are now framed, will ensure a level playing field throughout the Union and guarantee the access required, or whether they will allow national courts to hide behind proportionality analyses or the Commission's own practices to maintain the obstacles to effective private enforcement identified in the Directive's recitals.

This chapter presents the Directive's provisions on disclosure, and provides an analysis of these rules against the backdrop of the Commission's own practices and the ECJ's case-law on public access to cartel files and publication of infringement decisions. It is concluded that although the rules will require national courts to assess these questions against a new set of rules, the discretion left to the courts will allow them to carry on more or less as usual should they so desire.

## II. TAKING THE RISK OF GOING TO COURT

As noted by the Commission in the Green Paper preceding the proposal for the Directive,[6] actions for damages in antitrust cases regularly require the investigation of a broad set of facts. In order for a court to award damages, the cartel victim will have to prove (i) the existence and extent of the cartel; (ii) that the actions of (each of) the cartel members have caused the applicant harm, as well as (iii) the amount of the harm caused. This is no doubt an uphill battle, and probably a partial explanation for why the survey conducted by the Commission in the wake of the *Courage* ruling revealed a state of 'total underdevelopment' throughout the European Union.[7]

The Directive introduces a number of provisions that seek to remedy these problems and encourage individuals to make use of private action before national

[5] Commission Proposal for a Directive of the European Parliament and of the Council on certain rules governing actions for damages under national law for infringements of the competition law provisions of the Member States and of the European Union, COM(2013) 404 final, 2013/0185 (COD) 13.

[6] Green Paper (n 2).

[7] In the Green Paper, the Commission notes that while Community law demands an effective system for damages claims for infringements of antitrust rules, 'this area of law in the 25 Member States presents a picture of "total underdevelopment"'.

courts. First of all, there is now a rebuttable presumption of harm. According to Article 17(2) of the Directive, cartel infringements shall be presumed to cause harm, and the Commission has also published a guidance for national courts on how to quantify such harm.[8] Second, where several undertakings infringe the competition rules jointly, they shall be held jointly and severally liable for the entire harm caused by the infringement.[9] Third, not only are national courts bound by the decisions and rulings of the EU judicature, but Article 9 of the Directive also declares that where a national competition authority or court has established an infringement, such a finding shall be binding also on the court hearing the damages claim. Where the action for damages is brought before a court in another Member State, the finding of an infringement must constitute at least prima facie evidence of an infringement.

Even considering these attempts at invigorating the private enforcement system, filing a damages claim is not without risk. The burden of proof may not be as heavy to bear as it used to be, but the cartel victim will still need to collect a substantial amount of evidence in order to be successful in court. To use the words of Riley and Peysner, running a competition case – and particularly a damages case – in a national court is not for the fainthearted. The time that such cases take can be lengthy, the demands for documentary and economic evidence considerable and the costs substantial.[10] Ideally, the potential claimant would want to access at least some evidence already before taking matters to court in order to properly assess the chances of success. A company considering a follow-on action may therefore attempt to access evidence from the competition authority investigating the case. However, the rules on public access have not been harmonised and, despite the Court's rulings in cases such as *Pfleiderer*[11] and *Donau Chemie*,[12] the chances of accessing evidence from national competition authorities vary between Member States.

As for the Commission's case files, it has proven difficult for cartel victims to access the documents contained therein. This being said, and as will be discussed in more detail later in this chapter, the Commission has recently chosen another route to further transparency and allow cartel victims to gather relevant information, and that is through the publication of longer and more detailed infringement decisions. Even though these 'new' and extended versions

[8] Communication from the Commission on quantifying harm in actions for damages based on breaches of Article 101 or 102 of the Treaty on the Functioning of the European Union, 2013/C 16/07. The Communication is accompanied by a more comprehensive and detailed practical guide drawn up by the Commission's services, 'Commission Staff Working Document, Practical Guide, Quantifying harm in actions for damages based on breaches of Articles 101 or 102 of the Treaty on the Functioning of the European Union' C(2013)3440.

[9] Art 11 of the Directive (n 3).

[10] A Riley and J Peysner, 'Damages in EC Antitrust Actions: Who Pays the Piper?' (2006) 31 *European Law Review* 748, 749.

[11] Case C-360/09 *Pfleiderer AG v Bundeskartellamt* EU:C:2011:389.

[12] Case C536/11 *Bundeswettbewerbsbehörde v Donau Chemie AG and Others* EU:C:2013:366.

of the Commission's decisions may not always provide the evidence required to file a successful cartel damages claim, they may nevertheless help victims narrow down and specify any request for disclosure of or access to documents, thereby also increasing the chances of accessing the evidence required. However, as will be discussed in section V below, these attempts by the Commission have met steep resistance from the addressees of the infringement decisions, who are claiming that the extended versions should not be made public due to the confidential information allegedly contained therein. Thus, anyone who chooses to await the publication of a more detailed Commission decision before taking matters to court will need to be patient and will also risk having to wait in vain. The remaining option is for the cartel victim to take matters to court and convince the national courts to order disclosure. This is where the Directive comes into play.

## III. THE DIRECTIVE'S PROVISIONS ON DISCLOSURE

The Directive governs actions for damages before national courts. Recognising that access to evidence is key to achieving effective private enforcement, it contains a number of provisions on disclosure. Article 5 of the Directive deals with disclosure in general while Article 6 adds further requirements in situations where the evidence is sought from the file of a competition authority. As noted by Wils, the competition authorities' case files are obvious locations for potentially relevant evidence.[13] Yet, both Recital 29 and Article 6(10) of the Directive make competition authorities the last possible resort for obtaining evidence. The Directive provides that they shall only have to disclose evidence where such evidence 'cannot possibly be obtained from another party or from a third party'. The rationale behind this approach being that competition authorities have limited resources, and should focus those resources on the core task of detecting and punishing competition law infringements.[14]

### A. Evidence Held by Other Parties or Third Parties

The main provision on disclosure is thus Article 5. The Article requires Member States to ensure that national courts, in proceedings relating to damages actions, are able to order defendants or third parties to disclose relevant evidence, provided that the claimant is able to present 'a reasoned justification containing reasonably available facts and evidence sufficient to support the

[13] WPJ Wils, 'Private Enforcement of EU Antitrust Law and its Relationship with Public Enforcement: Past, Present and Future' (2017) 40(1) *World Competition* 3, 31.

[14] ibid.

plausibility of its claim for damages'. The wording of the provision prompts a number of reflections.

First, Member States are only required to enable national courts to order disclosure of evidence. There is thus no obligation on the part of the courts to actually do so.[15] It is worth noting that the Commission's initial proposal did actually require national courts to order disclosure in certain circumstances. Article 5(2) of the proposal required disclosure where the party requesting disclosure (i) could show that evidence in the hands of another party or a third party was relevant, and (ii) had specified either items of evidence or categories of evidence defined as precisely and as narrowly as possible. The legislator has thus taken a deliberate step back, and left it to the national court to decide whether or not to order disclosure.

Second, the provision applies 'in proceedings relating to an action for damages'. A narrow reading suggests that it is only when the claimant has actually brought a damages claim before a national court that the provision is triggered, leaving pre-trial disclosure outside the scope of the Directive. Such a narrow reading is supported by the fact that the initial proposal did not make any reference to proceedings relating to actions for damages, but simply imposed an obligation on Member States to enable national courts to order disclosure where the claimant had fulfilled the criteria listed in Article 5(1).[16] As discussed above, cartel damages cases are both complex and fact-intensive (read costly), and one would imagine that most cartel victims would want to access the evidence while still assessing their chances in court. However, those situations are not expressly governed by the Directive, leaving it open for Member States to exclude pre-trial disclosure, which would be unfortunate. Given that the current version differs from the Commission's proposal in this respect, there is reason to believe that at least some Member States considered the initial wording to be too far-reaching, and will thus apply a restrictive approach to the Directive's obligations.

Third, the victim must present a reasoned justification containing 'reasonably available facts and evidence sufficient to support the plausibility of its claim for damages'. Indeed this requirement is perfectly reasonable – defendants should not have to risk the costly, burdensome and undesired work of gathering and disclosing evidence unless there is reason to suspect that they have participated in a cartel, and that the cartel activity has caused the claimant harm. However, one cannot disregard the fact that the provision, as it is now framed, will discourage some victims from taking matters to court and that the national courts which do get to deal with these questions may interpret the requirements of the provision in a variety of ways.

[15] Directive Proposal (n 5).

[16] The criteria are that the claimant has presented reasonably available facts and evidence showing plausible grounds for suspecting that he, or those he represents, has suffered harm caused by the defendant's infringement of competition law. See Art 5(1) of the Directive Proposal (n 5).

Article 5(2) governs the specificity of the requests for disclosure. According to the Article, national courts should not be prevented from ordering disclosure where the applicant has managed to limit the request to specified items of evidence or relevant categories of evidence circumscribed as precisely and as narrowly as possible based on reasonably available facts. As noted by Wagner-von Papp, the wording of the Article caters to the restrictive Continental jurisdictions where disclosure rules tend to have two major limitations; disclosure will usually only be ordered if the applicant has requested disclosure of specified pieces of evidence, and these pieces of evidence have to be identified fairly precisely.[17] Through the introduction of 'categories of documents' the legislator seeks to increase the chances of disclosure also in Continental jurisdictions. However, it is not clear from the wording exactly how narrowly these categories must be defined, and although this requirement is perfectly reasonable, it may nevertheless discourage those victims that have not seen the file of the competition authority and do not know which documents to request. As noted by Dunne, the Directive emphasises that only 'relevant' evidence is subject to the disclosure requirement and, at least in the recitals, indicates a degree of suspicion in respect of requests relating to categories of evidence rather than specified pieces of evidence.[18] Indeed, Recital 23 states explicitly that '[p]articular attention should be paid to preventing fishing expeditions'. Given the above, there is a likelihood that national courts, even within the same Member State, may interpret the requirement in different ways. This concern is further underlined by the ECJ's case-law on access to the Commission's cartel files, which is discussed further in section IV.B below.

Any risk of divergent applications is further heightened by Article 5(3), which requires national courts to carry out a proportionality analysis and to limit disclosure of evidence to that which is proportionate. When doing so, the national court shall consider (i) the legitimate interests of all parties and third parties concerned; (ii) the extent to which the claim or defence is supported by available facts and evidence; (iii) the scope and cost of disclosure; and (iv) whether the evidence in question contains confidential information and the arrangements in place to protect such information. Imposing a proportionality restriction is of course both appropriate and necessary. Few would argue that disclosure should be arbitrary or disproportionate. However, a proportionality analysis involves a number of steps and inherently allows the national courts a certain room for manoeuvre, as it requires them to balance certain interests or rights against each other in order to determine which

[17] F Wagner-von Papp, 'Access to Evidence and Leniency Materials', available at: ssrn.com/abstract=2733973. See also DA Woods, A Sinclair and D Ashton, 'Private Enforcement of Community Competition Law: Modernisation and the Road Ahead' (2004) *Competition Policy Newsletter No 2*, 34.

[18] N Dunne, 'The Role of Private Enforcement within EU Competition Law' (2014) 16 *Cambridge Yearbook of European Legal Studies* 143, 163.

interest should be allowed to prevail in any specific situation. This balancing exercise is strongly evaluative, and unless it is applied in a transparent and consistent fashion, may be open to criticism.

Given the wide discretion provided for in Article 5 of the Directive, there is thus an apparent risk that at least some national courts will refrain from changing their previous practices and that the desired level playing field will not materialise.[19] This risk is further emphasised by Article 6, which adds additional requirements in those situations where national courts consider the possibility of ordering disclosure of documents held by competition authorities.

## B. Evidence Held by Competition Authorities

The Directive contains a number of additional provisions, which apply where the evidence requested may only be disclosed by a competition authority. As mentioned earlier, Article 6(10) imposes an obligation on the Member States to make sure that national courts only request disclosure from competition authorities when no party or third party is reasonably able to provide that evidence. In those situations, Article 6 applies alongside Article 5 and adds a number of additional conditions that need to be met in order for any evidence to be disclosed.

Whereas Article 5 governs proceedings relating to an action for damages, Article 6 appears to become applicable already at an earlier stage. The Article requires Member States to ensure that Article 6 is applied alongside Article 5 in those situations where, for the purpose of actions for damages, national courts order disclosure of documents held in the file of a competition authority. This apparent discrepancy seems odd, given that the first option should be to seek an order for disclosure from the cartel members, which, according to Article 5, requires that there are ongoing proceedings before a national court. However, while Article 5 was given a new and narrower wording during the legislative negotiations, Article 6 remains unaltered in this respect. Time will tell what practical implications this may have, although one would expect the Court to favour consistency and coherence in its interpretation of the rules. It will be interesting to see whether any cartel victim will argue that pre-trial disclosure should be ordered from a competition authority's case file on the grounds that the national rules do not allow national courts to order disclosure from cartel members until proceedings have been initiated.

Where a national court is considering the possibility of ordering disclosure from a competition authority's case file, it will have to consider some additional factors when carrying out the proportionality analysis. First of all, Article 6(4) requires the court to consider whether the request has been formulated specifically

[19] For a further discussion on this, see Wagner-von Papp, 'Access to Evidence' (n 17).

with regard to the nature, subject matter or contents of documents submitted to a competition authority or held in the file thereof, rather than by a non-specific application concerning documents submitted to a competition authority. Given that Article 6 should apply alongside the requirements in Article 5, a number of questions arise.[20] Article 5 requires the applicant to request disclosure of specified items of evidence or relevant categories of evidence circumscribed as precisely and narrowly as possible on the basis of reasonably available facts and in the reasoned justification. Although the provision opens up for broader disclosures than those limited to specified documents identified in advance, the wording of the Article suggests that the applicant shall be able to provide some guidance on which documents it wishes to have disclosed. However, when reading Article 6(4), which, it is presumed, aims at adding an extra requirement to the court's assessment, another picture emerges. The court should determine whether or not it is dealing with a 'non-specific application'. This triggers the obvious question whether the court is not required to do that already under Article 5.

Article 6(4) requires national courts to consider 'whether the party requesting disclosure is doing so in relation to an action for damages before a national court', presumably suggesting that the court should be more inclined to order disclosure where court proceedings are already ongoing. Why this is the case is difficult to see. If an applicant fulfils the requirements in Article 5 – and can thus both show a reasoned justification and limit the request to specified documents or categories of documents circumscribed as narrowly as possible – there is no reason why the court should be less inclined to order disclosure from the file of a competition authority on the sole ground that there are no ongoing court proceedings. One would assume that pre-trial disclosure would help keep down the costs of court proceedings.

National courts are also required under Article 6(4)(c) to consider the need to safeguard the effectiveness of the public enforcement of competition law. Given the ongoing debate on the possible effects that extensive disclosure rules may have on cartel members' willingness to cooperate with competition authorities, the provision may be interpreted as a reminder to national courts to bear this relationship in mind when considering disclosure of documents held by a competition authority. Should this be the case, the placing of the provision is unfortunate, as national courts should preferably also consider this when ordering disclosure from defendants or third parties. However, the recitals allow for another interpretation of the provision. According to Recital 21, the effectiveness and consistency of the application of Articles 101 and 102 TFEU require a common approach across the Union on the disclosure of evidence that is included in the file of a competition authority and that such disclosure should not unduly detract from the effectiveness of the enforcement of

[20] See wording in Art 6(1).

competition law by a competition authority. This suggests that the national courts shall ensure that the disclosure is not unduly burdensome. A competition authority with limited resources should not be forced to spend a considerable part of those resources on matters of disclosure. It is true that the process of granting requests for access is burdensome, and that national competition authorities in Member States with extensive transparency rules, spend considerable resources on these matters. The Commission's recent proposal for a Directive empowering national competition authorities reveals that some Member States struggle with limited resources, and the concerns expressed in the Directive may therefore be legitimate (the Proposed ECN+ Directive).[21] However, the question is whether the right way forward is to limit disclosure rather than increasing the resources allocated to competition law enforcement.

Article 6 of the Directive imposes a number of additional obligations on national courts. Article 6(5) prevents them from ordering disclosure of the following documents until after the competition authority has closed its proceedings by adopting an infringement decision or otherwise:

- information that was prepared by a natural or legal person specifically for the proceedings of a competition authority;
- information that the competition authority has drawn up and sent to the parties in the course of its proceedings, and
- settlement submissions that have been withdrawn.

Thus, this prohibition only applies to a limited number of documents and during a limited period of time; that is until the competition authority has adopted an infringement decision. Article 6(6), on the other hand, imposes an absolute ban which is not limited in time. According to the Article, national courts may under no circumstances order disclosure of leniency statements or settlement submissions.

This brief presentation of the Directive's provisions on disclosure allows us to the draw the conclusion that although the Directive will definitely force national courts to carefully consider applications for disclosure, the wording of the provisions grants leeway to those courts that wish to adopt a restrictive approach. Anyone hoping for a radical change will thus have to rely on the ECJ to interpret the provisions in a more extensive manner. However, given the Court's case-law on access to evidence or information from the Commission, there is a risk (or chance for that matter) that the interests of ensuring effective public enforcement of the competition rules will be allowed to prevail. In the following section, two rulings from the ECJ, one concerning a request

[21] Commission proposal for a Directive with the aim to empower the competition authorities of the Member States to be more effective enforcers and to ensure the proper functioning of the internal market, COM (2017) 142 final, 2017/0063 (COD).

for information under Regulation 1049/2001 (the Transparency Regulation)[22] and the other concerning the publication of detailed versions of the Commission decisions, will be given. These practices may not only affect cartel victims' possibilities to access evidence, but may also have an impact on the willingness of national courts to order disclosure under the Directive.

## IV. ACCESSING THE COMMISSION'S CASE FILE

Anyone considering filing a damages claim will first need to assess the likelihood of success. In those situations where the Commission has investigated the competition law infringement, the cartel victim might therefore want to access the Commission's file in order to determine whether or not to go ahead with a lawsuit. Article 15(3) TFEU, Article 42 of the EU Charter on Fundamental Rights (the Charter) and the Transparency Regulation all aim at ensuring public access to the documents held by the EU institutions. Yet, the Commission has managed, effectively, to close the door on any attempts to access its cartel files. In a number of decisions, endorsed by the ECJ, it has relied on the exemptions to the right of public access established in the Transparency Regulation, and refused access to its files. This section will give first a brief overview on the rules of public access to documents held by the EU institutions before presenting the *EnBW* case, concerning the granting of access to the Commission's cartel case file.

### A. Public Access to Documents in the EU

After years of debate on the lack of transparency in the EU, the notion of openness has become not only one of the new guiding principles of the functioning of the EU machinery but also one of the foundations of democracy in the Union. The principle of transparency is set out in Article 15(3) TFEU and Article 42 of the Charter grants any EU citizen, and any natural or legal person residing or having its registered office in the EU, a right of access to European Parliament, Council and Commission documents. The modalities governing third parties' access to Commission files are laid down in the Transparency Regulation. Like Article 42 of the Charter, the Regulation provides citizens and legal persons of the Union the right of access to the documents of the EU institutions. This right does not only cover documents that have been drawn up by the institutions themselves, but also documents that fall into their possession. However, the right of access is not absolute. Article 4 of the Transparency Regulation provides for a number of exceptions.

[22] Regulation (EC) No 1049/2001 of the European Parliament and of the Council of 30 May 2001 regarding public access to European Parliament, Council and Commission documents.

The exceptions invoked by the Commission in this type of case are primarily those found in Article 4(2) and 4(3). According to Article 4(2), the institutions shall refuse access to a document where disclosure would undermine the protection of commercial interests of a natural or legal person, including intellectual property, court proceedings and legal advice, or the purpose of inspections, investigations and audits, unless there is an overriding public interest in disclosure. According to Article 4(3), access to a document, drawn up by an institution for internal use or received by an institution, which relates to a matter where the decision has not been taken by the institution, shall be refused if disclosure of the document would seriously undermine the institution's decision-making process, unless there is an overriding public interest in disclosure. The Commission has been prone to invoke these exceptions when receiving requests from third parties to access its files, be it requests to access an entire file or just the statement of contents.[23] One of the more recent rulings is the one in *EnBW*.

### B. The Court's Ruling in *EnBW*

The *EnBW* case concerned the Commission's refusal to grant access to its cartel case file and the possibilities of relying on a general presumption of confidentiality when doing so. EnBW considered itself to have been affected by a cartel operated by producers of gas-insulated switchgear. Relying on the Transparency Regulation, EnBW sought access to all the documents in the Commission's case file. Following discussions with the Commission, EnBW later withdrew its application and made a fresh application where it excluded three categories of documents, namely all documents (i) dealing exclusively with the structure of the undertakings concerned, (ii) relating exclusively to the identity of the addressees of the cartel decision, and (iii) that were drawn up wholly in Japanese.[24] The Commission rejected the request through a formal decision. According to the Commission, the documents all fell under the scope of the exception provided for in the third indent of Article 4(2) of the Transparency Regulation. Some of the documents in the category of internal documents also fell under the exception laid down in Article 4(3).[25] The Commission did not consider there to be any overriding public interest in disclosure. According to the Commission, all the documents in the file were fully covered by the aforementioned exceptions, and partial access could thus not be granted. EnBW brought an action for the annulment of the Commission decision before the General Court. Finding, inter alia, that the Commission was not entitled to rely on a general presumption that all the documents in the file were covered by the third indent of Article 4(2) of

[23] See eg Case T-437/08 *CDC Hydrogen Peroxide v Commission* EU:T:2011:752.

[24] Case C-365/12 P *European Commission v EnBW Energie Baden Württemberg AG* EU:C:2014:112, para 14.

[25] See above for the text of the two provisions.

the Transparency Regulation, the General Court annulled the contested decision in its entirety.[26] The Commission appealed.

In its ruling, the ECJ started by stressing the fact that Article 255(1) and (2) EC (now Article 15 TFEU) provided that any citizen of the Union, and any natural or legal person residing or having its registered office in a Member State, were to have a right of access to the documents of the EU institutions.[27] The Court further recalled that the Transparency Regulation is designed to confer on the public as wide a right of access as possible to the documents of the institutions. Having established the main rule, the Court moved on to the exceptions. Here, the Court declared that where the exceptions in Article 4 of the Transparency Regulation applied, the institutions must refuse access unless there is an overriding public interest in disclosure. The Court further declared that according to well-established case-law, the institution concerned must provide explanations as to how access to a certain document could specifically and actually undermine the interest protected by an exception in Article 4. Having said that, the Court continued and declared that it is open to the institution concerned to base such decisions on general presumptions that apply to certain categories of documents, as considerations of a generally similar kind are likely to apply to requests for disclosure relating to documents of the same nature.[28] The Court declared that it had already acknowledged the existence of such presumptions in four particular cases, and that all four cases were characterised by the fact that the request for access covered not just one document but a set of documents.

In that type of situation, the Court continued, the recognition that there is a general presumption that documents of a certain nature are covered by the exceptions in Article 4 of the Transparency Regulation enables the institution concerned to deal with a global application and to reply thereto accordingly. The present case entailed that type of situation, the Court noted.[29] As the Commission was likely to gather commercially sensitive information during the course of a competition law investigation and as the protection of commercial interests was closely linked to protecting the purpose of the investigation in these cases, the Court declared that a general presumption should apply.[30] Furthermore, the Court noted, the case was still pending before the General Court. According to the Court, a proceeding under Article 101 TFEU cannot be regarded as closed once the Commission's final decision has been adopted.[31]

In its appeal, the Commission had argued for a harmonious interpretation of the Transparency Regulation and the Antitrust Regulations. The ECJ agreed,

[26] Case C-365/12 P *EnBW* (n 24) para 28.
[27] ibid, para 61.
[28] ibid, para 65.
[29] ibid, para 69.
[30] ibid, para 81.
[31] ibid, para 99.

declaring that the Antitrust Regulations and the Transparency Regulation are on the same footing in the EU legal order, and that, accordingly, they should be applied consistently. If the purpose of the Transparency Regulation is to confer a right of access to the EU institutions' documents, the extent of such access should depend on the activities of the institution. According to the ECJ, the Commission's activity in antitrust proceedings does not require the same level of disclosure as compared to the legislative activities of the EU. Moreover, the exceptions set forth in Article 4 of the Transparency Regulation cannot be interpreted without taking account of the Antitrust Regulations' specific rules on access to the file. Here, the ECJ noted that, according to the Antitrust Regulations, in principle only the parties to cartel proceedings have a right to access the Commission's files. The ECJ thus found that if third parties, such as EnBW, were able to access the Commission's files through the Transparency Regulation, the specific system put in place by the Antitrust Regulations would be jeopardised. The Commission's investigative powers, which mostly rely on the information given by companies, would be undermined by the lack of guarantee that the documents submitted (voluntarily or not) by investigated companies would be treated with the highest degree of confidentiality.

Consequently, the ECJ concluded that the Commission was entitled to rely on a general presumption, stemming from the Antitrust Regulations, that the documents in a cartel file fell within one or more of the exceptions in Article 4 of the Transparency Regulation. The Commission could thus apply a blanket approach to a third party's broad and unspecified request, thereby sparing itself a fastidious document-by-document review of its voluminous cartel files.

The Court did take notice of the fact that EnBW sought access to the documents in question with the intention of later filing a damages claim. While acknowledging that any person is entitled to claim compensation for the loss caused by breach of the competition rules, and that such rights strengthen the enforcement of Article 101 TFEU, it did not consider such general considerations to be capable of prevailing over the reasons justifying the refusal to disclose the documents in question.[32] Furthermore, the Court noted that in order to ensure effective protection of the right to compensation, there is no need for every document relating to cartel proceedings to be disclosed to a claimant.[33]

This may be true, but how is the claimant to know which documents are actually necessary to prove the case? The *EnBW* case raises a number of questions of relevance to the present chapter. The Court discusses the relationship between the Transparency Regulation and the Antitrust Regulations at length. Although neither of these Regulations will come into play when a national court considers the possibilities of ordering disclosure of documents held in the file of national competition authority, it is fair to assume that at least some courts

[32] ibid, para 105.
[33] ibid, para 106.

will glance at the Court's jurisprudence and draw inspiration from these cases. This might discourage courts from ordering disclosure, especially in those situations where the request concerns a 'set of documents'. It is clear from the wording of the Directive, that national courts should be able to order disclosure of categories of documents, but at the same time avoid letting companies venture out on 'fishing expeditions'. The Court's ruling in *EnBW* will not provide any guidance to the national courts in this respect.

An additional reflection concerns the protection afforded where a case is still pending before a national court. In *EnBW*, the ECJ acknowledged that there is a general presumption that each and every one of the documents belonging to the Commission's case file are covered by the exceptions in Article 4(2) and/or 4(3) of the Transparency Regulation, and that access must therefore be denied until such time as the case is finally closed. The Directive, on the other hand, only protects a limited number of documents during the course of an investigation. The prohibition in Article 6(5) of the Directive only extends to certain categories of documents and during a limited period of time; that is until the competition authority has adopted an infringement decision or otherwise closed its proceedings. The ECJ, on the other hand, allows the Commission to rely on the presumption for all the documents in the file and until such time as the case has finally been adjudicated by the courts. This being said, the *EnBW* ruling should not be used to propose a more extensive ban on disclosure, as that would fit badly with the principle of proportionality and the Court's acknowledgement that the presumption of confidentiality is rebuttable. However, it may encourage some national courts to refuse disclosure also for documents other than those listed in the provision.

In the following section, another line of the Court's case-law relevant to disclosure and access to evidence will be discussed. Following requests from cartel victims,[34] the Commission has recently shown its willingness to publish more lengthy and detailed infringement decisions allowing possible cartel victims to access relevant information and circumscribe any requests for information properly.

## V. ACCESSING INFORMATION THROUGH THE COMMISSION'S INFRINGEMENT DECISIONS – THE *EVONIK DEGUSSA* CASE

Article 339 TFEU and Article 28 of Regulation 1/2003 prevent the Commission from disclosing any information covered by the obligation of professional secrecy. At the same time, Article 30 of Regulation 1/2003 requires the Commission to

[34] According to CDC Damages Claims, it was following its request to the Commission to disclose confidential parts of its Hydrogen Peroxide cartel decision that the Commission finally agreed to re-publish a more detailed, non-confidential version of that decision. See www.carteldamageclaims.com/competition-law-damage-claims/accessing-information-cases.

publish infringement decisions, and Article 15 TFEU obliges the Commission to ensure the transparency of its proceedings. The Commission has to reconcile these potentially conflicting obligations when it comes to the publication of non-confidential versions of its decisions.

Article 30 of Regulation 1/2003 thus requires the Commission to publish its cartel decisions.[35] The publication shall state the name of the parties and the main content of the decision, including any penalties imposed. When doing so, the Commission should pay regard to the legitimate interests of undertakings in the protection of their business secrets. Traditionally, the public versions of the Commission's decisions have been rather succinct. In recent years, however, the Commission has endeavoured to publish longer and more detailed versions, which could potentially facilitate matters for cartel victims. Although longer versions of the decisions will not necessarily provide the sufficient amount of evidence, they may still help cartel victims to limit their requests in such a way that the Commission may actually grant access and/or the national courts may order disclosure. The attempts by the Commission to publish the full details of cartel decisions have met steep resistance from the addressees of the Commission's infringement decisions. The recent case of *Evonik Degussa* deals with this matter.[36]

In May 2006, the Commission adopted an infringement decision against 16 companies active in the hydrogen peroxide and perborate sector found to have participated in a cartel. Evonik Degussa had been the first company to report on the cartel, and had thus received immunity from fines. In the course of 2007, a first non-confidential version of the infringement decision (the PHP Decision) was published on the Commission's website. Four years later, the Commission informed Evonik Degussa of its intention to publish a new, more complete, non-confidential version of the PHP Decision, setting out the entire content of that decision save for any confidential information. The Commission asked Evonik Degussa to identify the information that it considered confidential, and which should thus be excluded from the public version.

Perhaps not too surprisingly, Evonik Degussa considered that the PHP Decision contained both confidential information and business secrets, and objected to the proposed publication. In support of the objection, it claimed that the extended version of the PHP Decision contained a significant amount of information provided in relation to the leniency application, including the names of a number of its collaborators as well as information concerning its business relations. Evonik Degussa argued that the proposed publication would infringe the principles of legitimate expectations and equal treatment and would be liable to have an adverse effect on the Commission's investigations.[37]

[35] ie decisions made pursuant to Art 23 of Regulation 1/2003.
[36] Case C-162/15 P *Evonik Degussa GmbH v European Commission* EU:C:2017:205.
[37] ibid, para 21.

The Commission agreed to delete all the information that would allow directly or indirectly the identification of the source of the information communicated pursuant to the 2002 Leniency Notice[38] and the names of Evonik Degussa's collaborators. As for the rest of the information covered by the objection (the contested information), the Commission did not consider that it should be granted the benefit of confidentiality. Evonik Degussa referred the matter to the Hearing Officer who in his turn rejected the request for confidentiality. This decision was challenged before the General Court, but was dismissed as unfounded.[39]

Evonik Degussa appealed, alleging inter alia an infringement of Article 339 TFEU, Article 30 of Regulation 1/2003, Article 4(2) of the Transparency Regulation as well as the right to privacy as provided by Article 8 of the European Convention on Human Rights (ECHR) and Article 7 of the Charter. Moreover, it alleged an infringement of the principles of the protection of legitimate expectations and legal certainty. According to Evonik Degussa, the General Court had erred in law when holding that the contested information was neither confidential nor protected for reasons other than its confidential nature. First of all, the company argued against the General Court's view that the contested information had lost its confidential nature merely due to the passage of time. The Court did not accept this argument, noting that information which was secret or confidential, but which was at least five years old, must as a rule be considered historical and therefore as having lost its secret or confidential nature unless, exceptionally, the party relying on that nature was able to show that the information still constituted essential elements of its commercial position or that of interested third parties.[40] In the present case, Evonik Degussa had not put forward any specific argument to show that, in spite of its age, the information still constituted essential elements of its commercial position or that of a third party.[41] The Court saw no reason to reach another conclusion than that of the General Court.[42]

As for Evonik Degussa's claim that the publication was contrary to the Transparency Regulation, the Court noted that the Regulation was not applicable in the present case, and that the case-law deriving from the Regulation could not be transposed to the context of the publication of infringement decisions. Evonik Degussa had also argued that the publication of the contested information included information from the 'statements made by a leniency applicant', and that such publication amounted to publishing verbatim quotations and

[38] Commission notice on immunity from fines and reduction of fines in cartel cases (2002/C 45/03). The notice was replaced by a new one in 2006 (2006/C 298/11).

[39] Case T-341/12 *Evonik Degussa GmbH v European Commission* EU:T:2015:51.

[40] Case C-162/15 P *Evonik Degussa* (n 36) para 64.

[41] All the contested information dated from more than five years previously, and some from more than ten years previously.

[42] Case C-162/15 P *Evonik Degussa* (n 36) para 67.

extracts from those statements, which, Evonik Degussa claimed, could not be permitted.[43] To this the Court responded that the publication, in the form of verbatim quotations, of information from the documents provided by an undertaking to the Commission in support of a statement made in order to obtain leniency differed from the publication of verbatim quotations from that statement itself. Whereas the first type of publication should be authorised, subject to compliance with the protection owed, in particular, to business secrets, professional secrecy and other confidential information, the second type of publication was not permitted in any circumstances.[44]

As regards the Commission's treatment of the information submitted by leniency applicants, the Court acknowledged that the Commission, in point 29 of the 2002 Leniency Notice, was aware that that notice would create legitimate expectations on which undertakings might rely when disclosing the existence of a cartel to it. In that regard, the Notice provides, first, in point 32, that normally, disclosure at any time of documents received in the context of that notice would undermine the protection of the purpose of inspections and investigations within the meaning of Article 4(2) of the Transparency Regulation. Secondly, in point 33, the Notice provides that any written statement made vis-à-vis the Commission in relation to that notice forms part of its file and may not be disclosed or used for any other purpose than the enforcement of Article 101 TFEU. The Commission had thereby imposed on itself rules as regards the written statements received by it in accordance with that notice. However, the Court noted, those rules had neither the object nor the effect of prohibiting the Commission from publishing the information relating to the elements constituting the infringement of Article 101 TFEU which was submitted to it in the context of the leniency programme and which did not enjoy protection against publication on another ground.

Consequently, the only protection available to an undertaking which has cooperated with the Commission is the protection concerning (i) the immunity from or reduction in the fine in return for providing the Commission with evidence of the suspected infringement which represents significant added value with respect to the information already in its possession; and (ii) the non-disclosure by the Commission of the documents and written statements received by it in accordance with the Leniency Notice. Based on these findings, the Court concluded that publication, such as that envisaged, under Article 30 of Regulation 1/2003 in compliance with the protection of professional secrecy did not undermine the protection afforded by the Leniency Notice, since that protection could relate only to the determination of the fine and the treatment of the documents and statements specifically targeted by that notice. The Court thus concluded that the General Court had not erred in law in the course of its

[43] ibid, para 80.
[44] ibid, para 87.

analysis of the treatment to be given to information communicated by Evonik Degussa. The company's arguments in this respect were thus rejected.[45]

Through the Court's ruling, it is now clear that information that is more than five years old is presumed to have lost its confidential nature. Furthermore, in line with the Directive, the Court has now established that although leniency statements deserve absolute protection from publication, nothing else relating to the leniency procedure does. This may provide some guidance to national courts and will hopefully lead to a more timely publication of detailed Commission decisions.

## VI. JOINING THE DOTS

Today, few question the benefits of effective competition policy. Instead, there is a widespread consensus in most democratic societies that measures should be taken to promote competitive markets, and that this in turn requires legislation that monitors, prevents and corrects anti-competitive behaviour.[46] Controlling competition between companies is an area where the EU is particularly powerful. However, the rulings in *Courage* and *Manfredi* revealed a weakness in the system. While the Court acknowledged that the full effectiveness of Article 101 TFEU required both public and private enforcement, the reality was another. In recent years, we have therefore witnessed an increased focus on private enforcement of the EU competition rules. As noted in the recitals to the Directive, it is indeed the view of the Union legislator that the full effectiveness of Articles 101 and 102 TFEU requires that anyone can claim compensation before a national court for the harm caused to them by an infringement of those provisions.[47]

As discussed above, the Directive introduces a number of provisions that aim at facilitating cartel victims' access to evidence. However, partly because the initial Directive proposal was amended during the course of the legislative process, the current rules cannot guarantee that cartel victims obtain the evidence they need. A narrow reading of the provisions suggests that pre-trial discovery is beyond the scope of the Directive. Furthermore, the requirement that the cartel victim should not only be able to present a reasoned justification for its claim, but also to specify the evidence requested are open to various interpretations by national courts. There is also a risk that national courts will be influenced by the jurisprudence of the ECJ and its willingness to allow the Commission to – when it receives a request for access which covers a 'set of

[45] ibid, para 99.

[46] Tellingly, by 2008, 111 countries had enacted competition laws, which is more than 50% of countries with a population exceeding 80,000 people: see OECD, *Fighting corruption and promoting competition* DAF/COMP/GF/WD(2014)53.

[47] Recital 3.

documents' rather than a specific document – rely on a general presumption that the documents held in its case file contain commercially sensitive material and should therefore not be disclosed. Add to that the requirement on the part of the national courts to carry out a proportionality analysis which should be based on, inter alia, the extent to which the claim or defence are supported by available facts and evidence, the costs of disclosure and the existence of confidential information among the requested documents. It is easy to see that the application of the rules laid down in the Directive may vary between the Member States unless and until the ECJ gives its view on their application.

In principle, there is no reason to object to the requirements stipulated in the Directive. The rules should be framed in such a way as to avoid 'ambulance chasers'; the courts should not be a place for fishing expeditions. This said, it is unfortunate that the wording of Article 5(2) as suggested in the Commission's initial proposal was not maintained, and that there is thus no obligation on the part of national courts to order disclosure in those situations where the party requesting disclosure can show that evidence in the hands of another party or a third party is relevant, and has specified either items of evidence or categories of evidence defined as precisely and as narrowly as possible.

Member States have a loyalty obligation under Article 4(3) TEU, and Article 4 of the Directive codifies the principles of effectiveness and equivalence, requiring Member States to ensure that national rules and procedures relating to the exercise of damages claims are designed and applied in such a way that they 'do not render practically impossible or excessively difficult the exercise of the Union right to full compensation for harm caused by an infringement of competition law'. This provision should in principle ensure that the Member States interpret, implement and apply the provisions of the Directive in such a way as to ensure that cartel victims may access the evidence necessary. However, the Proposed ECN+ Directive indicates that general obligations on the part of the Member States may not be sufficient to ensure effective competition law enforcement throughout the Union. That proposal reveals that despite the Member States' obligation to designate competition authorities in such a way that the provisions of Regulation 1/2003 are effectively complied with, many national competition authorities lack the means and instruments required to fulfil this obligation.[48] Given the non-binding character of the Directive's provisions, and the number of conditions that may need to be met in order for disclosure to be ordered, there is thus a clear risk that the regulatory framework surrounding access to evidence in cartel damages claims will fail to reach the stipulated goal.

[48] Proposed ECN+ Directive (n 21) p 2.

# Part III

# Solved and Unsolved Issues in Private Enforcement

# 10

# *Damages Actions in Article 102 TFEU Cases: The New Frontier for Private Enforcement*

ASSIMAKIS P KOMNINOS*

## I. INTRODUCTION

THE APPLICATION OF the EU competition rules in private litigation before civil courts, also known as 'private enforcement',[1] has developed exponentially over the last 15 years in Europe, especially following the modernisation reforms of 2004. The antitrust community tends to identify damages actions usually with cartels and follow-on claims, which are brought after the Commission and the national competition authorities (NCAs) have adopted an infringement decision.[2] On the other hand, not much attention is accorded to litigation involving non-cartel infringements of Article 101 TFEU and abuses of a dominant position under Article 102 TFEU. Notwithstanding this relative lack of attention, Article 102 TFEU has increasingly been the basis for private enforcement actions throughout Europe. Most of these actions are typically stand-alone, although the amount of follow-on Article 102 TFEU litigation is recently increasing. A number of these actions have resulted in damages awards or settlements, though many have failed, too. Irrespective of the final outcome, these cases are highly instructive and can offer many lessons and insights for public enforcement in the area of Article 102 TFEU.

* Dr Assimakis P Komninos, Partner, White & Case LLP, Visiting Research Fellow, University College London. The usual disclaimer applies. These are the author's purely personal views. The author wishes to thank Sebastian Multala and Rebecca Yourstone for helpful legal research in Swedish.

[1] See AP Komninos, *EC Private Antitrust Enforcement, Decentralised Application of EC Competition Law by National Courts* (Oxford/Portland, Hart Publishing, 2008).

[2] Although not falling under the definition of 'follow-on' claims (since there is no final infringement yet), many cartel-related civil claims for damages are now brought after a cartel investigation has been initiated and is still pending.

## II. DISTINCTIVE FEATURES OF ARTICLE 102 TFEU CIVIL LITIGATION

Claims for damages in abuse of dominance cases are different from cartel cases in four main respects:[3]

First, there is a marked difference in respect of the type of competition law infringement and the 'theory of harm' that lies in the heart of the damages litigation: ie whether the anticompetitive conduct in question is exclusionary or exploitative. The vast majority of Article 102 TFEU damages cases refer to exclusionary conduct. This is hardly a surprise, since exploitative cases, such as excessive pricing, are rare, especially before the competition authorities. Indeed, the very few cases of damages claims in exploitation cases are all stand-alone cases,[4] as opposed to inexistent follow-on cases.[5] On the other hand, most Article 101 TFEU damages litigation refers to exploitative conduct in the form of cartels. The exclusionary types of cases are not rare[6] but certainly fewer than cartel litigation.

Secondly, Article 102 TFEU cases differ from Article 101 TFEU cases in respect of the type of claimants. In the former cases, which almost exclusively rely on exclusionary conduct, the claimants are usually actual or potential competitors and rivals that suffered harm because of the dominant company's behaviour. It is extremely rare to see customers and, indeed, consumers as claimants, although the latter may suffer harm as a result of the elimination of competition and the possible price increase or the deterioration of quality and innovation that, according to the economic theory, follows from this. This fact may be due to a number of factors. Competitors are much closer to the exclusionary behaviour and can relatively easily articulate and prove harm due to their being foreclosed. In addition, competitors tend to be relatively large companies with more resources and access to information than customers and ultimately consumers. Then, their harm may be much more concrete and concentrated than the more distant and dispersed harm of customers and ultimately consumers. Indeed, establishing causation appears easier for competitors than for customers and consumers.

[3] See also similar points made by C Fumagalli, J Padilla and M Polo, 'Damages for Exclusionary Practices: A Primer' in F Etro and I Kokkoris (eds), *Competition Law and the Enforcement of Article 102* (Oxford, Oxford University Press, 2010).

[4] For a rare case in Germany, see OLG Frankfurt a.M., 21.12.2010, 11 U 37/09 (Kart) – *Arzneimittelpreise*, which relates to a 400% price increase in the pharmaceutical market. For a Greek case, see Eirinodikeio Thessaloniki n° 722/1983, 4 RHDE 187 (1984), where the court considered that a dominant undertaking (in that case, Olympic Airways, a legal monopolist) had abused its dominant position in imposing an unfairly high cancellation fee covering the whole price of an air ticket to an individual. The court ordered Olympic Airways to restitute to its client a certain percentage of the ticket price, to the extent of this constituting unjustified enrichment.

[5] The recent resurgence of excessive pricing cases pursued mainly by the national competition authorities and most recently the European Commission may change that.

[6] It is remarkable that the ground-breaking *Courage v Crehan* case of 2001 (Case C-453/99 *Courage Ltd v Bernard Crehan* EU:C:2001:465) was based not on an exploitative but rather an exclusionary theory of harm.

Thirdly, the type of compensable harm is different in Article 102 TFEU cases from cartel cases. In the latter situation, the damages claim will typically be for the cartel overcharge and in that sense, for the actual harm suffered as a result of the cartel (*damnum emergens*). While other types of harm in principle can also be compensated (*lucrum cessans* – loss of profit, loss of opportunity, etc), such cases tend to be rare. On the other hand, in Article 102 TFEU cases, loss of profit and opportunity tends to be the most typical type of compensable harm.[7]

Fourthly, Article 102 TFEU damages litigation tends to be mostly stand-alone litigation, as opposed to follow-on, which is invariably the case of cartel litigation. Although there are some cases of follow-on claims, which are recently more numerous,[8] the vast majority of cases arrive at the courts absent an infringement decision of the Commission or the NCAs. This is explained by the identity of the claimants, who, as reported above, tend to be competitors and not customers. Competitors are far more likely to have knowledge of a possible infringement of Article 102 TFEU than customers. Certainly, this is the case in the area of exclusionary conduct. At the same time, competitors tend to be relatively strong undertakings with access to resources that allow them to engage in protracted litigation, in which they also need to prove the existence of a competition law infringement.

## III. THE CONDITIONS FOR ESTABLISHING CIVIL LIABILITY

The constituent elements of liability in damages for infringement of Article 102 TFEU are not different from those relating to infringements of Article 101 TFEU. The rationale behind damages litigation remains to restore the victim of the anticompetitive conduct to the financial position that it would have been in 'but for' the breach of the antitrust rules. To this end, the claimant must:

i. prove that there has been an infringement of Article 102 TFEU;
ii. prove that he/she has suffered harm (not necessarily the same as the anti-competitive effects mentioned in an infringement decision);
iii. prove a causal link between the infringement of Article 102 TFEU and any harm suffered; and
iv. quantify the measure of damages due.

[7] However, on some occasions, a competitor may have also suffered actual monetary loss apart from loss of profit as a result of an exclusionary conduct, eg when a margin squeeze abuse manifests itself in the form of charging an excessive price for an upstream input, an actual and direct extra cost has been imposed on the competitor. See further P Buccirossi, 'Quantification of Damages in Exclusionary Practice Cases' (2010) 1 *Journal of European Competition Law & Practice* 252, 254. Of course, in that case, the claimant may also claim loss of profit, if it had no other option but to pass the overcharge on to its customers and, as a result, it lost market share.

[8] In France, there are a number of follow-on cases in the area of mobile telephony. See eg R Amaro, 'Le contentieux indemnitaire des pratiques anticoncurrentielles (janvier – décembre 2015)' (2016) 1 *Concurrences* 251, 256–57.

### A. Standing

It is to be noted that in EU competition law, standing is not a condition in itself, because the rather rich case-law of the Court of Justice makes it clear that 'any individual' can claim damages for harm suffered as a result of a competition law violation, if the above conditions are fulfilled. The definition of 'any individual' includes consumers and not just competitors.[9] Indeed, it would have been an anomaly to speak of 'consumer welfare' in the application of Article 102 TFEU while not giving standing to sue to consumers, who are the ultimate beneficiaries of the competition rules.[10]

Of course, that does not mean that national courts do not occasionally adopt a more restrictive approach to standing. For example, in Germany, courts are particularly resistant to accepting the EU principle of a broad standing. In one case, a court excluded the shareholders of competitors from the protective scope of Article 102 TFEU. The claimants alleged that they had suffered harm due to the lower share price and the dilution of shares following capital increases in the company that was allegedly a victim of exclusionary conduct. According to the German court, the protective scope of Article 102 TFEU is limited to market participants such as competitors, customers/clients and consumers – not shareholders.[11] Such an interpretation sits in stark contrast with the Court of Justice's pronouncements in *Courage/Crehan*, *Manfredi*, *Kone*[12] etc. Instead of imposing limitations on standing, which as a matter of EU law would be unlawful, the national courts can approach these questions through the causal link. Indeed, causation would have been a better ground to treat claims of remoteness of harm. National laws, depending on the legal tradition to which they belong, employ notions of foreseeability and remoteness and provide that the claimant bears the burden of proving that the defendant's unlawful conduct caused the harm and that it is the predominant cause of the claimant's loss. A shareholder's claim is likely to fail that condition.

### B. Proving the Article 102 TFEU Infringement

Proof of the competition law infringement is not much of an issue in follow-on cases. As a result of Article 16(1) of Regulation 1/2003, as recently interpreted

[9] See eg Joined Cases C-295/04 to C-298/04 *Vincenzo Manfredi et al v Lloyd Adriatico Assicurazioni SpA and others* EU:C:2006:461, paras 63–64.

[10] See further M Ioannidou, 'Enhancing the Consumers' Role in EU Private Competition Law Enforcement: A Normative and Practical Approach' (2011) 8(1) *Competition Law Review* 59, 66, touching upon the link between the substantive standard of consumer welfare and procedural measures allowing for increased consumer participation.

[11] OLG Düsseldorf, 02.07.2014, VI U (Kart) 22/13 – *Telegate/Telekom*.

[12] Case C-557/12 *Kone AG et al v ÖBB-Infrastruktur AG* EU:C:2014:1317.

by the Court of Justice and national courts,[13] a Commission decision relating to proceedings under Article 101 or 102 TFEU has a probative effect in subsequent actions for damages,[14] since national courts cannot take decisions running counter to such Commission decision. In *Otis*, the Court of Justice considered Article 16 of Regulation 1/2003 as an expression of the division of powers within the European Union between, on the one hand, national courts, and on the other, the Commission and the EU courts.[15] Thus, 'because of its obligation not to take decisions running counter to a Commission decision finding an infringement of Article 101 TFEU, the national court is required to accept that a prohibited agreement or practice exists'.[16] The same principle applies to Commission decisions finding an infringement of Article 102 TFEU.

The implementation of the EU Damages Directive[17] has now fundamentally changed the legal reality and effectively extended the same state of affairs to the effect of infringement decisions of NCAs (and final judgments of national courts reviewing those decisions). The Directive has made a distinction between the effect of NCAs' decisions on follow-on litigation in the same Member State and the effect of an NCA decision on follow-on litigation in a different Member State. Thus, in the first case, under Article 9(1) of the Directive, the finding of an infringement should be deemed to be irrefutably established. Recital 34 of the Directive explains that '[t]he effect of the finding [of infringement] should, however, cover only the nature of the infringement and its material, personal, temporal and territorial scope as determined by the competition authority or review court in the exercise of its jurisdiction'. In the second case, under Article 9(2) of the Directive, the finding of an infringement in Member State A may now be presented before the national courts of Member State B, in accordance with the national law of the latter Member State, as at least prima facie evidence that an infringement of competition law has occurred. That finding can be assessed, as appropriate, along with any other evidence adduced by the parties.

Of course, there are some limits as to what has been 'irrefutably established' and which parts of an infringement decision are binding on civil courts. It happens that sometimes competition authorities venture into some statements

[13] See eg LG Köln, 17.01.2013, 88 O 1/11, *NetCologne/Deutsche Telekom*, where the German court interpreted Art 16 of Council Regulation (EC) No 1/2003 of 16 December 2002 on the implementation of the rules on competition laid down in Articles 81 and 82 of the Treaty [2003] OJ L1/1 as requiring a national court to follow all the Commission's findings relating to fault and not just to the finding of an infringement.

[14] Case C-199/11 *Europese Gemeenschap v Otis et al* EU:C:2012:684, para 51.

[15] ibid, para 54.

[16] ibid, para 65.

[17] Directive 2014/104/EU of the European Parliament and of the Council of 26 November 2014 on certain rules governing actions for damages under national law for infringements of the competition law provisions of the Member States and of the European Union [2014] OJ L349/1.

as to the harm produced by certain anticompetitive conduct, although the quantification of such harm may not be required in the specific case. In *Enron*, the UK Office of Rail Regulation had found that EWS was in breach of Article 102 TFEU for abusing its dominant position, by charging Enron discriminatory prices for access to its rail freight services without having any objective justification. In a follow-on action, the Competition Appeal Tribunal (CAT) held that there was no liability in damages for lack of causation.[18] On appeal, the English Court of Appeal ruled that tribunals overseeing damages claims are bound by the facts contained in an antitrust decision, but stressed that these have to be clear statements and not 'stray phrases'.[19] In that case, the courts accepted that they were bound by the regulator's findings with regard to antitrust liability but that the question of civil liability was open. In the end, the court held that causality benchmarks were not met. The claimant did not have the necessary prerequisites in order to enter the market (ie supply arrangements) and had no previous experience in the industry. Based on the above, the claimant failed to prove that 'but for' the infringement, a different outcome would have resulted, in which the claimant would not have suffered loss (or would have suffered a lesser loss).

Obviously, proving the infringement is more important in stand-alone cases, which, as mentioned above, constitute the vast majority of Article 102 TFEU damages litigation. In those cases, the burden of proof will generally lie with the claimant. As far as Article 102 TFEU is concerned, although Article 2 of Regulation 1/2003 makes no distinction whatsoever and places the overall legal burden of proof on the Commission or the claimant, the case-law suggests that the dominant company must prove, on its part, the possible existence of an objective justification, including efficiencies counteracting any actual or likely negative effects on competition.[20] This effectively means that the legal burden of proving the defence is on the dominant undertaking.

In stand-alone cases, on occasions, courts have sought support from their respective NCAs. For example, in France, in 2005, the Tribunal de grande instance of Paris seized the French competition authority with a request to define the relevant market and opine whether there was a dominant position. The court relied on Article L462-3 of the Code de commerce, which provides for this procedure of cooperation with the competition authority. The case shows some of the challenges and opportunities facing a court deciding

[18] *Enron Coal Services Ltd v English Welsh & Scottish Railway Ltd* [2009] CAT 36.

[19] *Enron Coal Services Ltd v English Welsh & Scottish Railway Ltd* [2011] EWCA Civ 2.

[20] Case T-201/04 *Microsoft Corp v Commission* EU:T:2007:289, paras 688 and 1114; Case C-209/10 *Post Danmark A/S v Konkurrencerådet (Post Danmark I)* EU:C:2012:172, para 42. See also 'Communication from the Commission – Guidance on the Commission's enforcement priorities in applying Article 82 of the EC Treaty to abusive exclusionary conduct by dominant undertakings' [2009] OJ C45/ 7, para 30. *cf* E Rousseva, 'Efficiency Defences under Article 102 TFEU: Retrospective and Prospective', *Tendances*, (2014) 2 *Concurrences* n° 14–21.

*inter partes*, when it seeks to bring in as *amicus curiae* or as expert the competition authority. One of the litigants requested the competition authority not to limit its response to the definition of the relevant market and to the finding of dominance, but also to opine on the question of abuse. However, the competition authority declined to be drawn into the full array of the dispute and decided to respond strictly to the questions submitted by the court. In that sense, the competition authority saw itself as a body similar to the Court of Justice or the French administrative courts when they decide on preliminary references made by other courts.[21] This did not mean that the authority rendered a totally abstract opinion. On the contrary, it heard both parties on the question of market definition and addressed their arguments one by one.[22] This sits in stark contrast with the approach of the European Commission, which in similar situations does not hear the parties and simply sends its rather abstract views to the national courts that have requested its assistance.[23]

## C. Harm and Quantification

The claimant must then prove that he/she has suffered harm and that the latter is causally linked with the infringement. These are separate conditions but in real life are examined together. As discussed above, harm in exclusionary abusive practices takes usually the form of loss of profit for competitors.[24] This can be caused by reduced revenues, because the excluded competitors may sell less quantity. At the same time, on certain occasions, actual harm may have also been suffered, for example when the dominant company has imposed an excessive price for a necessary input.

This is the main battleground in Article 102 TFEU litigation. Civil courts generally apply lower evidentiary standards for causation and proof of harm in cartel cases than in exclusionary abuse cases, which are far more demanding for claimants. Indeed, one can even speak of a certain 'asymmetry' between the two types of cases.[25]

[21] See A Krenzer, 'Private Schadensersatzklagen wegen Kartellverstoßes – Die französische Perspektive' in W Möschel & F Bien (eds), *Kartellrechtsdurchsetzung durch private Schadenersatzklagen?* (Baden-Baden, Nomos, 2010) 31.

[22] Conseil de la concurrence, Avis n° 05-A-20 du 09.11.2005.

[23] Commission Notice on the co-operation between the Commission and the courts of the EU Member States in the application of Articles 81 and 82 EC [2004] OJ C101/54, paras 19 and 29. On this question, see generally Komninos, *EC Private Antitrust Enforcement, Decentralised Application of EC Competition Law by National Courts* (n 1) 106–07.

[24] See also Case C-27/17 *AB flyLAL-Lithuanian Airlines, in liquidation v Starptautiskā lidosta Rīga VAS et al*, Opinion of Advocate General Bobek EU:C:2018:136, para 68.

[25] See L Prosperetti, in 'Antitrust Marathon V: When in Rome – Public and Private Enforcement of Competition Law' (2013) 9 *ECJ* 503, 534.

Even in cases of follow-on litigation, the national case-law shows that defendants have much better chances before the civil courts that adjudicate on damages claims than they have before competition authorities. This can be explained because of the different tasks and methodologies of competition agencies and civil courts. Competition authorities in Europe, when enforcing the law, do not usually resonate in terms of 'quantifiable harm', in the same way as courts do in private actions. Instead, authorities resonate in terms of 'anticompetitive object' and 'anticompetitive effect'.

The underlying rationale behind 'anticompetitive object' is that economic evidence generally shows that certain conduct is detrimental to competition because it causes or is likely to cause anticompetitive harm. For this type of cases, there is no need to analyse the existence of effects or certainly of harm suffered by specific market players. At the same time, even when competition authorities find that certain conduct is anticompetitive by actual or potential effect, this does not necessarily imply the existence of quantifiable and compensable harm, in the sense of tort law. Besides, the more general concept of 'anticompetitive harm', to which competition authorities are better attuned, is seen in an all-encompassing and abstract manner, unlike the concept of 'harm' employed in the context of civil litigation, which is direct, concrete and personalised. In other words, the former is more representative of harm done to the economy or the market[26] than of specific harm to certain persons, such as competitors, customers, consumers, etc.

Another issue is that not necessarily all abuses of dominance foreclose and ultimately cause harm to competitors. It is possible that an abusive practice may have caused harm to competitors that are as efficient as the dominant company, but not to less efficient competitors. For example, such less efficient competitors may have never been able to compete on the same scale as the dominant company, because of costs, quality and brand strength.[27] An additional challenge for the courts is that the abuse of dominance may have resulted in excluding potential competitors, who may have been deterred from entering the market. It will be very difficult to prove harm in such situations, since the new entrant may have never had activities on the specific market concerned and there is an inherent lack of observable data on its performance on that market.[28]

[26] In such cases, the Court speaks of 'impact on the market'. Of course, even this type of harm/impact, which is useful in terms of allowing an authority to increase the fine imposed on the infringer, must be grounded on specific, credible and adequate evidence. See Case C-534/07 P *William Prym GmbH & Co KG and Prym Consumer GmbH & Co KG v Commission* EU:C:2009:505, paras 79–82.

[27] See L Prosperetti, 'Estimating Damages to Competitors from Exclusionary Practices in Europe: A Review of the Main Issues in the Light of National Courts' Experience', Paper presented at the DG Comp Workshop on the quantification of antitrust harm in actions for damages, Brussels, 26 January 2010, 4.

[28] See Commission, 'Staff Working Document, Practical Guide on Quantifying Harm in Actions for Damages based on Breaches of Article 101 or 102 of the Treaty of the Functioning of the European Union' SWD(2013) 205, para 201.

Nor is it easy to identify a market share that the new entrant would have achieved after entering the market.

A more specific challenge is quantification. Claimants may fail to persuade the courts because their quantification methods may be flawed and unreliable. For example, they may take into account the wrong economic model or ignore important variables (such as the existence of an economic crisis) or project findings on the basis of wrong comparators. They may also be purely theoretical and not correspond to the economic realities of the market, the industry, and the timing under review. There have also been cases where the courts found errors in the claimants' econometric analysis and economic reports. These problems may lead to a complete or partial failure to prove the damages' quantum.

In the Spanish *Antena 3* case, the claimant alleged that the Spanish Football Association had its dominant position in managing football broadcasting rights by signing long-term contracts with other TV channels and excluding it. The Madrid Court of First Instance partially accepted Antena 3's claims for lost advertising profits and awarded EUR 25 million in damages,[29] on the basis of an expert's report submitted by Antena 3. The judgment, however, was subsequently overturned by the Madrid Court of Appeal,[30] because the Antena 3 experts' quantification of the damage was flawed. The court considered that Antena 3's loss of profit must be proved with rigour and that it was unacceptable to award damages where proof of such loss is based on a theoretical expert report that runs counter to reality.

In another case, the Madrid Commercial Court[31] rejected the claimant's flawed econometric analysis and awarded only a fraction of the damages claimed. The case had to do with the supply of data for telephone directory services. The dominant company was found to have made the entry onto the market of its competitors more difficult by providing them with inaccurate subscriber data. The claimant sought damages of EUR 6 million as compensation for additional expenditure incurred and for lost profits due to inaccurate and incomplete data. The court, however, dismissed the claimant's econometric analysis and awarded only EUR 670,000. It found that the econometric analysis had not properly taken account of a number of other factors explaining the claimant's poor performance in Spain.

On the other side of the coin, a German court awarded damages for lost profits without encountering serious problems when adjudicating on a claim brought by a competitor to a dominant company in the market for gas supply.[32]

[29] Juzgado de Primera Instancia nº 4 de Madrid, 07.06.2005, nº 125/2005, *Antena 3 TV v LNFP*.

[30] Audiencia Provincial Madrid, nº 25bis, 18.12.2006; upheld by Tribunal Supremo, Section nº 1, 14.4.2009.

[31] Juzgado de lo Mercantil nº 5 de Madrid, 11.11.2005, nº 36/2005, *Conduit Europe SA v Telefónica de España SAU*. The case is analysed and the civil court's approach criticised by M Martínez-Granado and G Siotis, 'Sabotaging Entry: An Estimation of Damages in the Directory Enquiry Service Market' (2010) 6(1) *Review of Law & Economics* 1.

[32] OLG Düsseldorf, 16.04.2008, VI-2 U (Kart) 8/06, *Stadtwerke Düsseldorf*.

The claimant was bidding for the supply of gas to a particular client but was foreclosed because of the dominant company's tying practices, which linked the district heating prices with the gas and electricity prices. The claimant had lost the bid because the dominant company threatened the client with an increase in its district heating price if it were to source gas and/or electricity from other suppliers. The claimant succeeded in proving that, based on its own supply costs, it would have been able to supply the contracted amount of gas and under normal circumstances a 5 per cent profit margin would have been expected.

To make it easier for national courts to quantify harm, the Commission has provided non-binding guidance on this issue in its Communication on quantifying harm in actions for damages based on breaches of competition law.[33] The Communication is accompanied by a Commission Staff Working Paper taking the form of a Practical Guide on quantifying harm in actions for damages based on breaches of EU competition law.[34]

The Practical Guide explains the strengths and weaknesses of various methods and techniques available to quantify antitrust harm. It also presents and discusses a range of practical examples, which illustrate the typical effects that infringements of the EU competition rules tend to have and how the available methods and techniques can be applied in practice. To a large extent, it is based on a 2009 Study commissioned by the Commission and includes quantification methods which can be divided into three main categories: comparator-based approaches, cost-based and finance-based analysis and simulation models.[35]

### D. Causal Link

Proving the causal link between the exclusionary conduct and the harm suffered, for example, by the competitors of the dominant company can be quite challenging. The exclusionary practice at issue may not be the sole factor responsible for the claimants' poor performance. The claimants may not have entered the market and/or expanded due to their inefficiency, lack of interest, potential self-limitations, or even because of neutral elements that are characteristic of the specific market structure. Another question is that the claimants may themselves be liable for any failure to enter the market or compete against the dominant company. Tort laws in Europe may not impose, to the same extent as in the US, a duty on victims of unlawful behaviour to mitigate their loss, but contributory fault remains a valid defence available to the dominant company.

[33] Commission, 'Communication from the Commission on quantifying harm in actions for damages based on breaches of Article 101 or 102 of the Treaty on the Functioning of the European Union' [2013] OJ C167/19.

[34] Commission, Practical Guide (n 28).

[35] See Oxera, A Komninos et al, *Quantifying Antitrust Damages: Towards Non-binding Guidance for Courts*, Study Prepared for the European Commission, December 2009.

In *Arkin*, a case concerning liner conferences and the alleged violation of Articles 101 and 102 TFEU, the English High Court found that the right test for causation was whether the breach of duty was the dominant or effective cause of the loss. On the basis of that test, the Court was required to consider whether the claimant was the author of its own misfortune by seeking to stay in a loss-making market.[36] In the end, the court decided that the claimant's own irrational pricing policy was the predominant cause of his business failure. Thus, the conduct of a claimant who continues trading, although he knows that his business is evaporating, may take the form of contributory fault, break the chain of causation and thus exclude the defendant's liability.

In *Verimedia*, a French case, a competitor sought damages following an exclusionary agreement.[37] The claim followed on from a 1998 decision of the then French Competition Council, which found that the defendants had voluntarily delayed the communication of information to the claimant necessary for it to conduct its activities in the market for media services. In its claim, Verimedia sought to recover damages as a result of loss of clientele. The Versailles Court of Appeal considered that, while the claimant was entitled to recover damages as a result of its loss of clientele, the quantum of those damages should be reduced due to the claimant's lack of knowledge of the market in which it was starting up, and the lack of precision of certain of its orders. The court therefore compensated the claimant only for the lost opportunity to penetrate the market quicker.

Then, the claimant may fail to prove that 'but for' the infringement, a different outcome would have resulted that would have been more positive for the dominant company's competitors. Here, the claimant will need to compare its profitability in the factual world, the world of the competition law infringement, with its hypothetical profits in the counterfactual world, the world where no infringement has taken place. Indeed, the claimant's counterfactual scenario may not be based on adequate and definite data. For example, even in a refusal to supply case, it may still be unclear what a competitor's sales and margins would have been absent the exclusionary behaviour.

A Swedish case exemplifies these difficulties.[38] In proceedings brought before the Stockholm District Court by competitors of VPC, the central securities depository in Sweden, the claimants argued that VPC's refusal to supply them with full CD-ROM copies of share registers constituted an abuse of a dominant position and that VPC should be ordered to pay damages. The court agreed that VPC had abused its dominant position, but awarded damages for half of the amount claimed, since full proof had not been presented by the claimants

[36] *Arkin v Borchard Lines Ltd et al (IV)* (QB (ComCt)) [2003] EWHC 687.

[37] CA Versailles, 12ème Ch. Sect. 2, 24.6.2004, n° 2/7434, *SA Verimedia v SA Mediametrie, SA Secodip and GIE Audipub.*

[38] Stockholm District Court, 20.11.2008, Cases n° T 32799-05 and T 34227-05.

with respect to the quantum of their damages. For example, in relation to rental and employee costs, the court considered that it could not be excluded that office space and staff could have been used by other parts of the claimants' business that were not affected by the abuse. Similarly, because the economy as a whole was in recession during the period when the abuse took place, the claimants were unable to precisely identify which part of the losses were the result of the defendant's abusive conduct, and which part was caused by the general economic downturn.

## IV. A SWEDISH CASE STUDY: *TELIA* FOLLOW-ON DAMAGES

### A. Introduction

#### *i. The Context of the Proceedings*

A Swedish follow-on case illustrates most of the above questions nicely. The case relates to a claim for damages brought by Spray Network Services AB (now Yarps Network Services AB – Yarps) against Telia Company AB (Telia) for an abuse of dominance on the wholesale market for ADSL broadband between 2000 and 2003. The abusive practices related to refusal to supply, discrimination and margin squeeze. Yarps' damages action against Telia (then TeliaSonera AB) was brought under the pre-2016 legislative regime. Up until the transposition of the EU Damages Directive in Sweden, through the entry into force of the Competition Damages Act (2016:964) in December 2016, the Swedish courts were previously bound neither by the Swedish competition authority's finding of an antitrust infringement, nor by the Swedish courts' decision to uphold such a finding.

#### *ii. Public Enforcement Proceedings*

In December 2004, the Swedish Competition Authority initiated proceedings against Telia before the District Court, to have it fined for an abuse of a dominant position.[39] It is in the context of that proceeding that the District Court requested the European Court of Justice for a preliminary ruling in the well-known *TeliaSonera* case. The preliminary ruling request concerned the criteria that need to be taken into consideration when determining whether pricing practices should be deemed to constitute an abusive margin squeeze. The Court of Justice delivered its ruling on 17 February 2011.[40]

[39] In Sweden, the competition authority does not have decisional powers to impose fines for violation of Swedish and EU competition law but must bring the matter to the District Court, which can impose such fines.

[40] Case C-52/09 *Konkurrensverket v TeliaSonera Sverige AB* EU:C:2011:83.

Following on from the Court of Justice's ruling the District Court found on 2 December 2011 that Telia had abused its dominant position through margin squeeze practices and for a duration of two years and eight months and consequently fined it SEK 144 million. The judgment was then appealed to the Swedish Market Court. The Market Court partially annulled the District Court's judgment and found that Telia had abused its dominant position through margin squeeze during limited time periods of between 8 to 19 months on a limited part of the market, and thus reduced Telia's fine to SEK 35 million.[41]

#### *iii. Private Enforcement Proceedings*

On 29 June 2006, Yarps initiated a damages action against Telia, for damages caused through Telia's abuse of dominance through margin squeeze, refusal to supply and discrimination from April 2000 until January 2003. Thus, the civil action partly concerned other forms of abuse and periods than the public enforcement proceedings.

The proceedings in the District Court were suspended on 6 September 2006, awaiting the *TeliaSonera* judgment from the Court of Justice, and resumed on 23 February 2011. In its judgment of 7 March 2016, the District Court found that Telia, by engaging in a margin squeeze from February 2002 to January 2003, had caused Spray and Tiscali damages of SEK 65 million. This judgment was appealed to the Court of Appeal by both Yarps and Telia. In the end, the Court of Appeal overturned the District Court's judgment.[42] The Court of Appeal's judgment is quite interesting in many respects.

### B. The Court of Appeal *Telia* Judgment

As explained above, since the private enforcement proceedings were subject to the procedural regime prior to the transposition in Sweden of the Damages Directive, the public enforcement proceedings (the Market Court's final decision, in particular) were not considered binding on Swedish civil courts, as far as the finding of an infringement was concerned. Therefore, the civil courts had to rule also on that point and this is what the Court of Appeal did. After defining national wholesale and retail markets for the provision of internet services, the court found Telia to have been dominant on the wholesale market, primarily on the basis of its 70 per cent plus market share. It relied on the *TeliaSonera* ruling of the Court of Justice and agreed that a company does not have to be dominant on both the wholesale and retail market in order to engage

[41] Judgment A 8/11 of 12.04.2013 (MD 2013:5).

[42] Svea Hovrätt, 29.06.2017, T 2673-16 *Yarps Network Services AB (i likvidation) v Telia Company AB.*

in margin squeeze. However, the court went on to assess dominance on the retail market as well and found Telia's share during the relevant period to have fluctuated between 41 and 54 per cent. It concluded that this was a strong indication of dominance and that Telia in any case had a 'very strong position' on the retail market.

Yarps alleged that Telia had abused its dominant position in three different respects and for three separate periods: discriminating against and refusing to supply Yarps between April 2001 and autumn 2001, discriminating against and refusing to supply Yarps, or alternatively engaging in margin squeeze against Yarps, from autumn 2001 to February 2002 and engaging in a margin squeeze against Yarps from February 2002 to January 2003. The Court of Appeal dismissed the claim in relation to the first two grounds/periods. It found that Telia was not in a position in the first of the above periods to supply the service and Yarps had failed to prove discrimination or refusal to supply in the second of the above periods, since a price between Telia and Yarps was not agreed until 18 February 2002.

The Court of Appeal, citing paragraph 46 of the *TeliaSonera* judgment, agreed with the District Court that the starting point for assessing Yarps' margin squeeze claim was, primarily, Telia's pricing, costs and margin. Thus, it refrained from analysing Yarps' actual costs, relying instead on the 'as efficient competitor' test to assess Telia's conduct. It then compared the wholesale price per month applied by Telia to Yarps per private consumer access and Telia's own retail prices. According to the court, in order for a competitor to make a profit on similar facts, it needed an additional margin (on top of the price it pays the wholesaler, ie Telia in this case) to cover additional costs of providing the service, such as providing customer support and marketing functions.

In the private enforcement proceedings, the District Court had conducted a long run average incremental cost (LRAIC) analysis of Telia's costs and arrived at a threshold number of a margin that Telia needed in order to cover its own additional costs.[43] Using this margin as a point of reference, the District Court found that for a company as efficient as Telia, the margin provided for under Telia's agreement with Yarps would have been negative for a number of months. The Court of Appeal, however, held that sufficient and reliable data were required in order for an LRAIC (or any other economic assessment) to form an acceptable basis for assessing a margin squeeze, and that the District Court's LRAIC analysis did not meet this requirement. Instead, the Court of Appeal agreed with the Market Court (in the public enforcement proceedings) and preferred Telia's to Yarps' analysis regarding the applicable reference margin.

[43] Interestingly, the threshold preferred by the Court of Appeal was 4 SEK higher than the one used by the Swedish Competition Authority.

That reference margin would be sufficient for an as efficient competitor to provide the additional services (although it left no room for profit). Thus, the margin was not negative.

The Court of Appeal then turned to assessing whether Telia's pricing practices were likely to hinder the ability of competitors at least as efficient as Telia to compete on the retail market for broadband connection services to end users. The Court of Justice in *TeliaSonera* had emphasised the need to assess each case of abuse on its facts, taking into consideration all the specific circumstances of the case.[44] In effect, the Court of Justice insisted on the necessity to follow an 'effects-based' approach.

Indeed, the Swedish court fully grasped the Court of Justice's invitation to analyse margin squeeze cases on the basis of an 'effects-based' approach and stated that

> it is apparent from the preliminary ruling that the circumstance alone, that the dominant company's pricing in purely mathematical terms leads to margin squeeze for competitors that are at least as efficient, is not in itself enough for the activity to be considered to amount to an abuse within the meaning of Article 102 TFEU.

The court made clear that, to establish that a margin squeeze is abusive, requires evidence of anticompetitive effects, although the effects do not have to be actual or even concrete (they may thus be potential). Anticompetitive effects may be proven in many ways, but the burden to do so is on the complainant. The Court of Appeal proceeded to test the evidence against Telia in a number of areas, concluding that Yarps had failed to show that Telia's pricing policy had anticompetitive effects on the market.

The Court of Appeal also dealt with the question whether Telia's services were indispensable to Yarps. The Court of Justice in *TeliaSonera* clarified that margin squeeze can be an abuse in its own right, independent of a refusal to supply and that indispensability as such is not a required condition.[45] The Court of Appeal accepted that and went on to assess whether Telia's service could be considered indispensable to Yarps despite the absence of a regulatory obligation to supply, as indispensability may give rise to a high probability of abuse.[46] The Court of Appeal found that the services concerned were not indispensable and, therefore, there was no high probability of abuse on this ground. Instead, a closer inspection of anticompetitive effects was required.

The Court of Appeal then considered that two parameters were critical, in order to determine whether there was an anticompetitive effect: first, the part of the market and importance of the customers that are affected and, second, the

[44] *TeliaSonera* (n 40) para 76.
[45] ibid, para 72.
[46] ibid, paras 70–71.

duration of the margin squeeze practices. The court's assessment was that Telia had imposed negative margins on Yarps for roughly 11 months and in relation to a fifth of customers. In comparison to other cases, such as *Wanadoo España* and *Slovak Telekom*,[47] the margin squeeze in this case was 'relatively short' and, while the share of the market affected by the margin squeeze was 'not insignificant', its scope did not provide a strong indication of anticompetitive effects. Furthermore, according to the court, the relevant activities took place in the early 2000s and, therefore, it should have been possible after all these years for Yarps to adduce more concrete evidence on the anticompetitive effect of the margin squeeze, which Yarps had failed to do.

Yarps argued that Telia's margin squeeze occurred at a crucial time in the migration from dial-up to broadband, and that absent the margin squeeze, Telia would not have captured as large a share of the market as it did. The Court of Appeal, however, pointed to contrary evidence that Telia's market share had in fact fallen from circa 70 per cent during the time the relevant practices were implemented to 65 per cent in 2004.

Finally, the Court of Appeal placed emphasis on the absence of any anticompetitive intent on the part of Telia. The court accepted that abuse is an objective concept and that intent should be irrelevant but also recalled that the Court of Justice in *TeliaSonera* had stressed the need to take into consideration all the specific circumstances of the case including the intent of the dominant company.[48] The Court of Appeal found that Telia had not intended to impose negative margins on Yarps. Telia was bound by a number of agreements that imposed on it terms that had been negotiated under very different (and overly optimistic) market conditions. It was proven that Telia was making a loss on these agreements and that the wholesale price charged to Yarps was likely a better reflection of the actual costs of providing the relevant services. Yarps, therefore, failed to show that Telia priced its services with the intent to exclude Yarps from the market.

As a result, on the basis of the above and after having taken into account 'all circumstances', the Court of Appeal held that Yarps had failed to satisfy the burden of proof incumbent upon it to show that Telia's conduct amounted to an abuse of dominance and, therefore, there were no anticompetitive effects and consequently no harm to be compensated.

## C. Analysis and Conclusions

The Swedish court's judgment is a good reminder of the difference of approach between competition authorities (public enforcement) and civil courts (private

[47] Commission Decisions of 04.07.2007 (Case COMP/38.784 – *Wanadoo España v Telefónica*) and of 15.10.2014 (AT.39523 – *Slovak Telekom*).

[48] *TeliaSonera* (n 40) para 88.

enforcement). The latter concentrate on anticompetitive harm in a much more concrete manner than the former. They must satisfy themselves that there is an infringement of Article 102 TFEU not in the context of a more abstract approach that is centred on the protection of competition on the market and on ensuring a competitive market structure, but rather in the specific context of a claim for damages, where the existence of an abuse of dominance must be causally linked with anticompetitive harm suffered by specific persons. In that sense, the civil courts are more likely to be particularly conservative in finding that there has been an abuse of a dominant position.

In the above case, of course, the Swedish court did not consider itself bound by the competition authority's or, indeed, the Market Court's findings on the existence of an abuse of dominance. The case was subject to the procedural rules prior to the transposition of the new Damages Directive in Sweden. Article 9(1) of the Directive, as explained above, provides that the finding of an infringement at public enforcement proceedings should be deemed to be irrefutably established at follow-on private enforcement proceedings.

However, the new rule is not expected to change fundamentally the practical reality. The Swedish case illustrates how antitrust and civil liability are intertwined and demonstrates the difficulties that can arise in distinguishing between the two concepts. Although they are theoretically separate, it can be difficult to decouple them in practice, especially in a case involving a claim for damages for exclusionary practices brought by the supposed victim of the exclusionary conduct. As stressed above, establishing in abstract terms a potential or even actual anticompetitive effect will not be good enough for the civil courts. Instead, they must satisfy themselves that the claimant has proven that it concretely suffered harm causally linked with the exclusionary practices. In the above case, the Swedish court engaged in an unrelenting application of the effects-based approach, precisely because it thought that without doing so it could have not fulfilled its task to render a robust finding on the existence or not of civil liability in damages and, ultimately, to award damages to the aggrieved party.

In that sense, the Swedish court's careful analysis of the evidence also demonstrates the risks inherent in the formalistic approach preferred by competition authorities when applying Article 102 TFEU. Although, the court relied on robust evidence showing the absence of any significant effects, this was not how the competition authority had analysed the case. Follow-on private enforcement cases in Article 102 TFEU cases represent a sort of ex post assessment of public enforcement decisions and their outcomes should not go unnoticed but rather be carefully monitored by the competition authorities, with a view to adopting the right approach when they themselves enforce unilateral conduct rules.

# 11

# *Implementing the Rules of the Damages Directive on Joint and Several Liability: The SME Derogation*

ANNA PISZCZ*

## I. INTRODUCTION

THE DAMAGES DIRECTIVE[1] embraces situations where several undertakings infringe the competition rules jointly. Such joint infringements are not limited solely to cartels, expressly mentioned in the first sentence of Recital 37 of the Preamble to the Directive. Also other horizontal agreements, vertical agreements, concerted practices as well as abuses of a collective dominant position belong to a general category of joint infringements.[2] Under Article 11 of the Directive, undertakings which have infringed competition law through joint behaviour are jointly and severally liable for the harm caused by the infringement of competition law; with the effect that each of those undertakings is bound to compensate for the harm in full, and the injured party has the right to require full compensation from any of them until he has been fully compensated. Although the transposition period for the Directive expired on 27 December 2016,[3] it was not until 2018 that some Member States finally

* Professor at the University of Białystok (Poland), Faculty of Law, Acting Chairman of the Department of Public Economic Law; legal advisor; piszcz@uwb.edu.pl, ORCID 0000-0001-7163-3292.

[1] Directive 2014/104/EU of the European Parliament and of the Council of 26 November 2014 on certain rules governing actions for damages under national law for infringements of the competition law provisions of the Member States and of the European Union [2014] OJ L 349/1.

[2] See also I Lianos, 'Causal Uncertainty and Damages Claims for the Infringement of Competition Law in Europe' (2015) 1 *Yearbook of European Law* 46; but see F Wijckmans, M Visser, S Jaques, E Noël, *The EU Private Damages Directive – Practical Insights. Minutes of the Closed Workshop 2015* (Cambridge – Antwerp – Portland, Intersentia, 2015) 54.

[3] See Directive 2014/104 (n 1) Art 21(1).

passed implementing legislation.[4] However, as a rule, Member States do not need to introduce the principle of joint and several liability (solidary liability) of multiple tortfeasors, as embodied in Article 11(1) of the Directive,[5] since it is already stipulated in their laws with regard to competition law damages. Whilst the analysis of the principle is thus not the focus of the present study, the transposition of the details contained in Article 11(2)-(3) of the Directive regarding limitations on joint and several liability of small and medium-sized enterprises (SME derogation/exception) is subject to detailed consideration, especially as these provisions are considered by commentators as ambiguous and difficult to interpret.[6]

In this chapter I will consider the background to the SME derogation, the SME status, the applicable conditions for the 'failing SME' exception and the extent of SME liability. The chapter concludes with anticipated consequences (future challenges) and an assessment of the derogation. The point of the analysis is both normative and descriptive. The comparative method is employed to some extent, as the topic may benefit from being examined in the light of comparative evidence drawn from various Member States.[7]

## II. EXCEPTION FOR 'FAILING SMES': BACKGROUND

The derogation in Article 11(1) of the Directive, provided for under its Article 11(2),[8] allows a special liability scheme in which an infringer that is a

[4] Greece, Portugal. See http://ec.europa.eu/competition/antitrust/actionsdamages/directive_en.html.

[5] Art 11(1) reads as follows: 'Member States shall ensure that undertakings which have infringed competition law through joint behaviour are jointly and severally liable for the harm caused by the infringement of competition law; with the effect that each of those undertakings is bound to compensate for the harm in full, and the injured party has the right to require full compensation from any of them until he has been fully compensated'.

[6] See eg A Vlahek and K Podobnik, 'Provisions of the Damages Directive on Limitation Periods and their Implementation in CEE Countries' (2017) 10(15) *Yearbook of Antitrust and Regulatory Studies* 171; S Peyer, 'Compensation and the Damages Directive' (2015) 15-40 CCP Working Papers, http://competitionpolicy.ac.uk/documents/8158338/8368036/15-10+CCP+Working+Paper/78f92b0e-6f92-4538-bca7-4f45e8de7b2b.

[7] This evidence mainly comes from the research conducted by the Law Faculty of the University of Białystok (UwB) and the Centre for Antitrust and Regulatory Studies of the University of Warsaw (CARS) on the harmonisation of private antitrust enforcement from a Central and Eastern European (CEE) perspective. As a result thereof, two conferences in Supraśl (Poland) were organised by the author of this chapter, ie A Piszcz (UwB), in cooperation with T Skoczny (CARS) in 2015 and 2017. Based on the results of the research, in June 2017 CARS published 11 national reports on the implementation of the Directive in all CEE countries in the form of a book: A Piszcz (ed), *Implementation of the EU Damages Directive in Central and Eastern European Countries* (Warsaw, University of Warsaw Faculty of Management Press, 2017).

[8] Art 11(2) reads as follows: 'By way of derogation from paragraph 1, Member States shall ensure that, without prejudice to the right of full compensation as laid down in Art 3, where the infringer

small or medium-sized enterprise (SME) shall be liable only to its own direct and indirect purchasers under certain specified requirements described in greater detail below. The derogation seems to be an example of a combination of a kind of *de minimis* rule[9] and a *sui generis* failing firm defence. The exception for 'failing SMEs' is constructed as a mixture of civil (private) legal provisions and regulatory rules. Unquestionably, it is not the first time an EU Directive has required national legislatures to intervene in private law for certain EU policy reasons. The afore-mentioned derogation, however, was not included in the Commission's proposal for a Directive which – in terms of joint and several liability – focused on liability limitations for immunity recipients. The early, and unsurprising, emphasis on the immunity recipients began to pave the way for more *leges speciales* to the general rule when the Commission's proposal for a Directive was examined by the European Parliament.[10] The SME derogation was inserted into the draft Directive almost at the last minute.

The rationale behind the derogation was not stated in the Preamble to the Directive; it is believed that the discrepancies between the national provisions implementing the derogation are partly due to insufficient information from the Commission about the goals underlying the rules of the Directive.[11] However, it can be assumed that the SME derogation was to be a form of support for SMEs by EU institutions.[12] It might have been driven by economic concerns

is a small or medium-sized enterprise (SME) as defined in Commission Recommendation 2003/361/EC (8), the infringer is liable only to its own direct and indirect purchasers where:

(a) its market share in the relevant market was below 5 % at any time during the infringement of competition law; and
(b) the application of the normal rules of joint and several liability would irretrievably jeopardise its economic viability and cause its assets to lose all their value'.

[9] A Piszcz in S Oliveira Pais and A Piszcz, 'Package on Actions for Damages Based on Breaches of EU Competition Rules: Can One Size Fit All?' (2014) 7 *Yearbook of Antitrust and Regulatory Studies* 227.

[10] See Draft European Parliament Resolution on the proposal for a Directive of the European Parliament and of the Council on certain rules governing actions for damages under national law for infringements of the competition law provisions of the Member States and of the European Union (COM(2013)0404 – C7-0170/2013 – 2013/0185(COD)), www.europarl.europa.eu/sides/getDoc.do?pubRef=-//EP//TEXT+REPORT+A7-2014-0089+0+DOC+XML+V0//EN.

[11] Critically on the lack of the statement in the Preamble, see A Jurkowska-Gomułka, 'How to Throw the Baby out with the Bath Water. A Few Remarks on the Currently Accepted Scope of Civil Liability for Antitrust Damages' (2015) 8(12) *Yearbook of Antitrust and Regulatory Studies* 68. On a likely cause of the discrepancies, see P Miskolczi Bodnár and R Szuchy, 'Joint and Several Liability of Competition Law Infringers in the Legislation of Central and Eastern European Member States' (2017) 10(15) *Yearbook of Antitrust and Regulatory Studies* 107–08.

[12] Even though they do not enjoy any specific support with regard to the public enforcement of competition law. The Commission Notice on agreements of minor importance which do not appreciably restrict competition under Art 101(1) of the Treaty on the Functioning of the European Union (De Minimis Notice) [2014] OJ C291/1 only states in fn 5 that 'agreements between small and medium sized undertakings (SMEs), as defined in the Commission Recommendation of 6 May 2003 concerning the definition of micro, small and medium-sized enterprises or any future recommendation replacing it (…), are also not normally capable of affecting trade between Member States' and refers to point 50 of Commission Notice – Guidelines on the effect on trade concept contained in

(however important they might be), even though it is disputed whether it is possible to recognise SMEs' economic importance or whether it should be deemed to be overestimated.[13] This is a matter of interpretation and, perhaps, this discussion can be criticised as such: how to say anything about any relevant tendencies or regularities (or lack thereof) in this regard if geographical and market-specific factors make it impossible?

In the literature, it has been argued that the level of antitrust fines is in relative terms more severe for smaller undertakings than larger ones and, moreover, smaller undertakings are also less likely, in practice, to be granted either immunity or a reduction in the level of fines.[14] The rationale for the SME exception is to avoid SMEs having to compensate all the harm that was caused by the infringement (including harm caused by other infringers).[15] Given the alleged role of SMEs (especially in smaller economies), their vulnerability to changes in markets and external factors as well as weaker access to tools helping them comply with the law, including competition law, the support for SMEs may be considered praiseworthy and laudable.[16] However, in the case of the civil liability limitation for 'failing SMEs', genuine concerns may be raised about its anticipated consequences. The derogation results in limitations on joint and several liability of certain infringers, while at the same time making it possibly more difficult for injured parties to get compensation[17] and modifying the way in which damages are distributed to the detriment of some infringers.[18]

## III. SME STATUS

When SMEs are favoured to the detriment of other infringers, inequality arises. What is particularly interesting about the SME derogation is, however,

Articles 81 and 82 of the Treaty [2004] OJ C101/81, which states that the reason for this presumption is the fact that the activities of SMEs are normally local or at most regional in nature; however, 'SMEs may be subject to Community law jurisdiction in particular where they engage in cross-border economic activity'.

[13] See Piszcz in Oliveira Pais and Piszcz, 'Package on Actions for Damages Based on Breaches of EU Competition Rules' (n 9) 227; but see Jurkowska-Gomułka, 'How to Throw the Baby out with the Bath Water' (n 11) 67–68.

[14] IS Forrester, 'Searching Beneath the Cherry Tree in the Garden: European Thoughts on How to Enhance the Task of Uncovering and Thereby Deterring Cartels' in CD Ehlermann and I Atanasiu (eds), *European Competition Law Annual 2006: Enforcement of Prohibition of Cartels* (Oxford and Portland, Oregon, Hart Publishing, 2007) 178–79.

[15] Wijckmans, Visser, Jaques and Noël, *The EU Private Damages Directive* (n 2) 55. However, as Schwab rightly observed regarding immunity recipients, it is hard to diagnose undue exposure to damages claims of a particular group of infringers (he saw no evidence to suggest that the Directive leads to immunity recipients being the first, or only target to be sued); A Schwab, 'Finding the Right Balance – the Deliberations of the European Parliament on the Draft Legislation Regarding Damage Claims' (2014) 5(2) *Journal of European Competition Law & Practice* 66.

[16] See also A Piszcz, 'Practical Private Enforcement: Perspectives from Poland' in M Bergström, M Iacovides and M Strand (eds), *Harmonising EU Competition Litigation: The New Directive and Beyond* (Oxford and Portland, Oregon, Hart Publishing, 2016) 218.

[17] Piszcz (n 9) 227.

[18] Jurkowska-Gomułka (n 11) 67.

that its scope literally does not extend to microenterprises.[19] Using the seemingly simple notion of 'SME' as a lens through which to depict the scope of the derogation, Article 11(2) of the Directive excludes microenterprises from the exclusion. Smaller enterprises seem to be treated unequally; therefore, one may see inequality within inequality for which there is no reasonable explanation. The above-mentioned provision makes microenterprises face the threat of being put at a significant disadvantage compared to the remaining subcategories of smaller enterprises, ie SMEs. The principal issue that arises is, thus, whether microenterprises are within the scope *ratione personae* of Article 11(2) at all.

Article 11(2) of the Directive makes reference to the definition of a small and medium-sized enterprise contained in Commission Recommendation 2003/361/EC.[20] A medium-sized enterprise and a small enterprise (and also microenterprise) are defined in Article 2 of the Annex to the Recommendation. The entire category of micro, small and medium-sized enterprises is made up of enterprises which employ fewer than 250 persons and which have an annual turnover not exceeding EUR 50 million, and/or an annual balance sheet total not exceeding EUR 43 million (Article 2(1)). Within this broad category, a small enterprise is defined as an enterprise which employs fewer than 50 persons and whose annual turnover and/or annual balance sheet total does not exceed EUR 10 million (Article 2(2)). Last, microenterprise status is maintained where an enterprise employs fewer than 10 persons and its annual turnover and/or annual balance sheet total does not exceed EUR 2 million (Article 2(3)).

Article 11(2) of the Directive is not well designed. Nevertheless, the majority of national legislatures copied the wording in Article 11(2), and in doing so, left national courts with the task of striving to provide a reasonable interpretation of the scope *ratione personae* of the SME derogation. This task may be considered difficult, especially given that, as a rule, exceptions (here, Article 11(2)) from general principles (here, Article 11(1)) should be construed and applied strictly, in a manner which does not undermine the application of the general rule; therefore, the use of functional (purposive) and systemic (rather than linguistic) interpretation is limited. You could argue that Article 2(2) of the Annex to the Recommendation ('a small enterprise is defined as an enterprise which employs fewer than 50 persons and whose annual turnover and/or annual balance sheet total does not exceed EUR 10 million') can be construed as meaning that it also involves microenterprises; undeniably a microenterprise employs fewer than 50 persons and its annual turnover and/or annual

[19] According to Art 2(3) of Commission Recommendation 2003/361/EC of 6 May 2003 concerning the definition of micro, small and medium-sized enterprises [2003] OJ L124/36, microenterprise status is maintained where an enterprise employs fewer than 10 persons and its annual turnover and/or annual balance sheet total does not exceed EUR 2 million.

[20] Commission Recommendation 2003/361/EC of 6 May 2003 concerning the definition of micro, small and medium-sized enterprises [2003] OJ L124/36.

balance sheet total does not exceed EUR 10 million. However, according to this interpretation, Article 2 of the Annex to the Recommendation should be treated as if its section 3 did not exist at all.

Furthermore, if the Directive stipulates that the joint and several liability for competition law infringements should be limited for small and medium-sized enterprises, it would be illogical to impose a stricter liability rule on microenterprises which are naturally even more vulnerable by virtue of their size than small and medium-sized enterprises. However, it is for the national courts to decide whether this argument *a maiori ad minus* can be applied to the restriction of the scope *ratione personae* of the SME derogation.

In the literature, it is accepted that 'rules of the Directive (...) must be implemented by the Member States only with regard to small and medium-sized enterprises' but '[i]t would (...) seem practical, for example, to declare those rules applicable also to microenterprises'.[21] This practical solution was welcomed by the Slovenian drafters in their work transposing the Directive; the Slovenian implementing text covered microenterprises and SMEs.[22]

The SME derogation may be enhanced during the transposition processes in other ways, too. As has been said above, Article 11(2) of the Directive makes reference to the definition of a small and medium-sized enterprise contained in the Recommendation. The EU legislature imposed a requirement to follow a non-binding act (Recommendation) via a reference to the latter made in a legally binding act (Directive),[23] even though the necessary identical definitions are also contained in a legally binding act, ie Commission Regulation 651/2014,[24] more precisely in Article 2 of Annex I of the Regulation.

Basically, three legislative techniques can be used in this situation. First, the reference can be copied as it is. This appears to have been done without reflection by the majority of national legislatures. Second, the reference can be corrected and made to reflect the Regulation instead of the Recommendation. This approach was chosen by the Slovak drafters.[25] Third, it is possible that a Member State does not employ a technique of reference to the external definitions at all. In that case, the obligation of the implementation of Article 11(2) of the Directive implies that a national legislature will lay down the definitions in national provisions. The Slovenian drafters favoured the inclusion in the national instrument of definitions modelled on those which appear in both the Regulation and the Recommendation.[26] In many ways, the latter technique may work

[21] Miskolczi Bodnár and Szuchy, 'Joint and Several Liability of Competition Law Infringers in the Legislation of Central and Eastern European Member States' (n 11) 103, 107.

[22] A Vlahek and K Podobnik, 'Slovenia' in Piszcz, *Implementation of the EU Damages Directive in Central and Eastern European Countries* (n 7) 280.

[23] See also O Blažo, 'Slovakia' in Piszcz (n 7) 254.

[24] Commission Regulation (EU) No 651/2014 of 17 June 2014 declaring certain categories of aid compatible with the internal market in application of Articles 107 and 108 of the Treaty [2014] OJ L187/1.

[25] See also Blažo, 'Slovakia' (n 23) 254.

[26] Vlahek and Podobnik, 'Slovenia' (n 22) 280.

better than the others. First, the result is that national provisions do not refer to a non-binding act. Second, staff headcount and financial ceilings determining enterprise categories (subcategories) under EU law have not been modified in recent years and there is a small chance that they will be changed. At the same time, the chances that the act to which the reference is made will be replaced by a new act without changes to the contents of the definitions seem much greater. Member States that applied the third technique are less likely to be in need of an update of the implementing provisions.

One further aspect concerning SME status is that Article 11(2) of the Directive does not concentrate at all on the period of time or moment at which the infringer needs to be an SME in order to be able to take advantage of the derogation. The requirement related to the market share must be met 'at any time during the infringement of competition law' (Article 11(2)(a)); but how about the SME status? How about staff headcount and financial ceilings determining SME category? When do they need to be met? At any time during the infringement? Or later on? During the lawsuit? At the moment of the use of the 'failing SME' defence? As a rule, Member States did not have the ambition to add any provisions that would clarify this. However, the Hungarian legislature added that the infringer must fulfil the requirement of being an SME during the whole duration of the unlawful behaviour.[27] Nevertheless, this addition, interpreted *a contrario*, may raise concerns as regards the lack of SME status at the moment of being held liable. You may wonder whether the opportunity to take advantage of the SME derogation by a larger enterprise that was an SME during the infringement – but is not so anymore – should not be considered abusive and contrary to the spirit of the Directive, in particular, to the right to full compensation.

## IV. APPLICABLE CONDITIONS FOR THE 'FAILING SME' EXCEPTION

In order to take advantage of the SME derogation, an SME infringer will need to prove it meets all four specific requirements, both positive and negative. These are cumulative requirements, and thus, if any of them are not satisfied, general rules on joint and several liability will apply. Following general principles, the burden of proof rests with the party who contends that a certain position or set of facts are true. Therefore, it will be incumbent upon an SME to prove exhaustively that it meets all four requirements.

The positive requirements are listed in Article 11(2)(a)-(b) of the Directive. The list combines a retrospective quantitative design (a) and a prospective qualitative design (b). The first positive requirement is, in fact, the threshold condition. The *de minimis* threshold for an SME infringer market share in the

[27] P Miskolczi Bodnár, 'Hungary' in Piszcz (n 7) 143.

relevant market is 5 per cent at any time during the infringement of competition law. Here, it may be noted that the threshold introduced by the Directive was set quite low. The EU legislature has not decided to define it as the level which corresponds to the thresholds applied for the purposes of public enforcement of competition law under the De Minimis Notice (10 per cent, 15 per cent and 5 per cent).[28] Anyway, in practice it can be difficult for national civil courts to assess conclusively whether the threshold condition is met. The assessment of an SME infringer market share in the relevant market at any time during the infringement is not something within the reach of an average civil court, susceptible to a simple solution. Therefore, this issue will appear on a list of issues for the experts to address not only in stand-alone damages actions but also in follow-on damages actions where a final decision binding on the national court[29] when determining the nature of the infringement and its material, personal, temporal and territorial scope[30] does not define the infringer's market share. All the above will result in consideration of the case being delayed.

The second positive requirement is that 'the application of the normal rules of joint and several liability would irretrievably jeopardise its economic viability and cause its assets to lose all their value'. In other words, the SME infringer must be in such a condition that its joint and several liability vis-à-vis injured parties other than its direct or indirect purchasers would be followed by its financial failure. Certainly, these are stringent (if not, in fact, prohibitive) conditions and, therefore, you can expect that the 'failing SME' defence will be accepted only in particular circumstances, such as the inability to pay.[31] It will not be easy for SMEs to meet and prove those conditions and, above all, to even interpret them.[32] The above-mentioned requirement is expressed in rather vague terms such as 'irretrievably' (ie how?),[33] 'economic viability' (how understood?) or 'to lose' the entire 'value' of 'its assets' (all of them?). The proof, if any, of such future circumstances and the causal relationship between them and the application of the normal rules of joint and several liability will be very difficult. The above vague wording is consistent with paragraph 35, sentence 3 of the Commission Guidelines on the method of setting fines.[34] Here, the pro-infringer provision is applied if its economic viability would otherwise be irretrievably jeopardised and its assets would lose all their value. It may be easier

[28] De Minimis Notice (n 12) paras 8 et seq.

[29] See Directive 2014/104 (n 1) Art 9.

[30] ibid, Recital 34, sixth sentence.

[31] In the literature, there are doubts regarding the practical feasibility of the SME derogation; see D Wolski in A Piszcz and D Wolski, 'Poland' in Piszcz (n 7) 221.

[32] Piszcz (n 9) 228.

[33] Interestingly, in the early version of the Slovenian implementing text the phrase 'undoubtedly jeopardise' was used (instead of 'irretrievably jeopardise'); see Vlahek and Podobnik (n 22) 280.

[34] Commission, 'Guidelines on the method of setting fines imposed pursuant to Article 23(2)(a) of Regulation No 1/2003' [2006] OJ C210/2.

to interpret provisions on the 'failing SME' defence drawing inspiration from what has been written about paragraph 35 of the Guidelines. However, the mere similarity of the two provisions does not support or explain the introduction of civil liability limitations for 'failing SMEs'.[35] The application of the Guidelines leads to the reduction of the fine; you could say that it is at the expense of a public budget, be it national or EU budget. The same cannot be said about civil liability limitations for 'failing SMEs'. In the latter case, unlike in the case of the public enforcement of competition rules, the application of the exception discussed above leads to the modification of the way in which damages are distributed at the expense of the remaining defendants: non-SME infringers and/or SME infringers that do not meet the requirements of Article 11(2)-(3) of the Directive.

Article 11(3)(a)-(b) of the Directive imposes two negative requirements of a retrospective design,[36] in addition to the general requirements covered by Article 11(2). First, the SME may not be a leader of the infringement of competition law or coerce other undertakings to participate therein (a).[37] Having regard to this requirement, it has been said in the literature that the liability rules for SMEs, while favourable to them, nevertheless facilitate deterrence from future infringements.[38] It may be assumed that, here, the requirement is assigned to this particular infringement in relation to which a lawsuit is brought and not any other infringements.

According to the second requirement (b), the SME may not be previously found to have infringed competition law, no matter how long ago it happened. Being found to have infringed competition law (as it can be assumed, by a final decision) makes the SME lose the right to the failing SME defence forever. This condition raises some concerns, especially in terms of the lack of any interaction with limitation periods. The broad terms in which the requirement in Article 11(3)(b) is framed entail that every infringement – even the least serious – prevents the SME from enjoying the derogation.[39] A source of initiative is also

[35] See also Jurkowska-Gomułka (n 11) 67.

[36] Art 11(3) reads as follows: 'The derogation laid down in paragraph 2 shall not apply where:

(a) the SME has led the infringement of competition law or has coerced other undertakings to participate therein; or
(b) the SME has previously been found to have infringed competition law'.

[37] Pursuant to para 28 of the Commission Guidelines on the method of setting fines (n 34), the role of leader in, or instigator of, the infringement is one of the aggravating circumstances that may result in the basic amount being increased. Therefore, the Commission's considerations on the above may appear in the decision and facilitate the proof in follow-on civil damages actions.

[38] Miskolczi Bodnár and Szuchy (n 11) 92; but see Jurkowska-Gomułka (n 11) 66 and S Peyer, 'Antitrust Damages Directive – much Ado about Nothing?' in M Marquis and R Cisotta (eds), *Litigation and Arbitration in EU Competition Law* (Cheltenham – Northampton, Edward Elgar Publishing, 2015) 41.

[39] Wijckmans, Visser, Jaques and Noël (n 2) 55.

among the concerns. How many times has it happened that an SME was a leader in, or instigator of, the infringement? Well, frequently non-SME infringers coerce smaller undertakings to participate in the infringement and/or take retaliatory measures against smaller undertakings with a view to enforcing the practices constituting the infringement. If, for any reasons, SME infringers are not put off participating in the infringement and follow the coercer, they may, after all, be found to have infringed competition law and lose the right to the failing SME defence forever. Furthermore, the analysed provision on 'recidivism' does not suggest whether the infringement of competition law must be found by a competition authority or a review court or it may also be found by a national court in proceedings for the private enforcement of competition law. A systemic interpretation of Article 11(3)(b) of the Directive would restrict infringements only to those found by a competition authority or a review court. It is noteworthy that Hungarian implementing provisions state that 'the SME has previously been found to have infringed competition law by the HCA [Hungarian Competition Authority – AP], or national competition authority of a Member State, or the Commission or by a court'; the decision must be legally binding and executable.[40]

## V. THE EXTENT OF SME LIABILITY

Under Article 11(2) of the Directive, an SME that meets the specified conditions shall be liable only to its own direct and indirect purchasers; at the same time, it shall not be liable to other infringers' direct and indirect purchasers unless those purchasers are its own purchasers. Some commentators' main emphasis is on the fact that direct and indirect providers are missing from Article 11(2).[41] In this respect, it is noteworthy that the literal extent of the liability of SMEs clearly – in terms of vis-à-vis whom they are liable – differs from that of immunity recipients' liability, since Article 11(4)(a) includes both purchasers and providers.[42] Moreover, Article 11 does not contain a provision resembling the provision in Article 12(4) stating that 'Member States shall ensure that the rules laid down in this Chapter [Chapter IV "The passing-on of

[40] Miskolczi Bodnár, 'Hungary' (n 27) 142–43.

[41] Miskolczi Bodnár and Szuchy (n 11) 105; M Petr, 'Czech Republic' in Piszcz (n 7) 92; A Piszcz, '*Quo vadis* CEE? Summary' in Piszcz (n 7) 302.

[42] Art 11(4) reads as follows: 'By way of derogation from paragraph 1, Member States shall ensure that an immunity recipient is jointly and severally liable as follows:

(a) to its direct or indirect purchasers or providers; and
(b) to other injured parties only where full compensation cannot be obtained from the other undertakings that were involved in the same infringement of competition law.

Member States shall ensure that any limitation period applicable to cases under this paragraph is reasonable and sufficient to allow injured parties to bring such actions'.

overcharges" – AP] apply accordingly where the infringement of competition law relates to a supply to the infringer'. It can therefore be inferred by way of logical reasoning *a contrario* that if the EU legislature intended to cover direct and indirect providers in Article 11(2), it would mention them explicitly in Article 11(2) or make an appropriate reference.

The lack of providers in Article 11(2) construed literally does not mean that a demand-side SME infringer does not bear liability for damages that arise at all; it only means that the general rules governing liability ('full' joint and several liability) instead of its specific rules apply to such an SME infringer. The EU legislature did not endeavour to explain the rationale for the application of the 'failing SME' exception only in the case of supply-side infringements and not demand-side infringements (eg buying cartels). There is no reason why a demand-side SME infringer should not be able to benefit from the advantages of the provisions in question. It must have been unintentionally omitted from the Directive. All in all, when drafting their national transposing provisions, Hungarian, Czech, Polish and Croatian drafters filled this gap.[43]

Naturally enough, commentators also focus on the second issue which is that provisions related to SMEs do not contain a provision similar to Article 11(4)(b) of the Directive relevant to immunity recipients according to which 'an immunity recipient is jointly and severally liable (…) to other injured parties [other than its direct or indirect purchasers or providers – AP] only where full compensation cannot be obtained from the other undertakings that were involved in the same infringement of competition law'.[44] The Czech, Slovenian, Estonian, Slovakian and Romanian legal drafters copied into national provisions related to SMEs the provision of Article 11(4)(b) relevant to immunity recipients, even though this is not provided for in the Directive.[45] This complement is considered compliant with the requirement for the SME derogation to be without prejudice to the right to full compensation.[46] The result of the lack of such supplementary provisions is that the injured direct and indirect purchasers (or providers) of infringers which do not meet the requirements of Article 11(2)-(3) of the Directive cannot effectively sue and take execution steps against a 'failing SME' infringer even where full compensation cannot be obtained from the other infringers.[47]

[43] Miskolczi Bodnár and Szuchy (n 11) 105; Petr, 'Czech Republic' (n 41) 92; Piszcz, '*Quo vadis* CEE? Summary' (n 7) 302. See also V Butorac Malnar, 'Croatia' in Piszcz (n 7) 67.

[44] Miskolczi Bodnár and Szuchy (n 11) 91, 104; Petr (n 41) 92; Vlahek and Podobnik (n 22) 280; E Pärn-Lee, 'Estonia' in Piszcz (n 7) 114; V Mircea, 'Romania' in Piszcz (n 7) 240.

[45] ibid. See also Blažo (n 23) 255.

[46] ibid, 255.

[47] A practical remark that can be made is that if the requirements provided for in the Directive are satisfied (ie the SME is failing), an SME will hardly have the assets to cover a claim submitted by another co-infringer; see Miskolczi Bodnár and Szuchy (n 11) 91–92. But see also concerns expressed by Kersting with respect to the limitation of civil liability of leniency applicants ('While it does generally make sense to privilege successful leniency applicants with regard to their civil

On the other hand, the argument is made that adding such provisions is impermissible, since SMEs have received preferential treatment in the Directive (even though it may not be objectively justified, particularly keeping in mind that compensation in damages might bring large enterprises into the same situation, ie they may risk their economic viability).[48,49] This is exactly the reason why Croatian drafters have not included such a provision in the implementing law.

Last, Article 11 of the Directive is not transparent about whether 'failing SME' co-infringers have the right to obtain a contribution from such an SME pursuant to Article 11(5), sentence 1.[50] Its application is not excluded in Article 11(2)-(3), nor do the latter provisions refer to Article 11(5), sentence 2 which limits the amount of contribution but only for an infringer which has been granted immunity from fines under a leniency programme. The consequence of this vagueness may be that it in fact extinguishes the potential for SMEs claiming rights under the SME derogation. In the literature, the view is held that, in the case of SMEs, the general rules on compensation among co-infringers apply.[51] This means that an infringer should have the right to recover a contribution from any other infringer, the amount of which should be determined in the light of their relative responsibility for the harm caused by the infringement of competition law (Article 11(5), sentence 1 of the Directive). Even though Article 11(5) neither chooses the method for the determination of that share as the relative responsibility of a given infringer, nor gives the examples of the relevant criteria thereof, Recital 37, sentence 3 of the Preamble exemplifies turnover, market share, or the role in the cartel as such criteria and states that the determination of the share is a matter for the applicable national law, while respecting the principles of effectiveness and equivalence. Interestingly, the Croatian drafters proposed to codify this provision in the Preamble into the national legal order.[52] The calculation of a contribution on the basis of the relative responsibility cannot be considered fair, however, where the liability of one of co-infringers is limited. The infringer who has paid more compensation than

liability, it is problematic to do so at the expense of the injured parties. (…) some victims can only claim compensation from successful immunity applicants if they prove that they cannot obtain full compensation from the other cartelists. This puts a significant burden on them which renders their right to full compensation less effective.'); see Ch Kersting, 'Removing the Tension Between Public and Private Enforcement: Disclosure and Privileges for Successful Leniency Applicants' (2014) 5(1) *Journal of European Competition Law & Practice* 4.

[48] Butorac Malnar, 'Croatia' (n 43) 68; see also Jurkowska-Gomułka (n 11) 67.

[49] Butorac Malnar (n 43) 68.

[50] Art 11(5) reads as follows: 'Member States shall ensure that an infringer may recover a contribution from any other infringer, the amount of which shall be determined in the light of their relative responsibility for the harm caused by the infringement of competition law. The amount of contribution of an infringer which has been granted immunity from fines under a leniency programme shall not exceed the amount of the harm it caused to its own direct or indirect purchasers or providers'.

[51] Petr (n 41) 92.

[52] Butorac Malnar (n 43) 66.

its share, shall have the right to recover a contribution from the 'failing SME' infringer, the amount of which should not be more than the amount of harm caused by the SME to its own direct or indirect purchasers, even if a contribution calculated on the basis of the relative responsibility is higher. Therefore, the contribution is 'capped' by the SME derogation. In such circumstances, the liability of the infringer who has paid more compensation than its share could be considered a kind of punitive liability.

## VI. ANTICIPATED CONSEQUENCES AND THE ASSESSMENT

The effective use of 'failing SME' defence will result in dismissing claims against the sued SME. The question arises as to whether such a court decision is binding irrespective of the fact that the SME ceases to meet the specified requirements later, in particular if it is not an SME and/or a failing entity any more. Would it be fair enough for injured parties (other than SMEs' direct or indirect purchasers, following the *verba legis* rule) that the 'failing SME' which effectively used the derogation in question before the court is protected forever? Should it not be possible for the injured parties to sue the SME after the SME ceased to meet the specified criteria? Depending on the answer to this, also *res judicata* concerns may be raised. Regardless of the above, you can expect that litigation will be more complicated, as claimants do not know whether the SME derogation will apply to the defendants when suing them in court; this will only be found out during the litigation process. Therefore, the incentives to sue SME infringers may be seriously reduced and the length as well as risks of civil proceedings may be seriously increased.[53] It will be interesting to see the practical application of the rules discussed here in the context of a given cartel involving both an immunity recipient and a 'failing SME'.[54]

Another challenge for the application of the rules analysed may result from the merger of the 'failing SME' derogation and the immunity recipient derogation, especially if there are differences between them. In practice, the 'failing SME' protection may clash with the protection of a larger undertaking that received immunity; especially larger undertakings advised by experienced law firms usually win the race to be the first through the competition authority's door in order to secure immunity.

The transposition of Article 11(2)–(3) of the Damages Directive has been a challenge for the national legislatures. The SME derogation turned out to be at odds with the existing national rules on joint and several liability (or, more specifically, joint and several liability for competition law infringements), resulting in

[53] See Peyer (n 38) 41–42.

[54] See also J Fitchen, 'Private Enforcement of Competition Law' in P Beaumont, M Danov, K Trimmings and B Yüksel, *Cross-Border Litigation in Europe* (Oxford and Portland, Oregon, Hart Publishing, 2017) 681.

it not being possible to implement it through a light-touch approach intended to minimise disruptions and retain as much as possible of the already existing conceptual frameworks. Some Member States limited themselves to what can be described as copying and others tried to rationalise the transposed provisions where possible.[55] No doubt, as a result, there are discrepancies between the national provisions implementing the SME derogation. This is one of the factors which may cause or aggravate the forum-shopping phenomenon.

The SME derogation has already received harsh criticism in the literature. It has been argued inter alia that Article 11(2) of the Directive seriously violates the effectiveness of EU competition law; as such, it has to be firmly and expressly disagreed with.[56] The derogation has also been considered contrary to the aim set out in the Directive, namely the protection of injured parties.[57] Commentators have found it debatable whether the exceptions are necessary and can be justified in the light of the principles of justice, reasonableness and good faith.[58] Anyway, it is postulated that the implementation of the exceptions to joint and several liability, including the 'failing SME' exception should be subject to review after a fixed period.[59]

[55] See examples in eg section III of this chapter.

[56] Jurkowska-Gomułka (n 11) 66.

[57] Miskolczi Bodnár and Szuchy (n 11) 92.

[58] V Mikelėnas and R Zaščiurinskaitė, 'Lithuania' in Piszcz (n 7) 194.

[59] Which is different from the review provided for in Dir 2014/104 (n 1) Art 20. Miskolczi Bodnár and Szuchy propose a review 'after a year'; Miskolczi Bodnár and Szuchy (n 11) 108.

# 12

# *Causation and Damage: What the Directive Does Not Solve and Remarks on Relevant EU Law*

KATRI HAVU*

## I. INTRODUCTION

THIS BRIEF CONTRIBUTION addresses issues of causation and damage in the context of competition infringement damages claims. The focus is on matters which remain relatively open under EU law, regardless of the partial harmonisation of rules related to damages disputes. National judiciaries hearing concrete damages cases must resolve a notable number of challenging details by combining vague EU law and complementing national rules. This chapter highlights some particularly tricky themes with respect to legally relevant causal links (between a competition infringement and alleged damages) and concerning relevant damage and its extent. A significant amount of academic articles and other texts have already been written on causation and damages issues in the competition infringement context,[1] including

* LLD, Adjunct Professor (Docent) of European Law and Assistant Professor (tenure track) of Private Law, University of Helsinki.

[1] See eg FG Wilman, 'The End of the Absence? The Growing Body of EU Legislation on Private Enforcement and the Main Remedies it Provides for' (2016) 53 *Common Market Law Review* 887, 887–909; J Stuyck, 'Damages for the Loss Caused by a Cartel: The Causal Link' (2015) 23 *European Review of Private Law* 459; I Lianos, 'Causal Uncertainty and Damages Claims for the Infringement of Competition Law in Europe' (2015) 34 *Yearbook of European Law* 170; E Clark and R Sander, 'Navigating the Quantum Minefield in Cartel Damages Cases' (2015) 6 *Journal of European Competition Law & Practice* 153; N Dunne, 'It Never Rains but it Pours? Liability for "Umbrella Effects" under EU Competition Law in Kone' (2014) 51 *Common Market Law Review* 1813; T Eger and P Weise, 'Harm and Damages as Economic and Legal Categories in Antitrust Law' in J Basedow, JP Terhechte and L Tichý (eds), *Private Enforcement of Competition Law* (Baden-Baden, Nomos, 2011) 31; AP Komninos, *EC Private Antitrust Enforcement: Decentralised Application of EC Competition Law by National Courts* (Oxford, Hart Publishing, 2008) 190–211; MO Mackenrodt,

by this author.[2] Therefore, the goal here is to avoid repeating earlier discussions or long introductions to the theme.[3]

As is well known, Directive 2014/104/EU[4] (the Directive) harmonised *certain aspects* of EU competition law related damages claims. The Directive does not provide any exhaustive discussions on damage, causal connection or fault.[5] The existing Directive provisions are remarkably vague as regards the significance, evaluation or establishment of these preconditions for damages liability.

When it comes to legally relevant causation and damage, the Directive provisions which are or may be of relevance – albeit non-exhaustive – include Article 3 on the right to full compensation and its elements, Article 2 on term definitions (including, for example, an attempt to define 'injured party'[6]), Article 11 on joint and several liability, Articles 12–16 on passing-on and related issues and Article 17 on quantification of harm. Moreover, there are interesting recitals in the Preamble of the Directive, such as Recital 11 on causation as well as 'other conditions' for compensation, Recitals 12–13 on standing, recoverable losses, interest and avoiding overcompensation and Recitals 39–41 and 43–47 concerning, inter alia, (proving) the existence and quantum of damages and the role of national law in that context.

Guidance by the Commission on quantifying harm (2013)[7] and, for example, the recent study on passing-on (2016)[8] may, prima facie, appear central to legal evaluations concerning causation and damage. However, they do not provide

'Private Incentive, Optimal Deterrence and Damage Claims for Abuses of Dominant Positions – The Interaction between the Economic Review of the Prohibition of Abuses of Dominant Positions and Private Enforcement' in MO Mackenrodt, B Conde Gallego and S Enchelmaier (eds), *Abuse of Dominant Position, New Interpretation, New Enforcement Mechanisms?* (Berlin, Springer-Verlag, 2008) 165.

[2] See eg K Havu, 'Practical Private Enforcement: Perspectives from Finland – Causal Links, the Principle of Effectiveness and Requirements for National Solutions' in M Bergström, M Iacovides and M Strand (eds), *Harmonising EU Competition Litigation: The New Directive and Beyond* (Oxford, Hart Publishing, 2016) 221; K Havu, 'Competition Restrictions, "Umbrellas" and Damages Claims – Comment on Kone' (2015) 8 *Global Competition Litigation Review* 134; K Havu, 'Horizontal Liability for Damages in EU Law – the Changing Relationship of EU and National Law' (2012) 18 *European Law Journal* 407.

[3] A reader not familiar with the discussion concerning conditions for liability in the competition infringement damages context may find contributions cited in the two preceding footnotes useful.

[4] Directive 2014/104/EU of the European Parliament and of the Council of 26 November 2014 on certain rules governing actions for damages under national law for infringements of the competition law provisions of the Member States and of the EU [2014] OJ L349/1.

[5] See also ibid, Recitals 11–13.

[6] ibid, Art 2: '"injured party" means a person that has suffered harm caused by an infringement of competition law'. The definition is vague and circular.

[7] Commission, 'Communication from the Commission on quantifying harm in actions for damages based on breaches of Article 101 or 102 of the Treaty on the Functioning of the European Union' [2013] OJ C167/19; Commission, 'Staff Working Document, Practical Guide on quantifying harm in actions for damages based on breaches of Art 101 or 102 of the Treaty on the Functioning of the European Union' SWD(2013) 205.

[8] Commission, 'Study on the Passing-On of Overcharges Final Report' (2016), a study prepared by RBB Economics and Cuatrecasas Gonçalves Pereira.

instructions on how to interpret or apply EU law but emphasise the role of national law while providing practical information relating to possible methods of calculation and assessment of damage.[9] The room for manoeuvre as regards how to legally classify the calculated amounts of money, in terms of the extent of relevant, recoverable damages, remains.

Other EU law complements the Directive provisions and related guidance documents. According to the Directive, the principles of effectiveness and equivalence, as well as the case-law of the European Court of Justice (ECJ), must be observed in competition infringement damages disputes.[10] This, together with the general principles of EU law, signifies that relevant EU law and guidance is found not only in the Directive (and soft-law documents) published by the European legislator, but also in rulings by the ECJ – and that there is relevant case-law even beyond the scope of competition cases. The line of case-law that stems from *Courage*[11] is vague, 'pointillist' and even partially contradictory concerning legally relevant damage and causation as well as the evaluations needed to confirm their presence. The ECJ's other guidance regarding, for instance, the procedural autonomy principles, full effect of EU law, practical effects and effective enforcement of competition provisions, and effective judicial protection may also be of relevance in competition infringement damages cases. In any case, all of the relevant EU law underlines the central position of national law – and the general, vague obligation to 'correctly' fill the gaps of EU law, producing court decisions that cohere with EU law.

The less than exhaustive nature of the Directive, as well as the complex body of possibly relevant EU law, naturally raises questions about acceptable decisions regarding damages and causation in cases heard by national courts. Even though the Directive underlines the requirement of full compensation, it may be challenging to evaluate, for instance, whether recoverable losses have been understood in a manner compatible with EU law, whether a finding that the causal link was broken before reaching some of the claimed losses is compatible with EU law, or whether other evaluations concerning establishing relevant damage and sufficient causation are too strict or permissive. Indeed, damages and causation decisions by national courts may be too strict (defendant-friendly) in a manner which contravenes the principles of EU law or the Directive, but the challenge is that in the current state of EU law, it is difficult to pinpoint clear limits of acceptability for the findings of national courts. Excessively permissive,

[9] See also discussion by, eg, J Drexl, Consumer Actions after the Adoption of the EU Directive on Damage Claims for Competition Law Infringements (2015) Max Planck Institute for Innovation and Competition Research Paper No 15-10, available at http://ssrn.com/abstract=2689521 20–21; Clark and Sander, 'Navigating the Quantum Minefield in Cartel Damages Cases' (n 1); V Mikelėnas and R Zaščiurinskaitė, 'Quantification of Harm and the Damages Directive: Implementation in CEE Countries' (2017) 10 *Yearbook of Antitrust and Regulatory Studies* 111.

[10] Directive 2014/104/EU (n 4), see in particular Art 4 and Recitals 11–12.

[11] Case C-453/99 *Courage Ltd v Crehan* EU:C:2001:465 (*Courage*).

claimant-friendly decisions may, when taken to the extreme, pose other problems as well as undermining the efficiency and welfare goals of EU competition law. The fact-intensity and the inherent need for *in casu* evaluation of damages and causation issues accentuate the problem of finding balanced outcomes that are also compatible with the requirements of EU law.

Below, this contribution explores four interrelated sub-themes pertaining to the challenge of correctly applying the combination of EU and national law to facts as regards legally relevant damage and causal connection.

## II. THE REQUIREMENT AND NOTION OF FULL COMPENSATION

The first of the sub-themes discussed here is the requirement and notion of full compensation. Even though the Directive and the competition infringement damages case-law underline the requirement, and discuss the recoverability of actual loss and loss of profit as well as the payment of interest, the relevant EU law is far from providing clear instructions on what should be compensated for in different circumstances. It is essential to notice that full compensation does not mean anything specific without a detailed picture of legally relevant damage and causal link. Additionally, an important aspect is when they should be considered established to a sufficient degree.[12]

In *Manfredi*, the concept of full compensation was not used, but what should be compensated was discussed, noting that damage sufferers must be able to seek compensation not only for actual loss (*damnum emergens*) but also for loss of profit (*lucrum cessans*) and interest.[13] In *Kone*, the ECJ explained that even damage potentially suffered by so-called umbrella customers could not be categorically excluded from the scope of the damages liability of infringers.[14] Nevertheless, it was noted in *Otis* that the causal connection between the infringement and damage should be 'direct'.[15]

The fact that EU law requires the possibility to seek *full compensation* was expressly mentioned in *Donau Chemie* and *CDC Hydrogen Peroxide*.[16] Nonetheless, these rulings do not explain the notion of full compensation other than by references, in *Donau Chemie*, to earlier competition infringement

[12] See also further K Havu, 'Full, Adequate and Commensurate Compensation for Damages under EU Law: A Challenge for National Courts?' (2018) 43 *European Law Review* 24.

[13] Joined Cases C-295/04–C-298/04 *Manfredi and Others* EU:C:2006:461 (*Manfredi*); see paras 59–64, 90–100.

[14] Case C-557/12 *Kone AG and Others v ÖBB-Infrastruktur AG* EU:C:2014:1317 (*Kone*). Umbrella customers are customers of competitors to competition infringers, and may incur damages due to the general increase in price level, attributable to the infringement.

[15] Case C-199/11 *Europese Gemeenschap v Otis NV and Others* EU:C:2012:684 (*Otis*) para 65.

[16] Case C-536/11 *Bundeswettbewerbsbehörde v Donau Chemie AG and Others* EU:C:2013:366 (*Donau Chemie*) paras 22–25; Case C-352/13 *Cartel Damage Claims (CDC) Hydrogen Peroxide SA v Evonik Degussa GmbH and Others* EU:C:2015:335, para 63.

damages cases.[17] In the case-law, the issue of causal link and required proof for establishing it is in practice entirely left to the laws of the Member States.[18]

In the Directive, full compensation is to some extent elaborated even though Article 3 on the right to full compensation (and on recoverable losses) mostly codifies case-law. According to the Directive, full compensation signifies placing a person who has suffered harm in the position in which that person would have been had the infringement of competition law not been committed. Further, without prejudice to compensation for loss of opportunity, full compensation under the Directive shall not lead to overcompensation.[19]

The Directive provisions do not define the relevant causal link between an infringement and damages or exhaustively regulate the evaluation of a causal link and establishing it. This also holds true for the details related to establishing and deciding the extent of legally relevant damage in a concrete case. The national laws of Member States, principles of EU law and case-law of the ECJ are highlighted as central legal sources with respect to these themes.[20] As discussed in the introduction, the studies and guidance published by the Commission as regards the quantification of damages and passing-on do not significantly change this overall picture when it comes to correctly applying the law. They do not entail guidance on interpreting, applying or fitting together relevant EU and national law, but rather explain economic aspects.

Nevertheless, the conceptions of legally relevant causation and damage are the other side of the coin of full compensation: they indicate what should be fully covered.[21] The non-exhaustive case-law together with the Directive signifies that, as a starting point, the role of national laws remains central and the national courts' room for manoeuvre significant. Additionally, more 'distant' ECJ cases (that is, case-law concerning other fields) may include relevant reasoning and further guidance on damage and causal link as concepts of EU law as well as on combining EU and national law in an appropriate way. Nonetheless, ECJ rulings in other damages liability contexts, too, are non-exhaustive. In general, 'causal link' under EU law refers to a breach of EU law being an immediate and exclusive, or at least necessary, cause of the alleged damage,[22] but this 'definition' is vague. Moreover, it is to some extent unclear how directly transferable reasoning from other lines of case-law is; in other words, how

[17] See *Donau Chemie* (n 16) paras 22–25.

[18] See *Courage* (n 11) paras 26–30; *Manfredi* (n 13) paras 61–64; *Kone* (n 14); *Otis* (n 15) para 65.

[19] Directive 2014/104/EU (n 4) Arts 3, 12, Recitals 11–13, 39–41, 43–47.

[20] ibid; see in particular Arts 3, 4, 12–17, and Recitals 11–13, 39–41, 43–47.

[21] See also further Havu, 'Practical Private Enforcement' (n 2) 222–228; Havu, 'Full, Adequate and Commensurate Compensation for Damages under EU Law' (n 12).

[22] See eg Joined Cases C-46/93 and C-48/93 *Brasserie du Pêcheur SA v Bundesrepublik Deutschland and The Queen v Secretary of State for Transport* EU:C:1996:79 (*Brasserie*); Case C-140/97 *Rechberger and Others v Republik Österreich* EU:C:1999:306; Case C-419/08 P *Trubowest Handel and Makarov v Council and Commission* EU:C:2010:147; Case C-45/15 P *Safa Nicu Sepahan Co v Council* EU:C:2017:402.

'binding' reasoning concerning full compensation, relevant causal link and damage in, for instance, Member State liability or EU liability cases is from the standpoint of a horizontal competition infringement damages case.[23]

In any event, the notion of full compensation has not been exhaustively defined in ECJ case-law in the sense of a discussion on its relationship with a relevant causal link and damage or required proof for establishing these.[24] Therefore, it is not clear under what kind of circumstances it would be acceptable for national courts to find that there is no relevant causal connection to a competition infringement, and thus no recoverable damage. This issue is central, for instance, where a court considers that other potential causes for lost profits have not been entirely excluded.

Additionally, central issues related, for example, to interest are open under EU law and the Directive. Inter alia, applicable interest rates currently seem to depend on national choices – the limits set for them by EU law principles are not entirely clear.[25]

The following sections further illustrate the challenges related to evaluating whether decisions by Member State courts on damage and causation comply with EU law. Particularly relevant aspects of 'general EU law' are the twin principles of effectiveness and equivalence (according to which national rules must not make relying on EU law practically impossible or excessively difficult and must not render the treatment of EU law-based claims less favourable than those based on national law),[26] and requirements for full effect and sufficient judicial protection. These 'outer limits' for national solutions have been repeatedly underlined by the ECJ in its preliminary rulings.[27]

[23] See further, eg, A Ward, *Judicial Review and the Rights of Private Parties in EU Law*, 2nd edn (Oxford, Oxford University Press, 2007) 251–52; IC Durant, 'Causation' in H Koziol and R Schulze (eds), *Tort Law of the European Community* (Wien, Springer, 2008) 47, 55–56; Havu (n 12); Havu, 'Horizontal Liability' (n 2) 411–425. As regards interesting Member State liability rulings, see, in addition to the previous note, eg, Case C-470/03 *A.G.M.-COS.MET Srl v Suomen valtio and Lehtinen* EU:C:2007:213; Case C-168/15 *Tomášová v Slovenská republika* EU:C:2016:602, paras 38–42. For interesting EU liability cases, see, in addition to the previous note, eg, Joined Cases C-104/89 and C-37/90 *Mulder and Others and Heinemann v Council and Commission* EU:C:1992:217; Joined Cases C-104/89 and C-37/90 *Mulder and Others v Council and Commission* EU:C:2000:38.

[24] See further Havu (n 12). Consider also, eg, N Reich, 'Horizontal Liability in EC law: Hybridization of Remedies for Compensation in Case of Breaches of EC Rights' (2007) 44 *Common Market Law Review* 705, 726–29; M Tomulic Vehovec, 'The Cause of Member State Liability' (2012) 20 *European Review of Private Law* 851.

[25] See Directive 2014/104/EU (n 4) Art 3. The question could be raised what kind of national solutions are problematic from the standpoint of the goal of full compensation, read together with, inter alia, the principle of effectiveness. For discussion and comparative remarks on national regimes, see eg G Monti (ed), 'EU Law and Interest on Damages for Infringements of Competition Law – A Comparative Report' EUI Working Papers Law 2016/11, https://papers.ssrn.com/sol3/papers.cfm?abstract_id=2753528; M Strand, 'EU och civilrättens splittring: Exemplet preskription och ränta vid skadestånd' (2017) 130 *Tidsskrift for Rettsvitenskap* 313.

[26] See eg *Manfredi* (n 13) paras 62, 96.

[27] See eg *Courage* (n 11); *Manfredi* (n 13); *Donau Chemie* (n 16); *Kone* (n 14). For interesting preliminary rulings touching upon full or sufficient compensation in contexts other than competition

## III. THE FULL EFFECT, EFFECTIVE APPLICATION AND PRACTICAL EFFECTS OF ARTICLES 101 AND 102 TFEU

The second sub-theme of causation and damages issues concerns the full effect (or full effectiveness, *effet utile*), effective enforcement and 'practical effects' of Articles 101 and 102 TFEU. These requirements have been emphasised by the ECJ but their exact significance in terms of appropriate national court decisions in damages disputes are to some extent obscure.

In *Courage*, the ECJ noted that:

> The *full effectiveness* of [the current Article 101 TFEU] and, in particular, the *practical effect* of the prohibition laid down in [Article 101(1) TFEU] would be put at risk if it were not open to any individual to claim damages for loss caused to him by a contract or by conduct liable to restrict or distort competition.[28]

Furthermore, in recent competition cases, the ECJ has underlined that it must be ensured that rules of national law 'specifically, in the area of competition law … do not jeopardise the effective application of Articles 101 TFEU and 102 TFEU'.[29] This latter statement appears in case-law as a kind of continuation of the 'procedural autonomy *dictum*' which highlights the principles of effectiveness and equivalence.[30] Nevertheless, as regards the evaluation of the conditions for damages liability – and causation in particular – the significance of underlining full effect, effective application or enforcement, and practical effects of competition rules is obscure.[31] Moreover, the interrelationships between these notions are not entirely clear.[32]

Different possible interpretations of the requirements and their practical implications are outlined concisely below. Some of the implications may seem extreme, and even partially problematic from the standpoint of the full compensation ideals of the Directive, but it is important to note the wide range of possible interpretation alternatives and prevailing ambiguity with respect to the meaning of the relevant passages in case-law.

The requirements focusing on full effect, effective enforcement and sufficient practical effects could be considered to imply an obligation on national courts

infringements, see eg Joined Cases C-397/98 and C-410/98 *Metallgesellschaft Ltd and Others* EU:C:2001:134; Case C-407/14 *Arjona Camacho v Securitas Seguridad España, SA* EU:C:2015:831; Case C-481/14 *Hansson v Jungpflanzen Grünewald GmbH* EU:C:2016:419 (*Hansson*).

[28] *Courage* (n 11) para 26. Emphases added. See also *Manfredi* (n 13) paras 60–64; *Donau Chemie* (n 16) paras 21–27.

[29] Case C-360/09 *Pfleiderer AG v Bundeskartellamt* EU:C:2011:389, para 24. See also Case C-439/08 *Vlaamse federatie van verenigingen van Brood- en Banketbakkers, Ijsbereiders en Chocoladebewerkers (VEBIC) VZW* EU:C:2010:739, para 57; *Donau Chemie* (n 16) paras 22, 27; *Kone* (n 14) paras 21–26; Case C-74/14 *Eturas UAB and Others* EU:C:2016:42 (*Eturas*) para 35.

[30] See eg *Kone* (n 14) paras 24–26.

[31] See, in particular, *Courage* (n 11) paras 25–29; *Manfredi* (n 13) paras 60–64, 90–100; *Kone* (n 14) paras 21–26, 32–34, 37.

[32] See eg *Donau Chemie* (n 16) paras 21–27; *Kone* (n 14) paras 21–26.

to opt for an extensive scope of granted damages. This interpretation would perhaps emphasise the sanction nature of damages awards and see significant damages liability as the realisation of the full effect, or practical effects, of the competition provisions.[33] Moreover, from the standpoint of individuals, receiving compensation for breaches of competition law can be seen as an important aspect of the full effect of EU law.[34]

Nevertheless, it can be noted that the goals of EU competition law might be undermined by overtly claimant-friendly approaches, especially if they make court decisions seem highly unpredictable and unjust. This is particularly relevant with respect to 'grey areas' of competition law prohibitions, such as those pertaining to vertical agreements and abuses of dominant position. Because of the fear of infringing competition law, undertakings may begin to refrain from behaviour that is actually allowed by EU competition provisions, and this may result in less efficient markets.[35]

The requirements of full effect and effective application or enforcement could also be interpreted as requiring an abstention from damages awards in cases of some remote or minor damages. In Europe, damages liability is not the most direct or effective way of catching and sanctioning competition infringements. Professional, efficient competition authorities and functioning public enforcement constitute the primary machinery for enforcing the EU competition provisions. Private litigation proceedings before national courts are resource-consuming, and it could be argued that at least some of the resources would be better allocated if invested in public enforcement.[36]

When damages claims are unlikely to be founded or unlikely to succeed because of, for instance, challenges in establishing a causal link, private enforcement should perhaps be discouraged in order to achieve more effective *overall enforcement* of competition law. Using resources for enhancing public enforcement instead of hearing a difficult private dispute can benefit the society as a whole and prevent competition infringement damages. For some, this may seem

[33] However, it is relatively clear that the main goal of damages liability under EU law in general and in the context of competition infringements is the compensation of the victim, not sanctioning. See Directive 2014/104/EU (n 4), eg, Art. 3, Recitals 3–7, 11–14, 22, 39, 44. For discussion on functions of liability, see eg C Van Dam, *European Tort Law*, 2nd edn (Oxford, Oxford University Press, 2013) 34–44; Havu (n 12); M Strand, *The Passing-on Problem in Damages and Restitution under EU Law* (Cheltenham, Edward Elgar Publishing, 2017) 364–69.

[34] See eg *Courage* (n 11) paras 23–29, *Manfredi* (n 13) paras 60–64, *Kone* (n 14) paras 21–26. See also, eg, regarding full effect and Member State liability, Joined Cases C-6/90 and C-9/90 *Francovich and Bonifaci and Others v Italian Republic* EU:C:1991:428 (*Francovich*).

[35] See further, eg, Mackenrodt, 'Private Incentive, Optimal Deterrence and Damage Claims for Abuses of Dominant Positions' (n 1) 188–89; A Devlin and M Jacobs, 'Antitrust Error' (2010) 52 *William and Mary Law Review* 75, 81, 128–30; K Havu, 'Private Enforcement of EU (Competition) Law – Remarks and Outlooks Regarding the Intertwinement of EU and National Law' (2014) 150 *Tidskrift utgiven av Juridiska föreningen i Finland* 55, 63–64.

[36] See further, eg, WPJ Wils, 'Should Private Antitrust Enforcement be Encouraged in Europe?' (2003) 26 *World Competition* 473; Mackenrodt (n 1) 188–89.

to contradict the way full compensation is underlined in the Directive. Nevertheless, the significant room for manoeuvre left for national systems as regards causation, extent of damage and required evidence may actually eliminate that contradiction. If no relevant causal link and damage are considered established, there is nothing that should be compensated (that is, there are no injured parties within the meaning of the Directive). Understanding the relevant causal link and damage narrowly supports excluding private litigants whose alleged damages are not clearly connected to competition infringements and whose claims would, therefore, be costly but not necessarily useful to adjudicate.

All in all, the significance of the requirements for full effect, effective application and practical effects of Articles 101 and 102 remains partially ambiguous when it comes to resolving details of damages claims. It is uncertain what kind of reasoning by national courts can be validly based on these requirements. National courts are under a general obligation to contribute to achieving the goals of EU law (Article 4(3) TEU). However, it may be challenging to determine what kind of decision genuinely contributes to achieving the aims of EU competition law, and which goals should be prioritised.

## IV. REMOTE DAMAGES, AND LONG AND COMPLEX CAUSAL LINKS

The third sub-theme highlighted here is the issue of remote damages, long and complex causal links, and the position of very remote or hypothetical victims of competition restrictions. As appropriate (EU law-compatible) damage and causation evaluations are not evident, cases entailing these issues are likely to be challenging. The problems in this area are connected to the more general EU law ambiguities as regards how *easy* it should be to obtain compensation, which is a more intricate issue than whether claims by certain claimants or awards for certain damages should be possible.

The ruling in *Kone* was 'pointillist' and context-specific but interesting when it comes to remote claimants and damages, setting out that the *categorical exclusion* of the losses of the particular group of *umbrella customers* from the scope of damages liability of *cartelists* is precluded by EU law.[37] This is a clarification of an 'outer limit' set by EU law,[38] not a detailed discussion on requirements for actually finding a legally relevant causal link and damage.

Moreover, the position of groups such as customers who were entirely priced out of markets, that is, those who did not buy anything because of a competition restriction, or customers who did not buy because they would have been

[37] *Kone* (n 14).

[38] Under case-law of the ECJ and the Directive, anyone should be able to claim compensation, which explains the inappropriateness of categorical exclusion of certain types of damages or certain victims. See eg *Courage* (n 11), and Directive 2014/104/EU (n 4) Arts 1–2, Recitals 3, 11–13.

umbrella customers affected by umbrella pricing if they had, remains open. The same applies to the correct (EU law-compatible) evaluation of many other remote damages and lengthy, multi-step causal relationships. Additionally, the correct treatment of complex causal relationships in the context of less objectionable infringements, such as certain vertical restraints, could differ from the case of cartels, but EU law remains silent regarding the matter.

Challenges of dealing with complex or hypothetical causal links and remote damages entail questions such as whether employees of a negatively affected company should receive compensation for harm incurred due to a competition infringement, or whether shareholders of infringer companies should receive compensation under certain circumstances (a competition infringement may harm even the latter in many ways).[39] If yes, what kind of proof should be required of causation and the existence and extent of damage?

As to the burden of proof for damages liability, the Directive regulates this in the context of some particular matters, but the starting point is that based on the principle of procedural autonomy, national legal systems should govern this area. Issues of the evaluation of evidence are merely touched upon in passing in the Directive.[40] As with EU law-based claims in general, standards and thresholds of proof applicable to competition damages disputes are to a significant extent left to Member States to determine.[41]

An aspect affecting the 'correct' (EU law-compatible) treatment of long, multi-step or hypothetical causal links and remote damages is the chosen approach to functions of damages liability: focusing on the sanction or deterrence purpose of liability would more readily justify granting damages to broad groups of claimants. As noted above while discussing full effect, effective application and practical effects of Articles 101 and 102 TFEU, the Directive nevertheless emphasises corrective justice thinking and compensation as a primary goal for damages liability. Also, the Directive expressly rejects overcompensation. Nonetheless, as is also illustrated above, the case-law of the ECJ is not as straightforward as it underlines the full effect of EU law and appears to emphasize deterrence in addition to compensation.[42]

[39] For discussion, see eg Wils, 'Should Private Antitrust Enforcement be Encouraged in Europe?' (n 36); Eger and Weise, 'Harm and Damages as Economic and Legal Categories in Antitrust Law' (n 1). See also Strand, *The Passing-on Problem in Damages and Restitution under EU Law* (n 33) 316–18.

[40] See Directive 2014/104/EU (n 4) Arts 12–15, 17, and Recitals 39–41, 45–47. See also the following section of this contribution.

[41] See Council Regulation (EC) 1/2003 of 16 December 2002 on the implementation of the rules on competition laid down in Articles 81 and 82 of the Treaty [2003] OJ L1/1, Art 2, Recital 5; *Eturas* (n 29) paras 30–35; *Otis* (n 15) para 65. See also, eg, *Hansson* (n 27) paras 44–59; Case C-621/15 *NW and Others v Sanofi Pasteur MSD SNC* EU:C:2017:484; Case C-310/14 *Nike European Operations Netherlands BV v Sportland Oy* EU:C:2015:690. Case-law includes clarifications on, eg, the interpretation of the principle of effectiveness. For example, procedural rules may not de facto shift the burden of proof where the allocation of the burden of proof is regulated by EU law. Guidance is, in any case, far from exhaustive.

[42] See eg n 27 above and further, eg, *Francovich* (34). Harm actually sustained is, in any event, central in the ECJ's reasoning.

A further issue to be noted while discussing remote or hypothetical damages is the significance of EU law judicial protection requirements. Typically, these, such as Article 47 of the EU Charter of Fundamental Rights, are highlighted as a part of the discussion on victims of competition infringements. Nevertheless, it must be borne in mind that the general principle of effective judicial protection, and the obligation of Member States to provide judicial protection in EU law matters (Article 19(1) TEU), may also be relevant for the position of defendants. Awarding damages when not objectively justified is problematic from the standpoint of judicial protection of competition infringers. The challenge is, again, that EU law does not directly and in a detailed, practical manner address the issue of under which circumstances awarding damages is not justified.

## V. CAUSATION AND DAMAGE-RELATED PRESUMPTIONS AND FACILITATIONS

The fourth sub-theme of causation and damage issues concerns causation and damage-related presumptions and other rules that have as their goal the facilitation of damages claims. Some ambiguity prevails as regards the details of dealing with these elements of the Directive, and implementing national law, in Member State courts.

The Directive specifically regulates burden of proof with respect to passing-on: an infringer that invokes the passing-on defence must prove the existence and extent of the passing-on of the overcharge. Claims by indirect purchasers are facilitated by a rule according to which an indirect purchaser is regarded as having proven that an overcharge paid by a direct purchaser has been passed on to indirect purchasers where it is able to show prima facie that such passing-on has occurred.[43] This rebuttable presumption of passing-on applies unless the infringer can 'credibly demonstrate to the satisfaction of the court that the actual loss has not or not entirely been passed on to the indirect purchaser'.[44]

The provision concerning quantification of damage, Article 17(1), sets out that

> Member States shall ensure that neither the burden nor the standard of proof required for the quantification of harm renders the exercise of the right to damages practically impossible or excessively difficult. Member States shall ensure that the national courts are empowered, in accordance with national procedures, to estimate the amount of harm if it is established that a claimant suffered harm but it is practically impossible or excessively difficult precisely to quantify the harm suffered on the basis of the evidence available.[45]

[43] Directive 2014/104/EU (n 4) Arts 12–15, Recitals 39–41.
[44] ibid, Recital 41.
[45] See also ibid, Recitals 45–46.

Furthermore, Article 17(2) states that it shall be presumed that cartels cause harm (the presumption of harm), but the infringer may rebut that presumption.[46]

The Directive provisions dealing with the burden of proof and evaluation of evidence in the context of the existence and extent of legally relevant damage are not highly comprehensive or detailed. Further, there are no specific instructions for interpreting relevant EU law principles and, for instance, the concrete meaning of rendering the exercise of the right to compensation 'practically impossible or excessively difficult'. The room left for Member State legal systems as regards the evaluation of evidence and issues such as standards and thresholds of proof signifies, prima facie, that many kinds of national solutions are compatible with EU law.

However, the 'outer limits' set out by EU law are likely to be challenging to decrypt from the standpoint of a concrete case. The more general obscureness concerning the issue of what kind of findings on causation and damage comply with EU law also affects the conundrum of when presumptions should prevail and when they should be considered rebutted. A challenging problem may be, for instance: when is a national court's finding that the presumption of harm has been rebutted inappropriate, that is, rendering the obtaining of compensation practically impossible or excessively difficult so as to infringe the principle of effectiveness? Rebutting the presumption should not be so easy as to in practice fully remove the legal presumption. Nevertheless, a genuine possibility for successful rebuttal should exist.

Further, the practical relevance of the presumption of harm and of the possibility to base the award of damages on an estimation[47] depends on other causation and damage considerations. The presumption of harm is formulated in a vague manner in the Directive, and the extent of legally relevant, causally connected damage is still to be decided without concrete support and elaborate instructions from the part of EU law.[48] Additionally, the issue whether a court accepts estimating the quantum of damages is only relevant if sufficient causation is considered established: without causation there is no need to decide the amount of compensation.[49]

## VI. CONCLUDING REMARKS

This contribution has explored damages and causation as well as establishing these conditions for liability. Remarks on four interrelated sub-themes have been

[46] See also ibid, Recital 47, which does not provide further information on requirements for successful rebuttal.

[47] See ibid, Arts 17(1) and 12(5).

[48] See also ibid, Recital 47 ('This presumption should not cover the concrete amount of harm'). See also further the chapter by Pieter Van Cleynenbreugel in this volume.

[49] See also Directive 2014/104/EU (n 4) Arts 12–15, Recitals 45–46.

presented to illustrate intricacies pertaining to this area. EU law appears to leave notable room for manoeuvre for national legislation and Member State courts. The issue of how easy it should be to obtain compensation, or under which circumstances and to whom reparation should actually be granted, is not specifically addressed by EU law. Additionally, many aspects of relevant EU law may still be in the process of development.

National transposition measures based on the Directive mirror the openness of EU law. It is common that the national provisions addressing competition infringement damages only loosely, if at all, define causation and damage. Typically, the wordings of national Acts are similar to the vague Directive.[50] More detailed evaluations related to finding and establishing causation, harm and the extent of damages in different situations are left for courts. Judiciaries, in turn, must follow the evolving EU law and bear in mind that possible future clarifications are capable of overriding contradictory national legislation or interpretations.

The general principles of EU law, requirements related to judicial protection, and the obligation to secure full effect of EU competition provisions are always relevant in damages cases before national courts. These 'outer limits' for acceptable national court findings are partially cryptic and challenging to combine, weigh against each other, and apply to concrete cases. Moreover, EU case-law includes ambiguous passages the significance of which for practical damage and causation evaluations remains obscure.

Granting full compensation to *successful claimants* is not necessarily enough in order to comply with the goals of EU law and the Directive. Nevertheless, clarifications of, for instance, when a finding that causation has not been established breaches the EU law principle of effectiveness are still lacking. Furthermore, the issue of when damages awards are extensively claimant-friendly so as to compromise the position and rights of the infringer defendants (or, through over-deterrence, efficiency goals of competition law) is also intricate.

Relevant EU law will probably develop further sporadically in preliminary rulings as suitable requests arrive at the ECJ, and indeed, the best remedy

[50] See eg the Irish implementing Act: European Union (Actions for Damages for Infringements of Competition Law) Regulations 2017, available at: www.irishstatutebook.ie/eli/2017/si/43/made/en/pdf; the Spanish Competition Act: Ley 15/2007 de Defensa de la Competencia (LDC), §§ 71–73 and 76–79, available at: www.boe.es/buscar/act.php?id=BOE-A-2007-12946; the Swedish Competition Infringement Damages Act: Konkurrensskadelag (2016:964), available at: www.riksdagen.se/sv/dokument-lagar/dokument/svensk-forfattningssamling/konkurrensskadelag-2016964_sfs-2016-964; the Finnish Competition Infringement Damages Act: Laki kilpailuoikeudellisista vahingonkorvauksista (1077/2016), available at: www.finlex.fi/fi/laki/alkup/2016/20161077; the German Competition Act: Gesetz gegen Wettbewerbsbeschränkungen (GWB), §§ 33–33c, available at: www.gesetze-im-internet.de/gwb/BJNR252110998.html#BJNR252110998BJNG019300118; the Austrian Competition Act: Kartellgesetz 2005, §§ 37a–37f, available at: www.jusline.at/gesetz/kartg; the Estonian Competition Act: Konkurentsiseadus, §§ 78, 782–783, available at: www.riigiteataja.ee/akt/120122017007.

for the conundrums explored here is new preliminary ruling requests by national courts – which should note the genuine ambiguities of EU law. More detailed guidance by the ECJ would promote harmonising central aspects of damages claims. However, the possibility exists that also the ECJ, just like the EU legislators, intends to avoid in-depth instructions on fact-intensive causation and damage evaluations. After all, some opportunities to discuss these matters in detail have already presented themselves.[51]

[51] See in particular *Kone* (n 14). As regards, Member State liability, see eg *Brasserie* (n 22); the relatively fruitful-looking preliminary ruling questions are found in paras 8 and 14.

# 13

# *The Presumption of Harm and its Implementation in the Member States' Legal Orders*

PIETER VAN CLEYNENBREUGEL*

## I. INTRODUCTION

THE OBLIGATION IMPOSED on Member States to explicitly acknowledge that cartels are presumed to cause harm is one of the key novelties introduced by Directive 2014/104/EU (the Directive).[1] As a result of that presumption, for the purpose of damages actions, harm to consumers and competitors is presumed to be present whenever a cartel is in place. As a legal presumption, it would allow claimants to proceed more easily with their action and to obtain damages for competition law infringements more effectively.[2] Although the presumption of harm seems straightforward in both its purpose and focus, its exact scope of application, as a matter of both EU and Member States' national law, has not received much attention, especially in contrast with other rules and presumptions included in the Damages Directive. Insight into that feature is nevertheless more necessary now than ever if only to avoid the presumption becoming an empty shell devoid of practical use.

The purpose of this chapter is to shed light on the interpretation problems accompanying the presumption of harm in the wake of transposition of the Damages Directive. To that end, the second section of this chapter will explore the legal nature and the scope of application of the presumption of harm underlying the Damages Directive. That analysis allows the inference that underneath

* Professor of European Union law, Liège Competition and Innovation Institute, University of Liège, Belgium, pieter.vancleynenbreugel@uliege.be.

[1] Directive 2014/104/EU of the European Parliament and of the Council of 26 November 2014 on certain rules governing actions for damages under national law for infringements of the competition law provisions of the Member States and of the European Union, [2014] OJ L349/1.

[2] That position would allow claimants to exercise their right to full compensation more effectively, as stated in Art 1(1) of Directive 2014/104 (n 1).

the surface of a clear and logical presumption, Member States still retain an important degree of autonomy in shaping and transposing the presumption. Acknowledging this potential for varied transpositions, the third section will summarise how the presumption has been transposed in the laws of seven Member States. That overview, although not fully representative of the varieties in place at the level of the Member States, permits a focus on key remaining interpretation and application problems accompanying the presumption of harm. The chapter will therefore conclude that even after the transposition deadline, many open questions remain to be addressed and resolved on this subject matter in the years to come.

## II. THE LEGAL NATURE AND SCOPE OF APPLICATION OF THE PRESUMPTION OF HARM

According to Article 17(2) of the Directive, it shall be presumed that cartel infringements cause harm. This presumption, which forms part of a provision devoted to the *quantification* of harm, has been inserted in order, according to the Commission,

> to remedy the information asymmetry and some of the difficulties associated with quantifying harm in competition law cases, and to ensure the effectiveness of claims for damages, it is appropriate to presume that cartel infringements result in harm, in particular via an effect on prices.[3]

It goes beyond the purpose of this chapter to revisit the origins of the presumption of harm in the Damages Directive.[4] Suffice it to say here that the Commission only introduced the presumption in the wake of an economic study – which has been the object of criticism[5] – pointing at the quasi-permanent presence of harm for others when a cartel is in place.[6] Translating the findings of that study into law, the Commission opted for a legal presumption as phrased in Article 17(2) of the Directive. This section offers some background on the legal nature (A.) and the scope of application of the presumption (B.) before questioning the impact on both nature and leeway granted to Member States when transposing the presumption (C.).

[3] Recital 47 in Directive 2014/104 (n 1).

[4] For an analysis in that regard, see M Iacovides, 'The Presumption and Quantification of Harm in the Directive and the Practical Guide' in M Bergström, MC Iacovides and M Strand (eds), *Harmonising EU Competition Litigation: The New Directive and Beyond* (Oxford, Hart, 2016) 298–300.

[5] See C Weidt, 'The Directive on Actions for Antitrust Damages after Passing the European Parliament' (2014) 35(9) *European Competition Law Review* 438, 442.

[6] See Oxera and a multi-jurisdictional team of lawyers led by A Komninos, 'Quantifying Antitrust Damages – Towards Non-Binding Guidance for Courts', available at: http://ec.europa.eu/competition/antitrust/actionsdamages/quantification_study.pdf, and also Iacovides, The Presumption and Quantification of Harm in the Directive and the Practical Guide' (n 4) 299.

## A. Legal Nature

In formulating the presumption of harm, the Directive did not explicitly elaborate on the legal nature of such a presumption. The common definition of a presumption is an *act of accepting that something is true until it is proved not true*;[7] while a *legal* presumption refers to the inscription of such an act of acceptance in a legal instrument (statute, regulatory practice or precedent case). As a result, as a matter of law, it will be accepted that certain facts are true, unless you prove up to a certain legal standard that those facts are not correct in the specific case at hand.[8]

The adoption or recognition of legal presumptions is most likely to alter the *burden of proof* imposed on litigating parties. To the extent that constituent elements triggering the legal presumption have been proven, claimants will be deemed to have adduced, to a sufficient legal standard, proof that specific behaviour was engaged in. The defendant party subsequently bears the burden of proving that the presumption cannot apply to the factual situation at hand, by virtue of being rebutted or inapplicable. As such, reliance on presumptions generally has the effect of shifting the legal burden of proof from the claimant to the defendant party. Such effects may be inscribed in the law itself, as a legal consequence of the presumption at hand, or may factually follow from the application of the presumption in itself.[9] In the latter case, the burden of proof is not formally shifted, but the type of evidence to be adduced by either party will be centred on the scope and extent of the presumption at play in the specific case.

Legal presumptions also affect the *standard of proof* and the legal tests that need to be fulfilled in order for a certain kind of behaviour to be deemed present. Whereas, in general, the party claiming something has to prove its claim to a sufficient legal standard – *actori incumbit probatio* – presumptions have the effect of allowing such party to infer the proof of its claim from the presence of 'shortcut' elements. Those shortcut elements are then to be considered as sufficient indications of the presence of illegal or potentially illegal behaviour. In competition law, such shortcuts would point towards a presumption of harmful or anticompetitive intent on the part of businesses or to the presumptive existence of anticompetitive effects. In both instances, adducing elements that could

[7] A presumption is defined as 'a legal inference that must be made in light of certain facts. Most presumptions are rebuttable, meaning that they are rejected if proven to be false or at least thrown into sufficient doubt by the evidence. Other presumptions are conclusive, meaning that they must be accepted to be true without any opportunity for rebuttal', www.law.cornell.edu/wex/presumption.

[8] P Ibáñez Colomo, '*Intel* and Article 102 TFEU Case Law: Making Sense of a Perpetual Controversy', LSE Law, Society and Economy Working Paper 29/2014, www.lse.ac.uk/collections/law/wps/WPS2014-29_Colomo.pdf 15.

[9] F Castillo de la Torre, 'Evidence, Proof and Judicial Review in Cartel Cases' (2009) 32(4) *World Competition* 505, 516.

trigger the presumption thus suffices to infer anticompetitive intent or prima facie anticompetitive effects. As such, those presumptions facilitate the task of detecting, addressing and ending infringements in specific case situations,[10] without full evidence of illegal behaviour having to be adduced.

In that regard, an additional familiar distinction is also made between conclusive and rebuttable presumptions. A conclusive presumption means that the opposing or defendant party cannot rebut – through factual evidence – the claim made by the enforcement authority in a specific situation.[11] A rebuttable presumption operates in a slightly different fashion. In that situation, the offering of probable evidence triggers the presumption that sufficient evidence to hint at illicit practices is present. Such presumptions point towards situations where conclusions can be inferred on the basis of probabilities reflected in certain evidence.[12] Proof to the contrary could be adduced, most likely by the opposing party, following the application of the presumption. In case evidentiary materials are to be rebutted, it may suffice that the defendant or opposing party claims that evidence to the contrary may convincingly be offered, rebutting the presumption of evidence *à charge* with evidence *à décharge*.

The presumption of harm included in the Directive clearly fits the above-mentioned conceptual description of a legal presumption. It allows claimants to shortcut their analysis by acting on the belief that a cartel has indeed caused harm. As an evidentiary rule, the presumption of harm in Article 17(2) of the Directive is not conclusive. The Directive acknowledges explicitly that the infringer should be able to rebut the presumption, showing that the claimant concerned did not suffer harm as a result of the cartel. In its current set-up, the presumption additionally also has an impact on both the burden and standard of proof. On the one hand, the presumption allows a claimant for damages to limit his action to asserting evidence of a cartel and to proceed with the quantification of damages suffered. The applicant no longer needs to show that actual harm was suffered; it instead falls upon the defendant to prove that no harm was done to the applicant in the case at hand by engaging in cartelism. As such, the general obligation imposed on the applicant (*actori incumbit probatio*) to prove the existence of harm is replaced by an obligation on the defendant to prove that no harm was done in any circumstances. On the other hand, the operation of this presumption tends to modify the standard of proof required in order to successfully claim damages in the context of competition law infringements. Whereas, in traditional instances of non-contractual liability law, a claimant

[10] D Bailey, 'Presumptions in EU Competition Law' (2010) 31(9) *European Competition Law Review* 362. See also C Ritter, 'Presumptions in EU Competition Law', available at: https://papers.ssrn.com/sol3/papers.cfm?abstract_id=2999638, accessed 16 January 2018.

[11] See on such 'assumptions' A-L Sibony, *Le juge et le raisonnement économique en droit de la concurrence* (Paris, LGDJ, 2008) 535 and Ibáñez Colomo, '*Intel* and Article 102 TFEU Case Law' (n 8) 14.

[12] Bailey, 'Presumptions in EU Competition Law' (n 10) 363.

had to prove a fault, harm and a causal link between both, the presumption effectively lowers the standard to do so by considering that no evidence on the existence as such of harm has to be adduced. At the same time, however, the presumption does not discharge a claimant from the obligation to prove a causal link, and therefore, the extent of the harm caused.[13]

## B. Scope of Application

Although the presumption offers an evidentiary rule capable of shifting both the burden and altering the standard of proof, its scope of application is far from absolute. In its current set-up in Article 17(2) of the Directive, it is effectively circumscribed by two conditions limiting its applicability.

First, the presumption only applies in relation to cartels. The Directive defines a cartel as

> an agreement or concerted practice between two or more competitors aimed at coordinating their competitive behaviour on the market or influencing the relevant parameters of competition through practices such as, but not limited to, the fixing or coordination of purchase or selling prices or other trading conditions, including in relation to intellectual property rights, the allocation of production or sales quotas, the sharing of markets and customers, including bid-rigging, restrictions of imports or exports or anti-competitive actions against other competitors.[14]

Preamble 47 explains in that regard that 'it is appropriate to limit this rebuttable presumption to cartels, given their secret nature, which increases the information asymmetry and makes it more difficult for claimants to obtain the evidence necessary to prove the harm'. Although it logically follows on from this that unilateral abusive behaviour does not benefit from the presumption, it would be incorrect to state that the applicability of the presumption extends to all types of collusive behaviour covered by Article 101 TFEU. Indeed, the presumption only applies to the extent that a cartel is in place. From the definition of a cartel given in the Directive, it would seem that both horizontal and vertical agreements or concerted practices could enter the scope of a 'cartel' envisaged by the Damages Directive. At the same time, the Directive's definition does not seem to include decisions by associations of undertakings and does not offer a closed list of restrictive practices deemed to reflect the presence of a cartel. The examples stated in the Directive all seem to qualify as the most obvious 'restrictions by object', raising the question whether, as regards the Directive, other restrictions by object and 'restrictions by effect' prohibited by Article 101(1) TFEU would also qualify as cartels. As the definition leaves it

[13] See the chapter by K Havu in this volume.
[14] Art 2(14) of Directive 2014/104 (n 1).

open to Member States to qualify other types of behaviour as cartels, it would seem that there is nothing that impedes that transposed laws offer more detailed definitions in this regard. In any case, it will fall upon judges in Member States – and at the Court of Justice of the European Union – to interpret the definition of a cartel in accordance with EU law.

Second, the presumption only relates to the existence of harm emanating from a cartel. It does not allow claimants to escape from having to quantify the harm suffered. In that context, the presumption serves above all as an obligation on national judges not to dismiss cases for lack of proof of harm. From that perspective, the presumption of harm allows Member State judges to proceed more easily to the quantification stage, not losing time on questioning whether harm is in place. Article 17(1) of the Directive adds to this that Member State judges should be able to estimate the harm caused by the anticompetitive behaviour concerned. It would not, however, seem to prevent a judge from estimating that the harm done amounts to a quantified amount of zero. The quantification of damages remains a matter for Member States' jurisdictions, to be determined on the basis of national private law, albeit in accordance with the principles of equivalence and effectiveness.[15]

### C. Transposing the Presumption of Harm: Still Room for Member State Variation?

On the basis of the analysis of the nature and scope of the presumption of harm developed above, one might at first sight conclude that Member States do not have much leeway in shaping the presumption in their national laws. From that perspective, Member States have to provide for an evidentiary rule that lowers the standard required to prove harm for the applicant and need to put in place a legal framework that enables the defendant to rebut the presence of harm in the context of damages actions. On top of that, Member States have to impose such a presumption only in relation to cartels as defined in the Directive. Beyond those minimum requirements, however, there are three ways in which Member States still retain a degree of autonomy in how to transpose the presumption. It is interesting to note that the degree left to Member States enables them both to extend and to limit the scope of application of the presumption of harm.

Firstly, the Directive remains silent on the actual harm that is presumed. It would therefore not seem unlikely for a Member State to circumscribe or limit the presumption to a specific type of harm being incurred and to ask for other kinds of damage to be proven in a more explicit way by the claimant. Taking a hypothetical example, a national legislator would be able to limit the

[15] Art 17(1) of Directive 2014/104 (n 1).

presumption of harm to the establishment that cartels lead to only certain types of economic damage, eg reputational damage, to a claimant, quantifying the damages awarded on the basis of the national rules regarding those particular damages. The Directive only states that the principle needs to be accompanied by rules making the standard and burden of proof required for the *quantification* of harm not impossible or excessively difficult.[16] No reference is made to the existence of all kinds of harm, leading to the conclusion that the legislator could, in principle, limit the presumption of harm to a single type of harm.

Secondly, the presumption only applies in relation to cartels as defined by the Directive. The definition offered in the Directive outlines the minimum conditions under which certain agreements or practices are considered to be cartels. That definition is not exhaustive and could include practices not mentioned explicitly therein. Nothing would seem to prevent a Member State from adding certain categories of cartel-like behaviour to the definition in the Directive. In the same way, nothing would seem to impede that the presumption is also extended to include unilateral anticompetitive behaviour. The Directive does not impose maximally harmonised standards in this regard,[17] leaving room for Member States to extend the scope of the presumption of harm. As a result, Member States in this instance could opt for a more expansive interpretation of the presumption of harm.

Thirdly, the presumption is rebuttable indeed, but the Directive remains silent on what kind of rebutting evidence needs to be adduced and when this would be sufficient. Again, it will fall upon the Member States to lay down more detailed procedural rules. Those rules have to respect the principles of equivalence and effectiveness as a matter of EU law.

It follows from the above that although the presumption of harm has to be incorporated in the laws of the Member States, those states are free to tailor and operationalise the presumption to the specificities of their own legal order. It is therefore important to analyse how the presumption has been interpreted, in an attempt to uncover the remaining interpretation and application gaps any current set-up may result in at Member State level.

## III. THE IMPLEMENTATION OF THE PRESUMPTION OF HARM IN MEMBER STATES' LAWS: OPEN ISSUES

The transposition of the presumption of harm does not seem to have varied very much across different Member States (A.). The limited variety notwithstanding, the ways in which the presumption has been transposed still allow

[16] Again, in Art 17(1) of Directive 2014/104 (n 1); Art 17(2) does not refer to those principles.

[17] See the chapter by M Hjärtström and J Nowag in this volume.

for application and interpretation problems to remain in place. It goes without saying that those problems will have to be addressed at some point by Member States' courts and the Court of Justice of the European Union in the years to come (B.).

### A. Transposing the Presumption into the Law of the Member States

As far as the Directive is concerned, the presumption of harm has a rather specific role in a relatively limited context. It functions as a tool to permit national judges to proceed more easily to an estimation of harm in the specific context of a cartel. It was therefore to be expected that Member States would also transpose the principle in an equally narrow fashion. This section offers an overview of the way in which seven Member States (France, Austria, Germany, the Netherlands, Belgium, the United Kingdom and the Republic of Ireland) have translated the presumption of harm into their national laws on damages actions. Although this hardly offers a full overview, these seven Member States at least allow us to sketch the quasi-uniform and limited ways in which the presumption of harm has been transposed.

In France, Directive 2014/104 has been transposed by means of an Ordonnance of 9 March 2017, which has modified the French Code de Commerce.[18] According to newly inserted Article L. 481-7 of the Code, it is presumed that all '*ententes*' between competitors cause harm, until proof to the contrary is delivered (by the defendant). Neither the Ordonnance nor the Decree accompanying it[19] defines the notion of '*ententes*' explicitly. In a Report to the President of the Republic accompanying the new legislation, the French legislature nevertheless indicates that the notion of '*entente*' refers to all violations of Article L.420-1 of the Code de Commerce, which is the equivalent of Article 101 TFEU.[20] To the extent that this would be the case, not only cartels as defined in the Directive, but also other restrictive agreements, decisions or practices that do not as such constitute cartels, would trigger the presumption of harm under French law. In doing so, the legislator extends the scope of the presumption beyond what is implied in the Directive. At the same time, however, French law seems to limit the scope of the presumption to cartels 'between competitors' (*entre concurrents*). Although this feature is not defined, you could argue

[18] Ordonnance n° 2017-303 du 9 mars 2017 relative aux actions en dommages et intérêts du fait des pratiques anticoncurrentielles, available at: www.legifrance.gouv.fr.

[19] Décret n° 2017-305 du 9 mars 2017 relatif aux actions en dommages et intérêts du fait des pratiques anticoncurrentielles, available at: www.legifrance.gouv.fr.

[20] Rapport au Président de la République relatif à l'ordonnance n° 2017-303 du 9 mars 2017 relative aux actions en dommages et intérêts du fait des pratiques anticoncurrentielles, available at: www.legifrance.gouv.fr.

that this would imply that the presumption only applies in relation to horizontal restrictive practices, as has also been the case in Austria.[21] In addition, the Ordonnance defines clearly the types of harm that can be presumed: losses suffered because of overcharges or not being able to lower prices, profits forgone because of a lower volume of sales, the loss of a chance and moral losses.[22] In the absence of case-law, it remains to be seen what kind of losses can be presumed to directly flow from the existence of an '*entente*' under French law at this stage.

The Austrian transposition of the Directive resembles its French counterpart. According to §37 of the Austrian Competition Act, a cartel 'between competitors' is supposed to cause harm.[23] Although the Act incorporates the definition of a cartel developed in the context of the Damages Directive, it explicitly limits the scope of the presumption only to cartels between competitors (*zwischen Wettbewerbern*), which again seems to imply only horizontal agreements and concerted practices. In addition, Austrian law allows for the rebuttal of the presumption, but does not explain how it can be rebutted in detail. Austrian law also does not define the type of harm that a cartel is presumed to cause.

In doing so, both the Austrian and French legislators seem at first sight to rely on a narrower interpretation of the cartel notion than the one proposed by the EU Directive, which is not explicitly limited to horizontal agreements. It remains to be seen whether this interpretation is considered compatible with the definition of a cartel in the Directive, which does not prima facie limit its scope to horizontal agreements. This is undoubtedly a matter that will fall upon the Court of Justice to clarify shortly.

The German, Belgian and Dutch transpositions of the Directive have stayed closer to the letter of Article 17(2) of the Directive. According to §33 of the German Competition Act, a cartel is presumed to cause harm. That presumption could nevertheless be rebutted. The German Act has copied the definition of a cartel as proposed by the Damages Directive, and only applies that definition in the context of the presumption of harm.[24] The Belgian Act transposing the Directive also relies on the Directive's definition of a cartel, before stating that an infringement of competition law committed by a cartel is presumed to cause harm, unless the infringer succeeds in rebutting the presumption.[25] In the Netherlands, Articles 193k-m were added to the sixth book of its Civil Code.

[21] §37c Kartellgesetz 2005, available at: www.jusline.at/gesetz/kartg/paragraf/37c.

[22] Art L481-3 Code de Commerce.

[23] See n 21.

[24] §33, Gesetz gegen Wettbewerbsbeschränkungen (GWB), available at: www.gesetze-im-internet.de/gwb/BJNR252110998.html.

[25] Loi du 6 juin 2017 portant insertion d'un Titre 3 ' L'action en dommages et intérêts pour les infractions au droit de la concurrence' dans le Livre XVII du Code de droit économique, portant insertion des définitions propres au Livre XVII, Titre 3 dans le Livre Ier et portant diverses modifications au Code de droit économique (1), available at: www.ejustice.just.fgov.be.

Those provisions confirm that a cartel infringing competition law is presumed to cause harm, relying on the definition of a cartel as stated in the Directive.[26] No specific provision is made regarding the possibility to rebut the presumption or to the legal nature of the presumption as a matter of German, Belgian or Dutch law. In those three legal orders, the notion of harm is to be defined in accordance with the principles applicable in their non-contractual liability laws.

The United Kingdom shows a similar pattern of transposition. The UK transposing Regulations confirm the existence of a rebuttable presumption of harm in the context of cartels, relying fully on the cartel definition proposed by the Directive. The implementing legislation contains neither specific rules on the types of harm nor on the specific requirements to rebut the presumption. That matter remains to be determined in accordance with the principles and precedents applicable in tort law.[27] The Republic of Ireland transposed the presumption in the same way as the United Kingdom.[28]

The non-exhaustive overview offered here shows that most Member States included in the seven state regimes compared have relied on quite a literal transposition of the presumption as stated in the Directive. At the same time, however, diversified transposition developments can also be detected in France and Austria. At this stage, it would still be too early to state that the different transpositions also have an impact on how the presumption will be interpreted in practice. That is something that remains to be seen in the years to come. For now, you could conclude by saying that there exists variety in the interpretation of the presumption, albeit to a relatively limited extent.

### B. Open Issues Remaining after Transposition

Although the transposition of the presumption of harm has given rise to some varieties, the overall picture sketched in the previous subsection is that Member States have generally stuck to copying the presumption as stated in the Directive in their own national laws. It is nevertheless submitted that sticking to the presumption as crafted by the Directive is not entirely unproblematic, as the

[26] See Art 193k-l, inserted by Wet van 25 januari 2017, houdende wijziging van Boek 6 van het Burgerlijk Wetboek en het Wetboek van Burgerlijke Rechtsvordering, in verband met de omzetting van Richtlijn 2014/104/EU van het Europees Parlement en de Raad van 26 november 2014 betreffende bepaalde regels voor schadevorderingen volgens nationaal recht wegens inbreuken op de bepalingen van het mededingingsrecht van de lidstaten en van de Europese Unie (Implementatiewet richtlijn privaatrechtelijke handhaving mededingingsrecht), available at: https://zoek.officielebekendmakingen.nl/stb-2017-28.html.

[27] Point 13 of Sch 8A attached to the 1998 Competition Act, inserted by The Claims in respect of Loss or Damage arising from Competition Infringements (Competition Act 1998 and Other Enactments (Amendment)) Regulations 2017, available at: www.legislation.gov.uk.

[28] Part 5(2) of SI No 43/2017 – European Union (Actions for Damages for Infringements of Competition Law) Regulations 2017, available at: www.irishstatutebook.ie.

invocability and day-to-day application of the presumption is fraught with uncertainty. In terms of application and successful invocability, the nature of the harm caused and the interpretation given to the cartel definition remain points of contestation (i.). In terms of the day-to-day application by Member States' courts, issues arise regarding the rebuttal of the presumption and the practical implementation of the presumption in conjunction with the quantification of harm (ii.). In order to avoid the presumption of harm becoming an empty shell, highlighting those problems and addressing them will be a necessity in the years to come. This subsection summarises the challenges brought about by the presumption and offers suggestions on how to address them more directly.

### *i. Envisaged Invocation Problems*

As far as the possibility of successfully invoking the presumption of harm is concerned, at present two elements continue to pose problems to its successful and streamlined application across the European Union. With slightly more attention being paid to those issues at the EU level, however, the problems identified could be alleviated rather easily.

Firstly, the successful invocation and application of the presumption of harm can be limited by means of a strict interpretation of the notion of harm. Although the Directive prescribes that cartels are supposed to cause harm and that this harm relates in principle to a rise in prices or not being able to lower prices,[29] it does not require Member States to accept that cartels cause all kinds of economic, personal or moral harm. Indeed, it can be submitted that the open-ended nature of the presumption of harm only requires that Member States presume a certain kind of harm, the extent of which is subsequently to be quantified by the judicial body concerned in accordance with national law and the guidance principles offered in the notice on the quantification of harm.[30] To that extent, it is not unlikely that a court in a Member State legal order considers that a cartel is only presumed to cause certain types of harm, eg reputational harm and that other types of harm have to be adduced more explicitly. In the absence of a CJEU judgment explaining whether a limitation of the presumption of harm to reputational damage squares with the principle of effectiveness or of a modification to the Directive, Member States' courts in principle remain at liberty to interpret the presumption as they please. It would therefore not be unlikely that the presumption will be interpreted narrowly at best or be downplayed at worst. The French legislature has clearly defined the different types of harm that can be caused by a cartel. Perhaps linking a legislative or judicial definition of harm to the harm presumption across the different legal

[29] Recital 47 of Directive 2014/104 (n 1).

[30] See the Commission's guidance principles in that respect, available at: http://ec.europa.eu/competition/antitrust/actionsdamages/quantification_guide_en.pdf.

orders of the Member States legal orders more directly might be a good idea. The Commission could call upon the Member States to streamline their different private law approaches in that regard by means of a guidance document, even though the use of soft law is most likely to trigger objections, both from the point of view of EU law and the principle of legal certainty and from the point of view of national legal orders wanting to safeguard the integrity and coherence of their own private law system.

Secondly, questions remain regarding the relationship between the presumption and the cartel definition. As highlighted earlier in this chapter,[31] the Damages Directive offers a definition of a 'cartel' outlining different forms and types of behaviour that should be considered cartelist. The EU legislature has nevertheless made it clear that the types of behaviour included in that definition are not exhaustive.[32] Member States should therefore be at liberty to interpret the notion of a cartel more widely than the definition offered by the Directive. The French transposition seems to offer an example of this, as it has interpreted the notion of a cartel to include, on the one hand, more types of behaviour than those listed in the Directive's definition, while on the other, it only seems to limit them to horizontal business relationships.[33] To the extent that the definition of a cartel differs from Member State to Member State, it is most likely that the application and successful invocability rates of the presumption will differ as well. That in itself could give rise to some kind of forum shopping, as some Member States may tolerate the presumption of harm more easily. It remains to be seen to what extent the possibility of such forum shopping results in Member States' courts or legislators limiting the extent of the presumption of harm to instances covered by the cartel definition in the Directive or in continuing to extend the presumption beyond that definition in order to attract more damages claims in their courts.

### *ii. Envisaged Day-to-Day Application Problems*

In terms of the day-to-day application of the presumption of harm by national courts, the Directive also left two gaps that have not directly been addressed in the Member States' transpositions studied in this chapter.

Firstly, the conditions to be fulfilled in order to successfully rebut the presumption of harm remain unclear, which may have an impact on the invocability of the presumption. It would seem that Member States' legislators and judges remain at liberty to interpret the scope for rebuttal more widely or more narrowly, as long as the EU principles of equivalence and effectiveness are respected.[34] This is likely to give rise to a variety of rebuttal regimes that could

[31] See section II.B above.
[32] Art 2(14) of Directive 2014/104 (n 1) refers to 'practices such as, but not limited to'.
[33] See n 22.
[34] Art 4 *juncto* 17(2) of Directive 2014/104 (n 1).

make the presumption of harm inapplicable in practice. Neither the Directive nor the transposed legal regimes studied in this chapter directly address the rebuttal of the presumption. As such, its application at Member State level remains open for now. Again, a more streamlined Commission initiative, offering more concrete guidance on how to organise the rebuttal stage, would be a welcome addition to the legal regime in place.

Secondly, the application of the presumption of harm is closely related to the assessment to be made of the quantification of harm.[35] The presumption allows Member States' judges to proceed immediately with the quantification of the harm suffered, as the fact that harm has been caused is deemed to be established in a private damages action as long as the infringer does not succeed in rebutting the presence of harm. The Commission has adopted guidance on how to quantify harm and requires national judges to estimate the amount of harm if no exact quantification can be made.[36] In the same way, national competition authorities can be asked to intervene in quantification assessments.[37] The different models and techniques offered by the Commission in its practical guidance all assume that a cartel causes a certain kind of economic harm. However, as was stated above,[38] the presumption could in practice be limited to only certain heads of damages, eg damages for reputational harm. To the extent that the presumption is interpreted in this narrow fashion, the models and techniques outlined in the practical guidance offered by the Commission to quantify economic damage could still be discarded rather easily by the Member States' courts. Therefore, should the Commission update its guidance, it would seem appropriate to link it more explicitly to the presumption of harm and to be clearer on the types of harm that are to be presumed present. Doing so might discourage Member States' courts from discarding the guidelines and would offer at least some guidance to those courts. That is all the more relevant given the absence of CJEU case-law on the matter and the fact that it may take a few more years before the first references for a preliminary ruling on the interpretation of the Directive will emerge.

## IV. CONCLUSION

The presumption of harm included in Article 17(2) of the Damages Directive requires Member States' courts to presume that cartels cause harm, allowing claimants to immediately bring arguments relating to the quantification of such harm. The presumption, although very clear at first sight, leaves issues relating to its scope of application unresolved, allowing for varied transpositions

[35] See also Iacovides (n 4) 299.
[36] See n 30.
[37] Art 17(3) of Directive 2014/104 (n 1); see also the chapter by M Iacovides in this volume.
[38] Subsection III.A.i.

in Member States' private laws. This chapter has offered an overview of the legal nature and scope of application of the presumption, prior to analysing how the presumption has been transposed into the laws of seven Member States (France, Belgium, the Netherlands, Germany, Austria, the United Kingdom and Ireland). The overview leads to the conclusion that the presumption has been transposed rather literally in most legal orders, although France and Austria have added their own accents. It has therefore been submitted that the invocation and day-to-day application of the presumption of harm in disputes before Member States' courts are not entirely unproblematic. The chapter has highlighted some concerns and called for a more streamlined follow-up approach by the European Commission in an attempt to avoid the presumption from becoming an empty shell. The application of the presumption in the years to come will highlight the extent to which more guidance at EU level may indeed prove necessary.

# 14

# *Article 17(3) of the Damages Directive and the Interaction Between the Swedish Competition Authority and Swedish Courts*

MARIOS C IACOVIDES*

## I. INTRODUCTION

ONE OF THE explicit aims of the Directive on competition damages actions (the Directive)[1] is to make the quantification of harm resulting from violations of European Union (EU) competition rules easier for damages claimants.[2] One of the several ways envisioned by the Directive to achieve that aim is Article 17(3), according to which national competition authorities (NCAs) may assist national courts in quantifying the harm caused by anticompetitive conduct.

In this chapter, I focus on the transposition of Article 17(3) of the Directive in Sweden and make the argument that Sweden has not correctly implemented the Article in Swedish law. The topic is admittedly rather limited at first glance, but a discussion on the (non-)transposition of Article 17(3) of the Directive in Swedish law offers three significant insights which make pursuing it worthwhile.

* Dr Marios C Iacovides (marios.iacovides@juridicum.su.se) LL.B (King's College London), LL.M (Stockholm University), LL.D (Uppsala University) is Assistant Professor in European Law at Stockholm University and Legal Counsel at the Swedish Competition Authority. All opinions expressed in this chapter are strictly personal and shall not be interpreted as representing the position of the Swedish Competition Authority. The author would like to thank participants at the conference 'EU Competition Law and the New Private Enforcement Regime: First Experiences from its Implementation' in Uppsala in June 2017 for useful comments and ideas as well as M Strand for very useful feedback. All errors and omissions remain the author's.

[1] Directive 2014/104/EU of the European Parliament and of the Council of 26 November 2014 on certain rules governing actions for damages under national law for infringements of the competition law provisions of the Member States and of the European Union [2014] OJ L349/1.

[2] Directive 2014/104 (n 1) Recitals 14 and 46.

Firstly, it informs us about the nature and degree of interaction of the Swedish Competition Authority (SCA) with Swedish courts and tells us something about the relationship between the two. Secondly, it reveals some important procedural differences between private and public enforcement of EU competition rules in Sweden and exposes a certain tension between national rules of procedure, on the one hand, and the effective application of EU competition rules in Sweden, on the other. 'Effectiveness' is a requirement that follows both from well-established case-law of the Court of Justice of the EU (ECJ)[3] and from the Directive itself.[4] As a result, the second insight inevitably leads to a discussion on whether certain aspects of Swedish procedural law may be impeding the effective application of EU competition law. Thirdly, it explores different courses of action for Swedish courts and claimants that may find, like this author, that Article 17(3) has not been implemented correctly in Swedish law.

The rest of this chapter is organised as follows. Section II briefly presents the legislative history of Article 17(3) and offers a quick look into some of the *travaux préparatoires*. Section III discusses the aim of Article 17(3) as revealed by its broader context and soft law. Section IV offers some background on certain aspects of Swedish procedural law that are relevant for the chapter. Section V deals with the choice of the Swedish legislator not to introduce any specific provisions in order to transpose Article 17(3) into the Swedish legal order and puts forward this chapter's main thesis, namely that Article 17(3) of the Directive has not been correctly transposed into Swedish law. Section VI concludes.

## II. THE LEGISLATIVE HISTORY OF ARTICLE 17(3)

In order to be able to assess whether Article 17(3) has been correctly transposed in the Swedish legal order, the purpose of the Article needs to be understood. To do that, we first need to embark on a short excursus through the Article's legislative history and *travaux préparatoires*.

The Directive has as its legal basis the combination of Articles 103 and 114 TFEU. Adopting a Directive under those Articles is done under Article 289 TFEU, the ordinary legislative procedure, and in accordance with the procedures provided for under Article 294 TFEU. The legislative initiative rests with the European Commission (Commission).[5] A consultation process, in the form of Green and White Papers, usually precedes a Commission proposal for secondary

[3] See eg Case C-453/99 *Courage v Crehan* EU:C:2001:465, para 29; Joined Cases C-295/04 to C-298/04 *Vincenzo Manfredi v Lloyd Adriatico Assicurazioni SpA* EU:C:2006:461, para 62; and Case C-360/09 *Pfleiderer AG v Bundeskartellamt* EU:C:2011:389, para 30.

[4] Directive 2014/104 (n 1) Art 4.

[5] TFEU, Art 289(1).

legislation and the process that led up to the drafting of the Damages Directive was no exception in that regard. Nothing resembling Article 17(3) can be found in the 2005 Green Paper[6] or the 2008 White Paper.[7]

The earliest trace of the provision is contained in the external impact assessment study entitled 'Making antitrust damages actions more effective in the EU: welfare impact and potential scenarios' (impact assessment study) which accompanied the White Paper.[8] The impact assessment study contains a suggestion to create a cooperation mechanism between NCAs and national courts, whereby 'if the defendant's conduct appears as a serious infringement of competition laws, conducive to substantial harm to society, then judges might wish to activate a [NCA] as *amicus curiae* to quantify the harm caused by the defendant'.[9]

The impact assessment study identified problems with the proposal, predominantly because of the cost associated with involving the NCAs in proceedings for antitrust damages. As pointed out in the study, a public antitrust investigation does not typically involve quantifying the damage suffered by individuals. What NCAs look for is evidence that the allegedly anticompetitive conduct has harmed competition, or that it at least has the capacity or is capable of doing so. What qualifies as harm to competition in EU competition law, even following the onset of the 'more economic approach',[10] may be much broader than 'consumer welfare' and, in fact, may even be different from direct harm to customers or consumers as a group, let alone to individual customers or consumers. Therefore, the study suggested that intervention from NCAs with the purpose of assisting national courts in quantifying the harm caused to individuals would be economically viable only if the threshold for activating the procedure were very high. Therefore, the study suggested that such intervention should be reserved for cases with very high stakes.[11]

[6] European Commission, 'Green Paper on Damages Actions for Breach of the EC Antitrust Rules', COM(2005) 672 final (Brussels, 19 December 2005).

[7] European Commission, 'White Paper on Damage Actions for Breach of the EC Antitrust Rules', COM(2008) 165 final (Brussels, 2 April 2008).

[8] Report for the European Commission, Making antitrust damages actions more effective in the EU: welfare impact and potential scenarios (Brussels, Rome and Rotterdam, 21 December 2007), available at: ec.europa.eu/competition/antitrust/actionsdamages/files_white_paper/impact_study.pdf#page=441.

[9] Impact assessment study, ibid, p 200.

[10] The term 'more economic approach' is often used as shorthand for the modernisation of EU competition law that came about in the mid-90s through the integration of economic thinking and evidence in the Commission's enforcement of the rules. See MC Iacovides, *A 'More Economic Approach' to WTO Law's Relevant Market Definition, Trade Harm, and Quantification of Trade Effects and Countermeasures – A Normative Law and Economics Comparison with EU Competition Law* (Uppsala, Uppsala University, 2016) 44–45 and White Paper on the Modernisation of the Rules Implementing Articles 85 and 86 of the EC Treaty [1999] OJ C 132/1. See also B Bishop, 'The Modernisation of DGIV' (1997) 18 *European Competition Law Review* 481.

[11] Impact assessment study (n 8) 201.

The impact assessment study's suggestion for a cooperation mechanism between NCAs and national courts on the issue of the quantification of damages in difficult high stakes cases does not seem to have won favour with the Commission at the time. The Commission presented its legislative proposal (the Draft Directive) in June 2013.[12] The original Article in the Commission's proposal corresponding to Article 17 was at the time Article 16. That Article did not include any provisions regarding the possibility for NCAs to assist national courts in quantifying the harm. Neither was any such provision contained in any other part of the Draft Directive.

The Draft Directive was subsequently scrutinised and debated in the European Parliament and the Council. Readings by the Parliament and the Council form part of the ordinary legislative procedure and both co-legislators have the right to propose amendments to the Commission's proposal. The Council's 'general approach' did not propose an amendment to what was then Article 16 of the Draft Directive.[13] However, the Parliament proposed such amendments. Following the first reading, the Parliament suggested an amendment whereby a new sentence to (then) Article 16(2) appeared. The wording in the relevant part was as follows:

> Where requested, competition authorities shall provide guidance on quantifying the harm.

The Article was further reorganised during the so-called trilogues between the European Parliament, the Council and the Commission. The trilogues resulted in further amendments to the Parliament's proposed addition and the proposed amendment was given its own paragraph in the Article, resulting in the adopted version's Article 17(3). The compromise text was worded as follows:

> Member States shall ensure that, in proceedings relating to an action for damages, a national competition authority shall be able, if it deems it appropriate, to assist on the determination of the quantum of damages upon request of a national court.

Following linguistic adjustments, the Directive was adopted by the Council with the following final wording of Article 17(3):

> Member States shall ensure that, in proceedings relating to an action for damages, a national competition authority may, upon request of a national court, assist that national court with respect to the determination of the quantum of damages where that national competition authority considers such assistance to be appropriate.

[12] Proposal for a Directive of the European Parliament and of the Council on certain rules governing actions for damages under national law for infringements of the competition law provisions of the Member States and of the European Union COM(2013) 404 final.

[13] EU Council, Proposal for a Directive of the European Parliament and of the Council on certain rules governing actions for damages under national law for infringements of the competition law provisions of the Member States and of the European Union – Adoption of the general approach, RC 43/JUSTCIV 261/CODEC 2515 (15983/13), Brussels 27 November 2013, 44.

Following the conclusion of the trilogues, COREPER endorsed the final text. In its analysis of the final compromise text, the Council observed that Article 17(3) 'enables a NCA, at its discretion if it considers it appropriate, to assist on the determination of the quantum of damages upon request of a national court'.[14]

For reasons that will become apparent further on in this chapter, it is useful to ponder on the wording of the amendment proposed by the European Parliament and the two later formulations of Article 17(3) of the Directive during the legislative process. A graphic illustration of the wording is provided in Figure 1, for ease of comparison.

**Figure 1** Article 17(3)'s legislative history

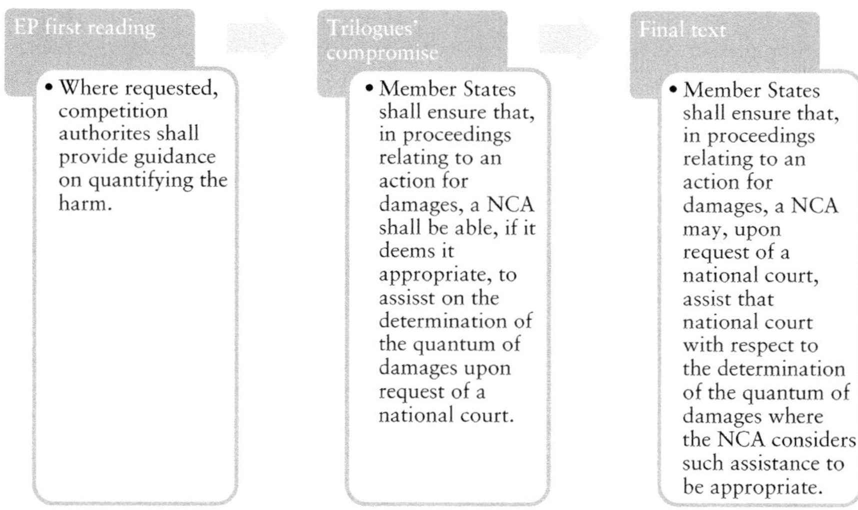


The comparison allows us to draw a few important conclusions. Firstly, the EU legislature chose explicitly to reformulate a vaguely worded 'where requested' with no indication of who the initiator of the request would have been, in order to put the initiative on making a request to the NCAs on the national courts. Secondly, the EU legislature chose to amend the originally proposed imperative 'shall' to make involvement of the NCAs simply possible ('shall be able') and finally only discretionary on the NCAs ('may […] where [it] considers such assistance to be appropriate'). Thirdly, possibly as a way of balancing the reduction in imperativeness, the EU legislature chose to change the nature of the NCAs' involvement, from providing 'guidance in quantifying the harm' to

[14] EU Council, Proposal for a Directive of the European Parliament and of the Council on certain rules governing actions for damages under national law for infringements of the competition law provisions of the Member States and of the European Union – Analysis of the final compromise text with a view to agreement, RC 6/JUSTCIV 76/CODEC 885 (8088/14), Brussels 24 March 2014, p 12.

'assist[ing] [...] with respect to the determination of the quantum of damages'. Fourthly, the final text made it clear that the said assistance is not to be provided to any of the parties, but to the national court that will have initiated the NCAs' involvement. Moreover, the EU legislature chose not to limit such requests in any way, for instance as the impact assessment study had suggested, to hard high stakes cases.

## III. THE AIM OF ARTICLE 17(3)

Beyond its legislative history, further clues as to the purpose of Article 17(3) can be discerned by looking at the whole of Article 17, and by viewing the Article in the broader context of the whole Directive and the soft law that accompanies it, as well as, naturally, the Preamble to the Directive.

Article 17(3) appears in Chapter V of the Directive, which is the chapter in the Directive that deals with the quantification of harm. Chapter V only contains one article, Article 17, consisting of three paragraphs. According to Article 17(1), Member States shall ensure that national courts can estimate the harm when it is excessively difficult or practically impossible for the applicant to do so. Member States must also make sure that the burden and standard of proof with regard to quantifying damages from violations of EU competition law shall not be such that exercising the right to damages becomes practically impossible or excessively difficult. Article 17(2) introduces a rebuttable presumption of harm in cartels. Seen in the context of the entirety of Article 17, it becomes clear that the purpose of Article 17(3) is to assist claimants further in quantifying the harm.[15]

As seen above, the goal of Article 17 of the Directive is to assist claimants in quantifying the harm they have suffered because of a violation of EU competition rules. That goal is, of course, compatible with the goal of the whole Directive, which is – broadly speaking – to encourage claims of damages and to facilitate private enforcement of EU competition law.

That said, other provisions of the Directive offer clarifications as to the extent of the goal. An important provision in this regard is Article 3 of the Directive. According to Article 3, Member States must ensure that claimants are able to obtain full compensation.[16] Full compensation for the purposes of the Directive is understood as the position in which the claimant would have been had the infringement of competition law not been committed and covers actual

[15] For a more detailed account of Directive 2014/104 (n 1) Art 17, see MC Iacovides, 'The Presumption and Quantification of Harm in the Directive and the Practical Guide' in M Bergström, MC Iacovides and M Strand (eds), *Harmonising EU Competition Litigation – The New Directive and Beyond* (Oxford, Hart Publishing, 2016).

[16] Directive 2014/104 (n 1) Art 3(1).

loss, loss of profit, plus the payment of interest.[17] However, full compensation under the Directive should not lead to overcompensation.[18] One way to avoid overcompensation according to the Directive is to account for passing-on, by putting in place appropriate procedural rules to ensure that compensation for actual loss at any level of the supply chain does not exceed the overcharge harm suffered at that level.[19] In turn, this is linked to the full effectiveness of the right to full compensation.

National courts – as Member State bodies entrusted with the effective application of EU law in their respective jurisdictions, including the Directive – must bear in mind the Directive's aversion to overcompensation. Hence, when they hear claims for damages from a claimant in a market with more than two levels, they must ensure that they do not award damages for harm that has been passed-on downstream, where the claimant is an intermediary buyer, or for harm that has been absorbed by the intermediary buyer, where the claimant is the final customer. Consequently, the caution not to overcompensate acts as a check on the goal of assisting claimants in the ways envisioned by Article 17 of the Directive.

The result is that, in certain situations, the interests of the Directive, EU competition law at large, and the national courts entrusted with applying the rules, will be independent from the interests of both parties in proceedings for damages. For instance, if the claimant inflates its claims in order to seek damages that are higher than the harm actually suffered, the goal of the national court to avoid overcompensation will not be aligned with the claimant's interests. In that situation, it is not entirely clear whether the court's interests will be aligned with the defendant's, as the latter's strategy will be to overestimate the amount of passing-on (for a direct purchaser) or to underestimate it (for a final customer) in order to avoid compensating the claimant fully. This is significant for the purposes of the chapter's thesis, as it suggests that a national court, in certain circumstances, might wish to activate the NCAs' assistance on its own motion rather than upon request from any of the parties. We will return to this point below, in section V.

In conjunction with the issuing of the Draft Directive, the Commission adopted a Communication on quantifying harm in damages actions (the Communication)[20] and issued a Practical Guide on quantifying harm in

[17] ibid, Art 3(2).

[18] ibid, Art 3(3).

[19] ibid, Art 12(2). For comprehensive coverage of the issue of passing-on in EU competition law, see M Strand, *The Passing-On Problem in Damages and Restitution under EU Law* (Cheltenham, Edward Elgar Publishing, 2017).

[20] Commission, 'Communication from the Commission on quantifying harm in actions for damages based on breaches of Article 101 or 102 of the Treaty on the Functioning of the European Union' [2013] OJ C167/19.

damages actions (the Practical Guide).[21] Further assistance on quantifying the passing-on, including a practical checklist with 39 steps for judges at national courts, is provided by the Study on the Passing-on of overcharges which was prepared for the Commission and made available in 2016.[22] These soft-law instruments reinforce the idea that the aim of Article 17(3) is to facilitate the quantification of damages by claimants, by making sure that national courts can instigate the assistance of the NCAs on the matter.

Recitals 45 to 47 in the Directive's Preamble provide further indications as to the purpose of Article 17 in general, but contain nothing expressly on the aim of Article 17(3). Recital 45 recalls that quantification of harm in competition law cases may constitute a substantial barrier to effectively claiming compensation from infringers, since quantifying harm is fact-intensive and costly and may require the application of complex economic models that would need to rely on data that are not easily accessible to claimants. The first part of Recital 46 continues with the rationale behind Article 17. It clarifies that the twin principles of equivalence and effectiveness place certain limits on the national procedural autonomy of Member States as to the quantification of harm. Those limits hinge on the intrinsic information asymmetries that exist between claimants and defendants, and the fact that quantifying the harm means assessing hypothetically how the market would have evolved but for the infringement, something that – like all counterfactuals – is inherently inaccurate. Based on those considerations, the latter part of Recital 46 and Recital 47 draw the conclusion that it is appropriate to introduce rules at the EU level to ensure that national courts have the power to estimate the quantum of damages, to enable NCAs to provide guidance on quantum where requested and to create a presumption that cartels result in harm, in particular via an effect on prices.

To conclude, the Article's broader context, the soft law that accompanies the Directive, and the relevant recitals in the Directive, show that Article 17(3) of the Directive is clearly intended to assist claimants in the quantification of damages stemming from violations of EU competition rules. The assistance that NCAs may provide to national courts regarding the quantum of damages is thought of as a further way of remedying the information asymmetry between claimants and defendants and the difficulties in collecting the necessary data and finding the evidence to substantiate the claim for damages.[23] Ultimately

[21] Commission, 'Staff Working Document, Practical Guide on Quantifying Harm in Actions for damages based on breaches of Article 101 or 102 of the Treaty on the Functioning of the European Union' SWD(2013) 205. See further, Iacovides, 'The Presumption and Quantification of Harm' (n 15).

[22] Final Report, 'Study on the Passing-on of Overcharges', available at: ec.europa.eu/competition/publications/reports/KD0216916ENN.pdf. According to Directive 2014/104 (n 1) Art 16, the Commission shall issue guidelines for national courts on how to estimate the share of the overcharge which was passed on to the indirect purchaser.

[23] On the difficulties associated with discovery in such cases, see H Andersson, 'The Quest for Evidence – Still an Uphill Battle for Cartel Victims', ch 9 in this edited volume.

then, Article 17(3) was enacted to further ensure the effectiveness of claims for damages and to make quantification of antitrust damages easier for claimants. However, that interest has to be balanced with the EU legislator's specific desire to avoid overcompensation and thereby the unjust enrichment of claimants to the detriment of claimants at a different level of the supply chain, as well as the desire not to subject the defendant to damages that go beyond full compensation, understood as actual loss, loss of profit, plus interest. The latter point is, admittedly, rather counterintuitive, as higher damages have a stronger deterrent effect. The intricacy lies of course in the fact that, at least in this author's opinion, enforcement of EU competition law – as the collective sum of private and public enforcement – ought to be *optimal*.[24] This requires reaching a delicate equilibrium between deterrence and punishment of anticompetitive practices, to which higher damages are conducive, with no excessive punishment that might result in defendants becoming incapacitated from competing further following an infringement, or the stifling of innovation.

## IV. SOME RELEVANT SWEDISH CONTEXT

The aim of this chapter is to examine whether Article 17(3) of the Directive needed to be specifically transposed into Swedish law by new provisions because the existing rules were insufficient. In order to do that, we not only need to understand Article 17(3) of the Directive, we also need to have an understanding of the relevant Swedish legal rules.

Before the transposition of the Directive into Swedish law, Chapter 3, section 25 of the Swedish Competition Act was the legal basis for private damages actions stemming from violations of the Swedish competition rules. The Directive was transposed into Swedish law by way of the Act on Competition Damages Actions (2016:964) (Konkurrensskadelagen, KSL). Following the enactment of the KSL, Chapter 3, section 25 of the Swedish Competition Act has been amended to make reference to the new Act.

Chapter 2, section 1 of the KSL establishes the right to damages for competition law infringements. The Patent and Market Court (PMD), a specialised chamber of the Stockholm District Court that inter alia hears competition law cases, is the exclusive forum in which to bring an action for damages based on that law.[25] Normally, in these cases, the PMD is quorate with two legally trained judges and two expert economist judges.[26]

[24] As pointed out to me by M Strand, *private* enforcement of EU competition law contains few traces of the American 'optimal deterrence' tradition. In that sense, my argument here can be understood as normative.

[25] c 5, s 1 of the Act on Competition Damages Actions (2016:964). Note, however, that damages actions, even those that stem from a competition law infringement, based on other laws (eg a breach of contract) can still be brought in other courts than the PMD. The composition of such courts does not include expert economist judges.

[26] c 4, s 4 of the Act on Patent and Market Courts (2016:188).

Swedish rules about procedure and evidence can be found in Rättegångsbalk (1942:740), the Swedish Code of Civil Procedure (the RB). While it is beyond the scope of this chapter to give a comprehensive overview of those rules, two provisions are particularly interesting for the purposes of the chapter's thesis, namely Chapter 35, section 6 (35:6 RB) and Chapter 40, section 1 of the RB (40:1 RB).

According to 35:6 RB, the '[p]resentation of evidence is the responsibility of the parties' and '[t]he court may on its own motion gather evidence only in cases which are not amenable to out-of-court settlement'.[27] The restriction on the courts' ability to gather evidence in cases that are amenable to an out-of-court settlement came about through the amendment of the RB in 2005. Private damages actions based on the new KSL are cases that are amenable to out-of-court settlement, meaning that in those cases the national courts are restricted by way of 35:6 RB from gathering evidence on their own motion.

At the same time, according to 40:1 RB, Swedish courts may request an expert opinion from public authorities, including of course the SCA. According to the provision '[i]f, for the determination of an issue the appraisal of which requires special professional knowledge, it is found necessary to call upon an expert, the court may obtain an opinion on the issue from a public authority'.[28] As a rule, expert opinions from public authorities, such as the SCA, do not entail an obligation to appear before the court to testify on the content of the expert opinion, in contrast to an expert opinion by individuals.[29] Therefore, as a rule, a written opinion from a public authority will be introduced into the case file and will be relied on as part of the body of written evidence in the case.

In the author's opinion, based on the principle that *lex posterior derogat priori*, the earlier drafted 40:1 RB will have to be interpreted in light of the more recently amended 35:6 RB. The implication is that in cases of private enforcement based on the new KSL, which are amenable to out-of-court settlement, the competent Swedish courts will be precluded from introducing evidence *on their own motion*, including expert opinions from the SCA, to the extent such opinions constitute evidence for the purposes of Swedish law. Such expert opinions may only be requested by the court if one of the parties initiates the procedures following from 40:1 RB.[30]

## V. THE NON-TRANSPOSITION OF ARTICLE 17(3) IN SWEDISH LAW

The Swedish Government deemed that Article 17(3) of the Directive did not require specific transposition into Swedish law, as it considered the existing

[27] Author's translation.

[28] Author's translation.

[29] c 40, s 8 of the Swedish Code of Civil Procedure.

[30] R Nordh, *Praktisk Process VI, Bevisrätt A – Allmänna bevisfrågor. Om ansvaret för bevisning, vittne, syn, sakkunnig m.m.* (Uppsala, Iustus Förlag, 2009) 91.

rules sufficient to achieve the Article's aim. Therefore, it did not introduce any provisions transposing the Article into the new KSL, nor did it propose any amendments to existing acts to that effect.

According to the Government's reasoning, which is set out in Government Bill 2016/17:9, the aim of Article 17(3) is to ensure that national courts have the necessary capacity and competences to quantify the harm. That capacity is already accomplished through the PMD's quorum rules, more specifically the inclusion of two expert economist judges on the bench. The Government added that, to the extent the court would consider that further assistance was required, the court could call on the SCA to provide assistance in accordance with 40:1 RB, if so requested by a party.[31]

It is submitted that the choice not to introduce a new rule in order to transpose Article 17(3) of the Directive into Swedish law was misguided for three reasons. Firstly, because the quorum rules are insufficient, secondly because Swedish courts are precluded from initiating the assistance on their own motion, and finally because it is unclear what criteria the SCA will apply to decide on the appropriateness of assisting the national courts. These are explored in the rest of this section.

### A. The Quorum Rules are Insufficient

As seen above, one of the Government's arguments in denying the necessity to transpose Article 17(3) of the Directive by introducing new provisions in Swedish law was that the specialised PMD court's quorum rules already provided the court with the necessary capacity to estimate the quorum of damages.

In this author's opinion, that argument is both irrelevant and superficial. It is irrelevant because the issue of the court's competence is entirely separate from the issue of what evidence and facts the court has before it. Clearly, the quorum rules cover the first, but do not necessarily solve the latter. The court can estimate the harm when it is impossible or excessively difficult for the claimant to do so, as follows from Chapter 35, section 5 of the RB. The court's competence in economics is, of course, an asset in that respect. Yet, the competence in economics is of no avail when the evidence before the court is such that it does not allow the court, despite its expert knowledge, to quantify the damages. Recall here that, as explained above, pursuant to 35:6 RB, the court is precluded from introducing evidence to the case file on its own motion.[32] Put simply, there is only so much that the expert economist judges will be able to do to estimate the harm if the evidence is thin or inadequate.

[31] Proposition 2016/17:9, 50–51.
[32] See further on this issue, s V.B. below.

Moreover, the argument is superficial, for two reasons. Firstly, it rests on the unrealistic assumption that in the majority of cases the two expert economist judges' competence would suffice to estimate the harm. In reality, it will depend a great deal on the type of knowledge of economics the expert judges hold. Good knowledge of macroeconomics and economic theory may not be sufficient or even relevant if the evidence in the case file is econometric, and it is not entirely clear that an economist has any advantage in that regard compared to a legally trained judge. Secondly, it disregards the fact that Swedish procedural rules allow for an action for competition damages to be brought in other courts than the specialised PMD court, where the action is based on other laws than the newly enacted KSL, even though this does not happen often. Those courts do not have expert judges sitting on the bench.

In contrast, NCAs, typically, and the SCA, in particular, employ a large number of economists, some specialised in macroeconomics, others in microeconomics, statistics, econometrics, or empirics. Moreover, NCAs have good expert knowledge of a variety of markets, gained through working on many cases that never reach the courts or become public knowledge, such as mergers that are cleared and investigations of complaints that do not result in prohibitions. As noted by the Swedish Bar Association, which used the opportunity offered to it during the legislative consultation phase to submit observations on the implementation of Article 17(3) of the Directive, the SCA's expert opinion on damages would add value because of its expertise and resources.[33] The expertise and resources are not always present at the national court, despite the PMD bench including two economists as judges. Even less so in courts whose bench is not comprised of a combination of judges and economists.

## B. Swedish Courts are Precluded from Initiating the Assistance on their own Motion

The argument about the insufficiency of the quorum rules and the internal capacity of courts – specialised or not – would have been less relevant if courts were able to call on the SCA on their own motion to assist them in the quantification of antitrust damages. Yet, as explained above, 35:6 RB precludes Swedish courts from doing so.

As we saw in section II, the original text proposed by the European Parliament for Article 17(3) simply used the passive voice 'where requested', without specifying by whom the requesting is done. This was later modified to clarify the point. Article 17(3) of the Directive states that the NCA becomes involved

[33] Sveriges advokatsamfunds yttrande R-2015/2089 av den 2 februari 2016 (N2015/04860/KSR), available at: www.advokatsamfundet.se/globalassets/advokatsamfundet_sv/remissvar/539931_20160203162626.pdf (in Swedish) 4.

in the quantification of damages 'upon request of a national court'. Clearly, the intention of the EU legislature was for the request to be made by the national court.

However, the Article is agnostic as to who *initiates* the national court's request and as to *how* the initiation is set in motion, arguably to avoid having to peek behind the veil of national procedural autonomy. Yet, one could assume that if the EU legislature had wanted to *limit* the possibilities of the national courts initiating the request on their own motion, it would have done so expressly in the Directive for the avoidance of doubt. Hence, since the Directive does not specify that assistance is to be provided only when the parties initiate the request, it is reasonable to deduce that it envisages that the request may be initiated by the national court on its own motion and not only at the request of the parties. As we saw above in section III, this possibility is significant, because under certain circumstances, both parties' interests may be different from the interests of EU competition policy and, hence, neither the claimant nor the defendant may have any incentive to make a request for the NCA's assistance. In other words, in certain cases, safeguarding the interests of EU competition law may depend on the national court requesting the assistance of the NCA in quantifying the damages.

Consequently, there is a difference between, on the one hand, what Article 17(3) of the Directive prescribes, and, on the other, the existing Swedish rules of procedure regarding who has the initiative to request the SCA's assistance. The situation created by not transposing Article 17(3) correctly puts the national courts in a difficult position. The predicament is that the national court would either have to find a way to reconcile applicable national law with the Directive's requirements and aim, or else disregard national law in order to give the Directive effect. Alternatively, it could choose to do nothing. In what follows, we elaborate on these three possibilities.

It is rather difficult to envisage that a Swedish court would go down the road of the first alternative. This alternative, which gives rise to what is known as the indirect effect of Directives, entails that in applying national law, whether the provisions in question were adopted before or after a Directive, national courts called upon to interpret it are required to do so, as far as possible, in the light of the wording and the purpose of the Directive, in order to achieve the result pursued by the latter and thereby comply with their obligations under EU law, including Article 288(3) TFEU. The duty is far-reaching and involves taking all appropriate measures, whether general or particular, to ensure the fulfilment of the Directive's aim. This duty stems from the secondary legislation itself, combined with the duty of sincere cooperation found in Article 4(3) TEU.[34] Nevertheless, the duty to interpret national law in conformity

[34] Case C-106/89 *Marleasing v La Comercial Internacional de Alimentacion* EU:C:1990:395, para 8 and Joined Cases C-397/01 to C-403/01 *Bernhard Pfeiffer et al v Deutsches Rotes Kreuz, Kreisverband Wanshut eV* EU:C:2004:584, paras 109–18.

with EU law does not stretch as far as to require the national court to interpret the law *contra legem*.[35] 35:6 RB is explicit in that in cases that are amenable to an out-of-court settlement, the court cannot introduce evidence on its own motion. The wording is clear and unambiguous, meaning that is not open to an interpretation that is in conformity with Article 17(3) of the Directive.[36] Moreover, it is in line with general principles of Swedish procedural law that all but eliminate the possibility for Swedish courts to *ex officio* raise issues or introduce evidence. Thus, to interpret 35:6 RB as allowing the court to initiate the involvement of the SCA and, thereby, to introduce evidence in the case on its own motion would clearly be *contra legem*. Therefore, it is not required by EU law.

The second option is for the Swedish court to set aside the national procedural rule that is contrary to Article 17(3) of the Directive.[37] Is that course of action conceivable? At first glance, it might be. EU law has supremacy over national law, irrespective of the status of the latter within the Member State.[38] Generally, the ECJ's case-law requires setting aside a national rule that is contrary to an EU rule and applying the latter instead, with no need for the national court to wait for the competent Member State court or authority to declare the national rule inapplicable, ineffective, unconstitutional and so on.[39] The requirement entails an obligation to set aside provisions of national law precluding national courts from pursuing an available procedure, in order to guarantee the effective application of EU law in their jurisdiction.[40] Alternatively, the requirement entails a possibility for national courts to 'create' procedures that are otherwise not available in the Member State, but only in situations where the party does not have recourse to any other available effective legal means.[41]

Along those lines, the argument could be made that the effective application of EU competition law, as expressed in several ECJ rulings[42] and Article 4 of the Directive, would require setting aside 35:6 RB, in order for the national court to request the SCA's assistance pursuant to 40:1 RB, on its own motion. The argument could be further supported by pointing out that it is already possible for Swedish courts to estimate the harm to a reasonable amount under

[35] Case C-212/04 *Konstantinos Adeneler and Others v Ellinikos Organismos Galaktos* EU:C:2006:443, para 110.

[36] Case C-555/07 *Kücükdeveci v Swedex* EU:C:2010:21, para 49.

[37] Case C-441/14 *Dansk Industri v Estate of Karsten Eigil Rasmussen* EU:C:2016:278, para 37 makes it clear that this is the course of action that the national court has to follow when it is impossible to interpret national rules *contra legem* to achieve compatibility with the EU rule.

[38] Case 4/64 *Flaminio Costa v ENEL* EU:C:1964:66; Case 11/70 *Internationale Handelsgesellschaft* EU:C:1970:114, para 3.

[39] Case 106/77 *Amministrazione delle Finanze dello Stato v Simmenthal SpA* EU:C:1978:49 and Case C-441/14 *Dansk Industri* (n 37) para 37.

[40] Case C-213/89 *R v Secretary of State for Transport, ex p Factortame* EU:C:1990:257.

[41] Case C-432/05 *Unibet (London) Ltd, Unibet (International) v Justitiekanslern* EU:C:2007:163, para 65; Case C-583/11 P *Inuit Tapiriit Kanatami et al* EU:C:2013:625, paras 103–04.

[42] See eg the cases cited above in n 3.

Chapter 35, section 5 of the RB where it is difficult or impossible for the claimant to provide full proof of the damage. Moreover, it should be noted here that the question of whether Article 17(3) of the Directive is (vertically or horizontally) directly effective is immaterial in this regard.[43] At the same time, the obligation on the national court applies *a fortiori* when the national court is seized of a dispute concerning the application of domestic provisions that have been specifically enacted to transpose a Directive intended to confer rights on individuals, as the Damages Directive.[44]

However, the Court's case-law would seem to preclude that very argument. In *van Schijndel*, the Court found that Union law:

> does not require national courts to raise of their own motion an issue concerning the breach of provisions of [Union] law where examination of that issue would oblige them to abandon the passive role assigned to them by going beyond the ambit of the dispute defined by the parties themselves and relying on facts and circumstances other than those on which the party with an interest in application of those provisions bases his claim.[45]

35:6 RB assigns to Swedish courts a passive role in cases amenable to out-of-court settlement. In the event that none of the parties in the proceedings has requested the court to initiate the SCA's assistance, it would seem an abandonment of that very passive role assigned to the court by virtue of the national rules of procedure, to take matters into its own hands in order to make the request.

The third and most likely option is for the PMD and other Swedish courts to do nothing. This is also the safest option, given that the parties will have no reason to challenge the fact that no request was made to the SCA for assistance in the quantification of harm. Clearly, a party that considers that the SCA's assistance would have been beneficial, would have initiated the request and the issue we are discussing in this subsection would simply not arise. Nevertheless, doing nothing *could* harm third parties in the exceptional cases where a third party is unable to claim damages from the infringer because the damages have already been fully awarded to other claimants, in light of the rule that the Directive should not lead to overcompensation.[46]

The question is whether such third parties would have recourse to any action for reparation in such circumstances. If not, this further reinforces the point that Article 17(3) of the Directive has not been correctly implemented in Swedish law.

[43] Case C-441/14 *Dansk industri* (n 37) paras 30–37. However, my understanding is that the rule still needs to have the qualities associated with direct effect, ie it will need to be clear, precise and unconditional as well as confer rights on individuals. On the issue of direct effect, see further below in this section.

[44] Joined Cases C-397/01 to C-403/01 *Pfeiffer et al* (n 34) para 112.

[45] Joined Cases C-430/93 and C-431/93 *Jeroen van Schijndel and Johannes Nicolaas Cornelis van Veen v Stichting Pensioenfonds voor Fysiotherapeuten* EU:C:1995:441, para 22.

[46] Directive 2014/104 (n 1) Art 3.

A first course of action would be an action for damages by such a third party against the Swedish state, arguing that the failure to transpose Article 17(3) of the Directive correctly has resulted in harm to it. Such an action would most probably fail. The claimant would have to meet the high threshold for state liability and prove that three cumulative conditions are met.[47] Firstly, the claimant would have to show that Article 17(3) is intended to confer rights on individuals. Yet that seems rather artificial, as the right claimed seems to be a right 'conferred' upon the national court, not the individual. Secondly, the claimant would have to show that the breach was sufficiently serious, which is not the case where the provision is capable of bearing the meaning understood by the Member State, or if there is a lack of consensus as to the meaning of the provision.[48] Thirdly, the claimant would have to show a direct causal link between the breach and the damage sustained. Even regarding this condition the claimant is in a rather difficult position, as the damage is sustained indirectly, through the awarding of damages to the first claimant by the competent national court.

A second course of action would be for the claimant to bring an action for damages against the Swedish state for a breach of EU law by the Swedish judiciary. The claim in this scenario would be that the failure of the Swedish court to ask for the assistance of the SCA in order to give full effect to Article 17(3) of the Directive by either consistently interpreting national law with the Directive or through setting aside 35:6 RB, has resulted in harm being caused to the third party. This action would also most probably fail. The same three conditions would have to be fulfilled as above, but the threshold would be even higher, since the second condition requires showing that the error is a *manifest* infringement of the applicable EU law.[49] Relevant factors to consider in that assessment include the degree of clarity and precision of the rule, whether the breach was intentional, whether the error was excusable, and whether the court had failed to make a preliminary ruling reference despite being bound to do so by virtue of Article 267(3) TFEU.[50]

A third course of action could materialise if the claimant were to bring an action for damages against the infringer under the KSL. One would expect the infringer to claim that damages have already been awarded to another party and that awarding damages to the second claimant would result in the damages exceeding the total amount of damages recoverable under the Directive. In other words, the infringer would be using Article 3(3) of the Directive as a shield. The claimant might claim that the judgment of the court in those earlier

[47] Joined Cases C-46/93 and C-48/93 *Brasserie du Pêcheur v Germany* and *R v Secretary of State for Transport, ex p Factortame (no 3)* EU:C:1996:79, para 51.

[48] Case C-392/93 *R v HM Treasury, ex p British Telecommunications* EU:C:1996:131, paras 43–44; Case C-278/05 *Robins v Secretary of State for Work and Pensions*, EU:C:2007:56, paras 78–81.

[49] Case C-224/01 *Gerhard Köbler v Republik Österreich* EU:C:2003:513; Case C-173/03 *Traghetti del Mediterraneo SpA v Repubblica Italiana* EU:C:2006:391, paras 42–44.

[50] *Traghetti*, ibid, para 43.

proceedings should be disregarded, as the failure of the court to initiate the assistance of the SCA entailed an infringement of Article 17(3) of the Directive. In effect, the claimant would be making a similar claim as the claimants made in *CIA Security* and *Unilever Italia*, trying to draw the benefit of a rule in a Directive horizontally as against another private party.[51] The difference making this even more exceptional than the already exceptional cases of indirect horizontal effect of Directives, is that the triggering event is not the failure of the state to comply with a Directive, but rather the failure of a national court to give effect to a provision of the Directive by setting aside a provision on national law. In effect, this third type of action contains the second type of case. Accordingly, it would also most probably fail.

Hence, the option of the national court doing nothing is safe, given that it would not be challenged by the parties themselves and that it would be all but impossible for third parties to challenge it, and even more so given the rarity of actions for infringement brought by the Commission under Article 258 TFEU.

As a consolation, it is worth pointing out that the third party could always try to recover its part of the damages from the first claimant, based on a claim of unjust enrichment, rather than pursue a claim against the state or the infringer.[52] Nevertheless, the point here was to show that the failure to transpose Article 17(3) of the Directive is problematic as it has the potential to harm at least some claimants and since those claimants would not have any effective means of redress to challenge the incorrect implementation of the Directive. This reinforces the thesis that the choice not to introduce a new rule in order to transpose Article 17(3) into Swedish law was misguided.

### C. It is not Entirely Clear that the SCA can Deem it Inappropriate to Assist the Court

The two reasons offered above are sufficient to show that Article 17(3) of the Directive has not been correctly transposed in Sweden. A final reason that supports that conclusion is that the failure to transpose the Article was a missed opportunity to provide guidance as to when the SCA deems it inappropriate to assist a Swedish court in the quantification of damages.

Recall that Article 17(3) of the Directive stipulates that the NCAs 'may' assist where the national competition authority 'considers such assistance to be appropriate'. This would seem to leave it entirely to the discretion of the NCAs to determine the merits of providing assistance. The question is whether the current Swedish rules are compatible with that.

[51] Case C-194/94 *CIA Security International SA v Signalson and Securitel SPRL* EU:C:1996:172; Case C-443/98 *Unilever Italia SpA v Central Food SpA* EU:C:2000:496.

[52] Strand, *Passing-on* (n 19) 356–59 and 366–67 opts for the use of the term 'windfall award' rather than 'unjust enrichment' and includes a discussion of US case-law on the matter.

As we saw in section IV, according to 40:1 RB, Swedish courts may ask for an expert opinion from public authorities. Providing expert opinion to the court is voluntary, except for persons 'who are obliged to assist as experts in their official capacity'.[53] According to the Government's reasoning, which is set out in Government Bill 2016/17:9, the SCA is not obliged to assist Swedish courts as an expert, because this is not expressly required by the regulations that set out the SCA's mission.[54] However, the SCA has a clear mission to work towards effective competition in the private and public sphere to the benefit of consumers. It is possible that the broadly worded mission affects the option of denying assistance. Moreover, the obligation to provide assistance to courts does not only follow from Chapter 40 of the RB but also from section 6 of the Administrative Procedure Act (1986:223), which stipulates that all public authorities have an obligation to provide assistance to other authorities[55] within the scope of their activities.

Moreover, it is not clear what criteria govern the SCA's deliberation on the appropriateness of assisting the national courts. Would it be in line with the spirit of the Directive and the purpose of Article 17(3) for the SCA to factor in budgetary constraints, the time it would take to provide assistance and the associated cost, the complexity of the case, and whether the case is a follow-on or a standalone action? It is rather telling that there are – as of now – no cases in which the SCA has appeared as an expert under 40:1 RB, although that possibility has always been available in Sweden. Moreover, the SCA has intervened in a domestic case on its own initiative under Article 15(3) of Regulation 1/2003 only once.[56]

Additionally, it is not clear what kind of assistance the SCA would provide. There are indications that the SCA considers that its role in assisting the national courts is not to quantify the harm, but rather to simply enlighten the courts as to the methods that could be used to do so.[57] Yet that seems hardly necessary, or of any value, given the Commission's detailed Guidance on Quantifying the Harm.[58]

To the extent a new provision, or an appropriate amendment, would have been introduced to transpose Article 17(3) of the Directive in the Swedish legal order, the Government Bill would have included some deliberations on the matters discussed in this subsection. Those preparatory works would have provided guidance on the conditions under which the SCA will make the

[53] c 40, s 4 of the RB (author's translation).

[54] Proposition 2016/17:9, p 52.

[55] Swedish courts are public authorities for the purposes of the Administrative Procedure Act.

[56] Opinion of the SCA to the Svea Court of Appeal of 25 March 2010 in Case Ö 1561-10 *Sodastream*, in accordance with Art 15(3) of Regulation 1/2003, available at: www.konkurrensverket.se/globalassets/aktuellt/nyheter/las-yttrandet-dnr-6322009-69724kb.pdf (in Swedish).

[57] See Sweden's country report for the OECD 'Relationship between public and private antitrust enforcement', DAF/COMP/WP3/WD(2015)4.

[58] Above, n 21. See further Iacovides (n 15).

choice of assisting the national courts in the quantification of harm and would have shed some light both on the expectations of the Swedish legislature and the SCA's own view of the matter. The failure to transpose Article 17(3) of the Directive was a missed opportunity in this regard too.

## VI. CONCLUSIONS

In this chapter, I examined whether Sweden has correctly implemented Article 17(3) of the Directive in Swedish law. Based on the legislative history of Article 17(3) and its aim as revealed by its broader context and soft law, it was submitted that Article 17(3) of the Directive has not been correctly transposed into Swedish law, mainly because Swedish procedural law precludes national courts from initiating the request for assistance to the SCA on their own motion.

The discussion regarding the transposition of Article 17(3) of the Directive into Swedish law shows that both Swedish courts and the SCA are quite passive in private damages actions for infringements of competition law. Moreover, the specialised competition courts in Sweden seem to be considered sufficiently competent to deal with issues of quantification without the assistance of the SCA. This misses the point that quantification is complex and that the SCA is often better placed than the national courts and the parties to estimate the harm caused by anticompetitive conduct.

The non-transposition of Article 17(3) of the Directive into Swedish law can prove to be detrimental to claimants in some exceptional cases. The discussion showed a certain tension between national rules of procedure on the one hand and the effective application of EU competition rules in Sweden on the other. It is submitted that it would have been much more appropriate if the tension had been resolved through legislation rather than court actions based on EU law principles, as it was shown that such actions would most likely fail.

# Index

INTRODUCTORY NOTE

References such as '178–79' indicate (not necessarily continuous) discussion of a topic across a range of pages. Wherever possible in the case of topics with many references, these have either been divided into sub-topics or only the most significant discussions of the topic are listed. Because the entire work is about 'damages', the use of this term (and certain others which occur constantly throughout the book) as an entry point has been minimised. Information will be found under the corresponding detailed topics.